Confrontation, Class Consciousness, and the Labor Process

Recent Titles in Contributions in Labor Studies

The Limits of Trade Union Militancy: The Lancashire Textile Workers, 1910–194
Joseph L. White

Coal, Iron, and Slaves: Industrial Slavery in Maryland and Virginia, 1715–1865
Ronald L. Lewis

American Workingclass Culture: Explorations in American Labor and Social History
Milton Cantor, editor

Working-Class Community in Industrial America: Work, Leisure, and Struggle in Two Industrial Cities, 1880–1930
John T. Cumbler

Organizing Dixie: Alabama Workers in the Industrial Era
Philip Taft, revised and edited by Gary M Fink

At the Point of Production: The Local History of the I.W.W.
Joseph R. Conlin, editor

Conflict and Accommodation: Coal Miners, Steel Workers, and Socialism, 1890–1920
Michael Nash

Division of Labor: A Political Perspective
Elliott A. Krause

Radicalism and Freethought in Nineteenth-Century Britain: The Life of Richard Carlile
Joel H. Wiener

Ideology and the Rise of Labor Theory in America
John A. DeBrizzi

White Collar Workers in Transition: The Boom Years, 1940–1970
Mark McColloch

Labor Migration in the Atlantic Economies: The European and North American Working Classes During the Period of Industrialization
Dirk Hoerder, editor

Proletarians and Protest: The Roots of Class Formation in an Industrializing World
Michael Hanagan and Charles Stephenson, editors

Confrontation, Class Consciousness, and the Labor Process

STUDIES IN PROLETARIAN CLASS FORMATION

EDITED BY
MICHAEL HANAGAN
AND
CHARLES STEPHENSON

CONTRIBUTIONS IN LABOR STUDIES, NUMBER 18

GREENWOOD PRESS
NEW YORK · WESTPORT, CONNECTICUT · LONDON

Library of Congress Cataloging-in-Publication Data
Main entry under title:

Confrontation, class consciousness, and the labor process.

(Contributions in labor studies, ISSN 0886–8239 ; no. 18)
Bibliography: p.
Includes index.
1. Labor and laboring classes—Addresses, essays, lectures. 2. Proletariat—Addresses, essays, lectures. 3. Industrial sociology—Addresses, essays, lectures. 4. Labor economics—Addresses, essays, lectures. I. Hanagan, Michael P., 1947– . II. Stephenson, Charles. III. Series.
HD4851.C63 1986 305.5'62 85–17734
ISBN 0–313–25140–1 (lib. bdg. : alk. paper)

Library of Congress Catalog Card Number: 85–17734
ISBN: 0–313–25140–1
ISSN: 0886–8239

First published in 1986

Greenwood Press, Inc.
88 Post Road West
Westport, Connecticut 06881

Printed in the United States of America

The paper used in this book complies with the Permanent Paper Standard issued by the National Information Standards Organization (Z39.48–1984).

10 9 8 7 6 5 4 3 2 1

Michael Hanagan's Dedication:

To Julia

Charles Stephenson's Dedication:

To Bill Malone and Brian Greenberg
Mentors and Friends

Contents

Figures and Tables

FIGURES

TABLES

Acknowledgments

For their help, advice, and encouragement during this long project we would like to thank Miriam Cohen, Betty Stephenson, John Cumbler, Robert Asher, John Merriman, and Charles and Louise Tilly. Chuck Sokolik, Len Smith, and Marianne Burke provided valuable help along the way. As typist and editor, Mrs. Mildred Tubby was absolutely crucial to the success of this project.

Confrontation, Class Consciousness, and the Labor Process

1

Introduction

Michael Hanagan and Charles Stephenson

An old cartoon from a socialist newspaper shows a group of seedy intellectuals and bohemians bunched together inside a factory, all looking intently at a tiny black splotch on the workshop floor. The caption reads, "Comrades, the point of production!" The cartoon captures succinctly two essential truths about nineteenth- and early twentieth-century Marxist thought. First, it calls to mind the importance of the labor process in Marxist theory. Phrases such as "organization at the point of production" or "class struggle at the point of production," have had a special resonance because Marx argued that changes in the labor process, specifically the contradiction between the means of production and the relations of production, were the major dynamic of modern political conflict and of political development. Second, the cartoon reminds us that typically Marxists paid little attention to the examination and analysis of what was meant by the "labor process." In 1954, John Plamenatz did not meet with a speedy and convincing reply when he claimed that Marx and Engels did not present a meaningful definition of the term "relations of production," and labeled this imprecision a "ghost battalion closing a vital gap in the front of Marxist theory."[1]

The last twenty years have witnessed a renewal of interest from a newer generation of scholars, both Marxist and non-Marxist, in conceptualizing and analyzing the labor process and the nature of work in capitalist society and their relation to worker militancy; in the process, our conception of the "labor process" and the way in which it influences workers has expanded greatly.[2] In its strictest sense, "labor process" includes three elements: the organization of the work process; the disposition of the tools; and the objects on which work is performed. However, these elements of the labor process are more complicated than they may seem at first sight. The organization of work can be differentiated according to modes of payment, methods of supervision, and levels of skill, and it can be manipulated by capital in its effort to appropriate control.[3] Workers can earn wages in the form of "subcontracting payments," "piece" rates, or "straight" rates; they can labor under foremen, under fellow workers, in "semi-autonomous" work groups, or by themselves; they can be highly skilled, semi-skilled, or unskilled. Moreover, workers can own or lease all or part of the basic means of production, or all machines and tools can be owned by the employer.[4]

The tools used to produce commodities also are important in this formulation in so far as they determine the level and intensity of capital investment. Large investments in fixed capital mean that work must be continuous and regular; small investments cause it to be fluctuating and irregular. Finally, such factors as the nature of demand and the character of the raw materials can have an important influence on the rhythm and nature of work. Commodities that have an extensive and dependable market may create conditions for permanent long-term jobs, while commodities with a smaller and erratic market may permit only temporary employment and create conditions for cyclical migration. Additionally, the extent to which raw materials are relatively homogeneous and routinely obtainable also encourages the rational organization of work. Industries that transform raw materials that have already been processed mechanically are easier to transform toward "efficient operation" than industries that have to wrestle directly with nature.

While the rediscovery of the complexity of the labor process has been a significant aspect of contemporary labor history, the most important aspect of recent research has been the exploration of the social relationships based on the labor process. Such social relationships include the solidarities generated by particular kinds of technology and shop-floor labor organization and the shared identities created by common confrontation between industrial work experience and the previous work experience of proletarians. They also include the cultural institutions and social values that workers acquire in class-based leisure institutions or through their participation in political organizations in so far as these institutions and organizations shape workers' conceptions of the labor process.

Although they share a common interest in analyzing the labor process, the contributors to this volume differ in emphasis and in interpretation. Oliver Carsten emphasizes the independence and autonomy of the specific work experience of the skilled worker. Searching for a broader basis of solidarity, John Cumbler argues that the culture of all American workers must be shaped by the alienation and exploitation of capitalist labor organization; he stresses the shared feelings that arise in any capitalist workshop and the common class identification that results. In contrast, Alf Luedtke examines the ambiguous nature of the shop-floor experience and the variety of ways that workers may interpret their work life, and argues that forces outside the workplace are necessary in order for workers to develop a cohesive and unified interpretation of their work experience. But all these authors concern themselves with the formative role of work in shaping workers' cultures and traditions, and all are concerned with the relationship between the labor process and workers' lives outside the factory.

Considered together, these extremely provocative essays on the labor process in advanced capitalist countries reveal the importance of studying the relationship between the labor process and the solidarity that workers exhibit and the value systems that they hold. Increasingly, scholars concerned with the work experience are widening their conception of the influence of this process to include the recreational life of the workers, the recruitment patterns of the workforce, and the stratification systems within the industrial order. They are coming to realize that factors such as ethnicity must be linked to both the work process and the system of labor organization if the centrality of the labor process is to be maintained. On the other hand, scholars concerned with popular culture are recognizing the ways in which the labor process influences choices among culturally determined alternatives; consequently, they are looking more carefully at the work process and finding that much that was taken for granted as belonging to the autonomous realm of technological change actually belongs to the rich and diverse world of popular culture.

The essays in this collection, both those that deal with advanced capitalist nations and those that deal with nations that emerged from colonialism in the twentieth century, all consider the crucial issues concerning the relationship between labor process and worker militancy. Here it is useful to compare and contrast the new concern for proletarianization and labor process shared by historians of the advanced capitalist countries and those of the former colonial nations, and to assess the extent to which these essays suggest new directions for historians of the labor process.

The three essays on labor movements in advanced capitalist nations—by Carsten, Cumbler, and Luedtke—all suggest fresh avenues of research and perhaps even possibilities of synthesis. Their focus is less on the specific elements of labor process and more on the solidarities, attitudes, and conflicts that result from these processes. For example, Oliver Carsten concentrates on the solidarities generated on the shop floor. The "artisanal" workers that Carsten describes in Meriden were not only highly skilled workers; they also possessed a great deal of control over the work process and only with qualification could be equated with the "proletariat." While few late nineteenth- and early twentieth-century artisans owned their own tools, still their considerable control over the work process rendered them very incompletely "subordinate" in the production process. Thus, although the workers Carsten describes were involved in large-scale capitalist industry, they retained many of the traditions of petty commodity production. They were able to do so because much in their method of production was identical to that of petty commodity production. Even though such workers labored in large factories, their techniques were those of small groups of skilled workers. Until the division of labor made inroads into their work methods, they remained only partly integrated into modern capitalism, at least in the way that modern capitalists desired. Carsten's emphasis on the role of the division of labor in defining worker identity stresses the role of labor process, yet his careful pursuit of the ways in which work determines the leisure-time patterns of workers opens up new lines of research for this approach.

The presence of artisanal workers in an advanced capitalist nation in the twentieth century will not surprise American or European labor historians. Following the lead of E.P. Thompson, George Rudé, and Albert Soboul in Europe, and Herbert Gutman, and David Montgomery in the United States, labor historians have begun more and more to show how work experience influenced the attitudes and culture of militant workers.[5] Usually the emphasis is placed on the solidarity of pre-industrial workers and the relative lack of solidarity among industrial workers. In Meriden, Connecticut Carsten shows that artisanal occupations generated an informal sociability that expressed itself in membership in fraternal societies—"a central part of a life style in which they had extended work-based solidarities beyond the workplace." When their position was threatened, these artisans already possessed a rich organizational world capable of responding and organizing to defend themselves. In contrast, industrial workers in New Britain lacked the skills that provided the basis for informal sociability. Additionally, they lacked the organizational richness of the nearby artisans, and this made them far less capable of fighting effectively to represent their interests.

Yet, even in Meriden, when the company decided in 1915 to extend "management rights" by crushing the closed shop and by introducing scientific management techniques, the workers could not stand against them, despite a protracted struggle. "The company clearly intended to end the traditional autonomy of the artisan," Carsten says; "scientific management offered an opportunity to break the workers' control of their jobs" and to entrench a group of "obedient skilled workers." Despite the reality that these artisanal workers represented ultimately little threat to the employers, management in Meriden, consistent with management elsewhere, intrinsically viewed worker autonomy as potentially threatening both to its own control of the work process and, in the end, to capital's control generally. In Meriden, as elsewhere, management determined to end that threat, and they did so successfully. "The memory of the strike in Meriden and its outcome," Carsten tells us, "was strong enough to inhibit union organizing for over fifty years."

John Cumbler also examines the relationship between work and the shaping of working-class culture. Cumbler focuses on how the everyday experiences of proletarian life, both on and off the job, shaped proletarian attitudes and argues that *all* proletarian experiences shared a common denominator of alienation and oppression. Even through "ethnicity" was a formative influence on the culture of a large section of the nineteenth and twentieth-century American working class, these ethnic characteristics were conditioned by the proletarian experience. Cumbler seeks to determine the circumstances under which ethnic culture might reflect or retard working-class sentiments. He focuses squarely on the proletarian experience itself and directly from it derives the elements of political resistance. In his chapter, Cumbler explores the roots of class consciousness among unskilled and semi-skilled ethnic proletarians. These workers of Irish and southern Italian origin lacked marketable skills and were cut off from the artisanal tradition of political militancy. Yet they were capable of asserting the importance of working-class issues against their own ethnic, middle-class community leaders; on more than one occasion, Irish bosses in Fall River were unable to turn out the vote for prominent anti-labor candidates.

Why did the ethnic working classes sometimes assert themselves in opposition to their community leaders? Cumbler argues that two factors were at work—first, the enduring presence of grievances created by the work experience of the capitalist factory or workshop; second, the structural conditions that promoted or hindered middle-class leadership within the ethnic community.

For Cumbler, the character of ethnic groups is affected strongly by the room for maneuverability possessed by its middle-class leadership. In analyzing the strengths and weaknesses of collective action among the ethnic working classes, he considers the way in which the ethnic group inserted itself into American society, as well as the class composition of the ethnic group. Ethnicity in its effects on working-class community has been viewed ambivalently by American historians. The intense emotional divisiveness generated by ethnicity often is identified as a major factor preventing a coalescence of a cohesive working-class movement in the United States. John Bodnar has gone so far as to suggest that a family-oriented insularity generated by immigrant cultures obviated the importance of workplace experiences.[6] Others have addressed the "trappings" of ethnicity as serving the stratified social structure. "The cues of felt ethnicity," Colin Greer said of twentieth-century America, "turn out to be the recognizable characteristics of class position in this society," useful to a "hierarchical class structure which expresses itself in ethnic categories."[7] An emphasis upon ethnicity reinforced one's "class" position but, critically, without communicating the *substance* of class. Some "class" issues—Sunday drinking, for example—were less threatening to middle-class power than other, work-related issues, such as hours or wages.

Cumbler suggests a variation of this view; he agrees that ethnic culture, while not necessarily divisive in a class sense, sometimes reinforced in the community's mind its own separateness and therefore became associated with working-class sentiments and was defended as part and parcel of ethnic working-class identity. Cumbler emphasizes the "contradictory pressures" upon ethnic communities and leaders: "Although the nature of the relationship between ethnicity and class identity changed over time," he says, "particular historical convergences" could result in a "contradictory mix" of outcomes. Cumbler, too, shows the need to examine the relationship between labor process and ethnic institutions and argues that together, work experience and ethnic institutions influenced the formation of class conflict and identity. For Cumbler, then, working-class experience and ethnic culture are not separable, but neither one is a simple reflection of the other.

Alf Luedtke is more skeptical than either Carsten or Cumbler about the relationship between proletarian experience and political consciousness. He looks at a group of metalworkers and scrutinizes carefully the ways in which work affected the formation of working-class culture. He shows how work experience promoted both a sense of collective identity and, at the same time, a corresponding sense of individualism. Most interesting, however, is the phenomenon of *Eigensinn*, the sense of self-will and self-reliance. Through his analysis of *Eigensinn*, Luedtke raises doubts about the ability of work experience to serve as a guide to political action. Luedtke asserts the need to look closely at the manner in which political action is related to shop-floor relations; his strong suggestion is that the relationship is not a derivative one.

Luedtke insists that workers' behavior often was not directed toward anything but gaining, briefly, more individual "space"—expressed by "horseplay" and "small joys": at those times "workers *neglected*, but mostly did *not directly interfere with* the ongoing work process. The boundaries between *Eigensinn* and calculated resistance remained blurred and fluid," he explains. But he warns against interpreting all such resistance as political; there may be a political content within horseplay, but it is one which must be developed consciously. "The *daily politics* were in no way fixated on resistance," Luedtke says. Many workers may have had a "concept of alternative political organization," but often they remained "'private' and 'self-willed'." Actual experience was ambiguous and could be expressed by apolitical as well as political behavior. The task of socialist parties was not simply to reflect workers' shop experience, but to select those elements of the shop experience that promoted solidarity and to expand them. More than either Carsten or Cumbler, therefore, Luedtke emphasizes the indeterminacy of the work experience, but he includes careful efforts to distinguish the range of possible interpretations generated within the work experience. For Luedtke, this range sets the limits within which other forces may seek elements to build or to shape workers' consciousness.

Together the Carsten, Luedtke, and Cumbler pieces raise key questions about the process of class formation within the industrializing European and American city. Although all three authors have different conceptions of the role of labor process in generating working-class conflict, they all agree in focusing on the importance of those structures that mediated between the workplace and consciousness. Carsten's argument suggests that the presence of large numbers of artisans might have had an important influence on the development of working-class protest. Cumbler argues that the nature of the link between the ethnic working class and the ethnic middle class was crucial. Finally, Luedtke suggests that forthrightly political intervention is needed for workers to fashion their shop-floor experiences into any meaningful terms. If they are right, the presence of artisans, ethnic middle-class leaders, and socialist parties were all of crucial significance for the growth of working-class awareness in advanced industrial countries during the nineteenth century.

All three essays that deal with working-class militancy in the advanced capitalist nations emphasize the essential ways in which labor process, shop-floor solidarities, and cultural experiences influence worker militancy. These essays only represent the latest development of an American and European historiography that has created a "new labor history" that borrows heavily from social history. Only twenty years ago, most labor historians studied formal labor organizations such as trade unions and socialist parties while concentrating their attention on the growth of the industrial proletariat.

Recently, labor historians outside the West have also become interested in the labor process. For almost two decades, labor historians of the former colonial nations have been strongly influenced by dependency theory and other interpretations that stressed the importance of international exchange relations in determining political developments rather than internal dynamics such as changes in the labor process. While the arguments of scholars like Andre Gunder Frank and Immanuel Wallerstein were invaluable in breaking with the stultifying stage models of earlier theorists, these arguments in turn neglected vital aspects of the historical process.[8] As Robert Brenner has pointed out, these theories did not attempt to explain why some nations were able to challenge seriously the existing worldwide division of labor while other nations were not.[9] A critique of existing theories of African development by Frederick Cooper concludes that "a much closer scrutiny of production is needed than the new-fangled concepts of articulation, dependency, and underdevelopment allow. Perhaps a return to those central but neglected aspects of the old Marxism—primitive accumulation, the labor process, and class struggle—might be salutary."[10]

What Cooper is suggesting is not a full-scale return to old-style Marxism, but the use of Marxist concepts within a non-deterministic framework of historical interpretation—in short, Marxist analysis shorn of its stage theory and its emphasis on inevitability. Cooper argues that historians need to consider the issues stressed by dependency theorists, but also to focus more on the dynamics of proletarianization. In his discussion of proletarianization, he includes the twin processes of primitive accumulation and of changes in labor organization. Cooper reminds us that the analysis of labor process is only one part of the study of class formation. The analysis of change in the work experience focuses on what happens inside the workplace, but primitive accumulation helps us understand the origins of both workers and of the workplace.

Cooper's discussion of proletarianization locates one important difference between labor historians in the advanced capitalist countries and those in the Third World nations. Those in the less-developed countries generally have included the study of accumulation as part of labor history itself. In the West, labor historians have tended to see accumulation as outside their field. Too often, they have yielded the study of primitive accumulation to demographers, economists, or to historians of migration or of ethnicity. "Primitive accumulation" refers to a dual process: first to the methods by which a small minority of individuals amassed control over productive resources; second to the process by which a large number of individuals were denied access to such resources. In the former colonial nations, the close connection between primitive accumulation and labor process is almost inescapable. Whether they study the slave economies, tribal societies, or the colonial or post-colonial periods, historians have found that the terms of primitive accumulation have helped shape the labor process and that the widely different conditions of capital accumulation and labor process in different regions of Africa and Asia can contribute in important ways to the understanding of the varying outcomes of historical change.

The great merit of these chapters on the former colonies is that they focus on the specificities of capital accumulation, labor process, and class struggle in a single case or in comparative perspective. Attention to concrete examples is crucial in the less-developed world, because there the process of accumulation was more prolonged and involved systems of labor organization more varied than in the advanced capitalist West.

These essays suggest that careful attention to clarifying and analyzing the diversity of labor processes and systems of capital accumulation can give us insight into particular labor histories. Following our contributors' example, we want to show the great flexibility of the concepts of proletarianization and labor process; they are analytical categories capable of focusing attention on a variety of important processes in many economic structures.

While these categories may be misleading if used in a highly generalized context, within the framework of specific times and places they can be most useful. The case of South Africa presented by Martin Murray and the four small Asian nations studied by Frederic Deyo present examples of relative capitalist success in the less-developed world in the twentieth century. In some ways they form a good parallel to the study of Germany by Luedtke and those of the United States by Carsten and Cumbler, which also provide examples of capitalist success in the nineteenth century. The essay by Murray presents a case where a colonial government played an extraordinarily forceful role in primitive accumulation and he details the resultant effects on the organization of labor. Deyo's essay takes up the theme of state intervention in the economy in a different context and shows that in the most successful of capitalist states in the Far East, the state has played a key role in organizing and directing the labor process. Finally, where Murray and Deyo emphasize the differences in accumulation and labor process between the advanced capitalist countries and the former colonies, Peter Gutkind's study of a struggle for control over the labor process among canoemen in West Africa reminds us that there may also be similarities to the West that have escaped notice.

The heart of Murray's article concerns the particular path of primitive accumulation in South Africa and the ways in which the native population protested against government policies. In regard to capital accumulation, the period of primitive accumulation was more abridged in the colonies than in Western Europe or the United States. Either in the form of outside investors or of white landowning farmers, capital accumulation came from Europe and the settlers used the colonial state to create a proletariat for them.

In terms of the formation of a workforce, proletarianization in Africa seems to fit Karl Marx's analysis even better than the English case that he himself studied. In discussing proletarianization in England, Marx emphasized the expropriation of cottagers and small peasants as a result of the Enclosure Laws. Now historians generally portray the most important consequences of legal enactments for English proletarianization in terms of the freeing of the grain trade or the lifting of protective industrial legislation.[11] This changed emphasis is important because modern-day historians, even Marxist historians, view proletarianization differently than did Marx. Marx pictured legal enactments creating a rural proletariat that became the basis for the industrial proletariat. Modern-day Marxists are more likely to emphasize the transformation of outworkers and artisans into proletarians. E.P. Thompson's *The Making of the English Working Class* relies heavily on the assumption that there is a continuity between the traditions of pre-industrial workers and industrial workers.[12] The identification of the group that formed the basis of the industrial proletariat bears on the kinds of traditions and attitudes that might be expected to be found within the embryonic proletariat.

Assumptions that hold for industrializing England need not hold elsewhere. Although Marx may have overemphasized the role of enclosures in creating a surplus proletariat available for industrial labor in England, the South African case seems to fit perfectly Marx's depiction of proletarianization. The South African Native Land Act of 1913 mandated wholesale and ruthless expropriations of the native population; through it a settler population in place utilized the government to create a rural labor force for its farms. "Scarcely any legislation has ever been enacted which has affected the Native population with so much dismay," Murray quotes a contemporary as saying of the act, "whose object is to prevent the Natives from ever rising above the position of servants to whites." Thus, Murray points out: "The agrarian class transformation that erupted" in South Africa early in this century was effected in large part by "the direct intervention of the state administration." The repressive legislation's creation of a proletarian population in itself weakened the basis for rural resistance to white, capitalist rule.

Perhaps most important of all, the overwhelming role of state power in South Africa in proletarianizing the population was to have a decisive effect on the political evolution of that nation. The political powerlessness of the native population in the face of overwhelming Western military and political power and the disregard for the rights of the natives, fed by Western racism and feelings of cultural superiority, enabled property owners of European origin to win goals achieved in very different ways in their home countries. In England, the Enclosure Acts marked a political triumph for landed groups struggling to check royal power—thus market domination went hand in hand with the struggle to limit state power. In South Africa, in contrast, the conditions of primitive accumulation created a massive rural proletariat completely subordinated to the employers; in the colonies, settler populations won economic victories in coalition with state administrators.

The role of the state in promoting accumulation and in enforcing labor discipline in the workplace is the major theme of Frederic Deyo's essay on industrialization and labor movements in "the Gang of Four"—Hong Kong, South Korea, Singapore, and Taiwan—a story of successful co-optation and repression of working-class movements in countries without a tradition of labor organization and where the state was prepared to sponsor industrial development. What all these countries have in common is government-controlled trade unions—a step beyond the company unions of the advanced capitalist nations—and an unmediated government participation in the exploitation and reduction to misery of the working-class population. Part of the result was (between 1960 and 1979) "the most rapid annual growth rates per capita of all developing nations."

In these nations, the trade-union movement is not simply regulated, but is itself an institutional tool for controlling the labor force. There, a national bourgeoisie has enforced laws and regulations that colonial rulers seldom were successful in enforcing. In order to promote capital accumulation to compete on the world market with advanced capitalist countries—undertaken in concert with advanced capitalist countries—the governments of these nations are carrrying out a ruthless exploitation of their own workforces. Also, in these countries as in the colonies, government officials clearly are haunted by the spectre of European Communist and socialist parties. Both colonial administrators and national bourgeoisies have before them the history of the European trade union and socialist movement; both are determined that it "won't happen here." Their pursuit of tightly controlled export-oriented industrialization has seen these countries already preside over a transition from "repressive to [authoritarian] corporatist labor controls," a neater form of organization, although one which reflects a continuing or increasing need for containment of labor protest."

Far more successfully than nineteenth-century nations, the modern capitalist nations described by Deyo have managed to industrialize without making concessions to independent working-class movements. Practically alone of all the articles in this collection, his piece does not record significant amounts of internal social conflict. Indeed, to a greater extent than in the nineteenth century, modern-day protest movements have been led by small elites who built mass-party structures that incorporated the masses without involving them in any way in decision-making processes. The result has been the rise of dictators and authoritarian regimes whenever crises threatened. "To the extent that the new Asian industrial working class is to act as an agent of social chage," Deyo concludes of their success so far, "its power will derive" for the foreseeable future "from its ability to disrupt, provoke, or support external forces, rather than to engage in autonomous social action."

While the role of the state in accumulation and in influencing the labor process is important, however, the labor process itself must not be neglected. Peter Gutkind's chapter in this collection reminds us that struggles over the labor process also took place in the pre-colonial world. His chapter on Ghanian boatmen responds impressively to the call to establish workers' pre-industrial heritage. He finds a long tradition of resistance, with examples of struggles by workers extending "back to the sixteenth century and probably further"—and in doing so shows that the struggles of workers in colonial Africa may be very similar to those of nineteenth-century skilled artisans. "Canoemen engaged in concerted action and protest," Gutkind says, and "labor (and class) consciousness found expression repeatedly in protest and activism." To a remarkable extent, he overcomes the formidable difficulties of working with outside sources in a non-literate society. One reason why Western labor historians have become so interested in artisans, truth be told, is that they were so much more literate than any other section of the working class. Save for the difficulties of getting at the boatmen's history, the story that Gutkind weaves is broadly similar to that discovered within their own countries by Western labor historians—skilled workers possess extraordinary solidarity, exhibit unusual militancy, and influence the formation of the modern labor movement in their country. Could the situation have been explained in their own terms, the silver "chasers" of Meriden would have understood quite well the plight of the canoemen of the Cape Coast.

The Gutkind essay also focuses attention on the relationship between skilled workers and unskilled workers in a way that invites comparative attention. If the recent history of Western labor is being rewritten in order to show the extent to which skilled workers shaped the course of the European and American labor movement, it seems in order to inquire about the role of skilled workers in the former colonies. The canoemen of the Ghana coast were not so very different in many ways from the Mississippi pilots described by Mark Twain; both groups banded together to defend their skilled positions from attack. In comparing the labor movements of advanced capitalist nations and of former colonial nations, perhaps the role of skilled workers needs to be considered more systematically.[13] In some ways, perhaps, the struggle of artisans and highly skilled workers helped create a historically specific context for industrial workers in Western Europe and the United States very different from that in the nations that emerged from colonialism in the twentieth century. In Ghana, the position of the canoemen was undermined decades before the formation of a permanent proletariat. Where industrialization occurred without the presence of large numbers of artisans or highly skilled workers, the political content of workers' struggles might develop very differently.

In summary, in the former colonies as in the advanced capitalist nations, the systematic effort to examine the related processes of capital accumulation and the transformation of the labor process helps historians put their fingers on some vital aspects of the growth and development of the labor movement.

Finally, this collection concludes with a review of experiences in workers' control in recent political experience. The article by James Petras and Rita Carroll-Seguin brings together themes of the two series of essays that have been discussed previously. The issue of workers' control arises naturally from the focus on labor process of the essays by Carsten, Cumbler, and Luedtke. Yet the experiments in workers' control have taken place in countries that have not known advanced capitalism and usually in nations that lacked developed labor movements of skilled workers with a tradition of control over the workplace. Most often, experiments in workers' control were enacted from on high by governments whose ties to the organized working class were quite tenuous; the theme of government intervention in the work process in former colonial countries is a theme of Murray, Deyo, and Gutkind. It is precisely the contradiction between the lack of an organized labor movement and the government support for workers' control in those countries that have experimented with workers' control, that forms the chief theme of the Petras and Carroll-Seguin article. They argue that this contradiction explains the relatively ambiguous record of such experiments.

Petras and Carroll-Seguin review some of the most important experiments in workers' control and argue that, in Algeria, Chile, Bolivia, Peru, and Yugoslavia, attempts to moblize the working classes by bureaucratic fiat or reformist co-optation have been unsuccessful. Most experiments in workers' control have resulted not from workers' initiatives as much as from the efforts of precariously established regimes to co-opt the working classes. In most of the states discussed in this essay self-management was achieved in the midst of unstable social and political as well as economic conditions and found arrayed against it "a class of displaced landlords, capitalists, bankers [and] generals" unsympathetic to new forms of organization and still sufficiently powerful with internal or external forces to threaten its stable development. Such regimes hope to prevent the working classes from playing a more active role in national political life, and they also hope that concessions in this area will spur industrialization by persuading workers to increase productivity without substantial changes in levels of capital investment. These efforts, however, are doomed. For when they are successful, the sphere of workers' control expands, and sooner or later brings workers into conflict with bureaucratic administrators or the national bourgeoisie. Perhaps as alarming for ruling groups, workers' control tends to be most successful in areas where workers are well organized and politically militant and, conversely, successful workers' control tends to increase the strength of militant workers' organizations rather than quieting them. The essay, therefore, focuses on "the transitory nature of co-participation."

In some ways the Yugoslav case is the most interesting of all. In contrast to other countries, the national bourgeoisie had long been expropriated when "workers' control" was instituted, and the Yugoslav Communist party had roots deep within the working class. While important aspects of "workers' control" remain alive there, the Yugoslav case shows that without participation in political decision making at the national level, workers viewed control in an instrumental way and used their new power to benefit regional working-class groups in the short term. Their inability to set long-run goals—which stems from their lack of political power—has as a consequence riveted the workers' focus on immediate benefits of production plans and investment allocation. Without organized democratic participation in national-level politics, local forms of "market socialism" tend to foster competition between municipalities and to divide segments of the working class. "Self-management has served to fragment the working class" say the authors, "and to encourage workers in individual firms to operate like capitalists."

The Petras and Carroll-Seguin essay provides just the right note for concluding our discussion of the essays in our collection. If Deyo reminds us that through strategies of direct intervention in the workplace and systematic co-optation of the workers' movement capitalist economies still may succeed in industrializing at least some smaller nations, the last chapter suggests that any real effort to incorporate workers into the industrialization process is likely to come as a result of workers' protest movements and political organization. Essentially, this essay suggests that every successful reorganization of production by politically able, class-conscious workers may be threatened by the prerogatives of political managers. "Without a successful transformation of the political structure and a comprehensive restructuring of the economy," they say, "worker-controlled enterprises are likely to be undermined." Thus workers' success in such situations depends not only upon the depth but also the breadth of prior artisanal experience. Indeed, Petras and Carroll-Seguin reinforce Luedtke's analysis when they conclude:

> The emergence of a class consciousness directed toward the direct control over the productive process is not an inevitable result of class struggle, but rather the specific outcome of political leadership and organization which is actively committed to this form of social organization.

Without an organized labor movement and without workers' participation in national politics, gains in productivity are not immediately forthcoming from efforts at "workers' control," and they may not come at all. In any event, no form of partial workers' control that limits workers' control to narrow sections of the economy or imposes serious limits on working-class decision making is likely to co-opt the labor movement and render the working classes quiescent. If the age of the "democratic revolution" is over, it is far from certain that the age of "bureaucratic revolution" or "authoritarian rule" is upon us. Indeed, if Petras and Carroll-Seguin are correct, the age of proletarian protest is far from over in many industrializing nations.

The analysis of "workers' control" movements by Petras and Carroll-Seguin also returns us to the question of the relationship between labor process and worker militancy with which we began. The argument of their essay is that if the demand for "workers' control" has any possibilities at all, it can only succeed by taking root in a militant workers' movement. In turn, the rise of workers' militancy may be strongly influenced by the particular methods of accumulation and the kinds of transformation occurring within the labor process.

But we do not return precisely to where we started. The focus on changes in the organization of work in the advanced capitalist nations has provided a whole series of interesting and plausible arguments about the relationship between shop-floor experience and worker militancy. The focus on both capital accumulation and labor process in the less-developed countries also has suggested a number of important reasons why these nations did not follow a Western model. In both sets of nations, the study of the work experience succeeds in locating some key explanations that at least partly contribute to our understanding of labor militancy.

While arguments that tie changes in the labor process to worker militancy seem to have a real explanatory power in the advanced capitalist countries, we also note the relatively larger role that arguments relating the terms of accumulation to popular militancy have played outside the West. But this may not represent a real difference in historical experience. We lament the relative failure of Western labor historians to tie their studies of the formation of the labor force to their studies of changes in the work process. Only recently have Western historians, such as Yves Lequin and John Bodnar, begun to study work process in the context of the processes of capital accumulation that forced workers to migrate to the workplace.[14] We think that such studies have real potential. We also agree with those historians who argue that the world of the workplace does not completely determine the lives and culture of the worker, but neither does it play only a minor role or no role at all. The world of the workplace is only one part of the larger world of work and industry from which the modern proletarian emerged, but it remains a critical part.

While the emphasis on the labor process has been a valuable contribution of labor historians in the advanced capitalist countries, the focus on the conditions of accumulation by labor historians in the less-developed countries contains many important insights. European and American historians can benefit from these studies. Most Irish and Italians came to the United States because of processes of agricultural transformation and the decline of rural industry in their own native lands. The same forces that pushed the Irish and Italians across the sea pushed German and French rural dwellers into the city. Little is known about the operation of these forces and the ways in which these forces intersected with the needs and conditions of capitalist industry. Perhaps a widened definition of what is meant by proletarianization and its relationship to labor process may cast new light on some of the oldest problems of labor history in the advanced capitalist countries.

NOTES

1. John Plamenatz, *German Marxism and Russian Communism* (London: Longmans, 1954), p. 27. For a Marxist response, see G.A. Cohen, *Karl Marx's Theory of History, A Defence* (Princeton, N.J.: Princeton University Press, 1980).

2. For recent explorations of the labor process in America and Western Europe see: Harry Braverman, *Labor and Monopoly Capital: The Degradation of Work in the Twentieth Century* (New York: Monthly Review Press, 1974); Michael Burawoy, *Manufacturing Consent: Changes in the Labor Process under Monopoly Capitalism* (Chicago: University of Chicago Press, 1979); Partick Friedenson, *Histoire des usines Renault*, 2 vols. (Paris: Editions du Seuil, 1972); David M. Gordon, Richard Edwards, and Michael Reich, *Segmented Work, Divided Workers: The Historical Transformation of Labor in the United States* (Cambridge: Cambridge University Press, 1982); Michael P. Hanagan, *The Logic of Solidarity, Artisans and Industrial Workers in Three French Towns, 1871–1914* (Urbana: University of Illinois Press, 1980); James Hinton, *The First Shop Stewards Movement* (London: Allen and Unwin, 1973); Patrick Joyce, *Work, Society, and Politics: The Culture of the Factory in Later Victorian England* (New Brunswick, N.J.: Rutgers University Press, 1980); David Montgomery, *Workers Control in America* (Cambridge: Cambridge University Press, 1979).

3. See, for example, Stanley Aronowitz's discussion in *False Promises; The Shaping of American Working Class Consciousness* (New York: McGraw-Hill, 1973); E.J. Hobsbawm, "Custom, Wages, and Work Load in Nineteenth Century Industry," in *Labouring Men*, ed. E.J. Hobsbawm (New York: Anchor, 1964), pp. 404–435; Bruce Laurie and Mark Schmitz, "Manufacturing and Productivity: The Making of an Industrial Base," in *Philadelphia: Work, Space, Family and Group Experience in the 19th Century*, ed. Theodore Hershberg (Oxford: Oxford University Press, 1981), pp. 43–92; Stephen A. Marglin, "What Do Bosses Do?" *Review of Radical Political Economics* 6:2(1974): 33–60; Bernard Mottez, *Systèmes de salaires et politiques patronales* (Paris: CNRS, 1966); Michelle Perrot, "The Three Ages of Industrial Discipline in Nineteenth-Century France," in *Consciousness and Class Experience in Nineteenth-Century Europe*, ed. John Merriman (New York: Holmes and Meier, 1980), pp. 149–168.

4. See David Montgomery, "Workers' Control of Machine Production in the Nineteenth Century," *Labor History* 17:4(1976): 485–509; E.J. Hobsbawm, "Artisans and Labour Aristocrats," in *Workers: Worlds of Labor*, ed. E.J. Hobsbawm (New York: Pantheon, 1984), pp. 252–272; and Raphael Samuel, "The Work-

shop of the World: Steam Power and Hand Technology in Mid-Victorian Britain," *History Workshop* 3(1977): 6–72.

5. Introductions to recent labor historiography in Europe and in the United States can be found in the following essays: David Brody, "Labor History in the 1970s: Toward a History of the American Worker," in *The Past Before Us, Contemporary Historical Writing in the United States*, ed. Michael Kammen (Ithaca: Cornell University Press, 1980), pp. 252–269; Roger Price, "The Labour Process and Labour History," *Social History* 8, n.1(Jan. 1983): 57–75; William G. Roy, "Class Conflict and Social Change in Historical Perspective," *Annual Review of Sociology* (1984): 483–506; and Charles Tilly, "Reflections on the Revolutions of Paris: An Essay on Recent Historical Writing," *Social Problems* 12(1964):99–121.

6. John Bodnar, *Workers' World: Kinship, Community, and Protest in an Industrial Society, 1900–1940* (Baltimore: Johns Hopkins, 1982), especially his conclusion. "Deeply conservative tendencies pervaded the American working class," Bodnar says; "Clearly, family obligations dominated working-class predilections and exerted a moderating influence on individual expectations and the formulation of social and economic goals" leading to "the predominance of family interests over personal ones." In terms of the work experience "regular employment remained the foundation of the [family] enclave itself"; other factors were present but "ancillary." (p. 166, 177, 185).

7. Colin Greer, ed., *Divided Society: The Ethnic Experience in America* (New York: Basic Books, 1974), pp. 34–35.

8. Some important dependency theorists include: Daniel Chirot, *Social Change in the Twentieth Century* (New York: Harcourt Brace Jovanovich, 1977); Andre Gunder Frank, *Capitalism and Underdevelopment in Latin America: Historical Studies of Chile and Brazil* (New York: Monthly Review Press, 1969); Immanuel Wallerstein, *The Modern World System: The Origins of the European World System in the Sixteenth Century* (New York: Academic, 1974) and his sequel, *The Modern World System II: Mercantilism and the Consolidation of the European World Economy, 1600–1750* (New York: Academic, 1980).

9. Robert Brenner, "The Origins of Capitalist Development: A Critique of Neo-Smithian Marxism," *New Left Review* n. 104(1977): 25–92.

10. Frederick Cooper, "Africa and the World Economy," *African Studies Review* 24, nos. 2–3 (June-Sept. 1981): 1–93, p. 17–18. See also his article, "The Problem of Slavery in African Studies," *Journal of African History*, 20, n. 1 (1979): 103–125.

11. A classic statement on English enclosures is the first chapter of Barrington Moore, *Social Origins of Dictatorship and Democracy: Lord and Peasant in the Making of the Modern World*, (Boston: Beacon, 1966); see also, Robert Brenner's "Agrarian Class Structure and Economic Development in Pre-Industrial Europe," *Past and Present* 70(1976):30–74.

12. E.P. Thompson, *The Making of the English Working Class* (New York: Vintage Books, 1963).

13. Mark Twain, *Life on the Mississippi* (New York: American Library, 1980), pp. 99–109.

14. Yves Lequin, *Les ouvriers de la région Lyonnaise*. 2 vols. (Lyon: Presses Universitaires de Lyon, 1977); Bodnar, *Workers World*, and also, John Bodnar, Roger Simon, and Michael P. Weber, *Lives of Their Own: Blacks, Italians, and Poles in Pittsburgh, 1900–1960* (Urbana: University of Illinois, 1982).

2

Brotherhood and Conflict in Meriden and New Britain, Connecticut, 1890–1920

Oliver Carsten

The Labor Day parade of 1892 in the industrial city of Meriden, Connecticut, was described by a local paper as "a great demonstration in every particular."[1] Almost 2,500 men and women marched and twenty-six local unions participated, the largest being the Buffers and Polishers Assembly of the Knights of Labor. Among the bands providing music for the parade were those of two fraternal organizations, the Turners, a German benefit and gymnastic society, and the Young Men's Total Abstinence and Benefit Society, a predominantly Irish, Catholic organization. That year, and in subsequent years, no Labor Day parade took place in the similar-sized industrial city of New Britain, Connecticut. On Labor Day, 1895, the New Britain local paper reported: "The stores closed at noon, but the factories with one or two exceptions, have been running all day."[2] And New Britain's fraternal society membership was considerably lower than that of Meriden. In New Britain, according to the survey conducted by the Connecticut Bureau of Labor Statistics in 1891, 18.5 percent of the town's population belonged to fraternal societies; in Meriden, 29.1 percent.[3]

This article will attempt to show that the combined strength of unions and fraternal societies in Meriden and their joint weakness in New Britain was more than just fortuitous. In Meriden, fraternal societies and unions were linked in a tight web of solidarities. Off-the-job sociability and on-the-job labor organization sustained each other, each forming a necessary and integral part of the community life of skilled workers. Once one of these twin poles had been destroyed, the other was so sapped that the culture they had sustained collapsed. New Britain, on the other hand, lacked the skilled workers necessary to sustain a high level of fraternalism or of craft unionism. Compared with the workers of Meriden, its workers were comparatively disorganized both on and off the job, and were largely at the mercy of the city's employers.

The study of life in the community, outside the workplace, has clearly been on the agenda of the "new" labor historians. But output in this area has remained relatively small, and there has been a general failure to explore mutual ties between work and sociability. Thus Herbert Gutman has criticized one study for failing to explore fully "the many familial, social and cultural networks of mutuality outside the workplace that sustained collective protest."[4] All too frequently, when they have examined sociability, historians have seen the potential for segmented leisure patterns to lead to divisiveness in the working class, and have ignored the possibility that even leisure pursuits that were somewhat divided along skill and ethnic lines could strengthen workers' ability to act collectively.[5]

There have been relatively few studies of the American working class that throw much light on the relationship between work and sociability. There is, however, one classic sociological study in this area. In *Union Democracy*, Seymour Martin Lipset, Martin A. Trow, and James S. Coleman demonstrate the connection between the leisure activities of the printers in the New York local of the typographical union and their participation in union affairs.[6] The ITU is notable for having a long-standing two-party system in which the two parties are divided along ideological lines and for the regularity with which the incumbent party is turned out of office by the rank and file. It is also notable for the vitality of its occupational community, one characterized both by formal organizations—benevolent organizations, newspapers, social clubs, athletic teams, and lodges—and by informal networks.

The authors of *Union Democracy* conclude that there is something in the nature of the printers' work that makes them prefer to socialize with fellow members of their craft. Among other factors, they single out the high status of printing relative to other working-class jobs, the value the printers attach to their craft, and the freedom from supervision on the job, which allows printers to socialize in the shops.[7] They also point to the influence on the printers' union of this tendency to socialize with each other; "The independent printers' organizations clearly work counter to the structural mechanisms which Michels identified as inherent in large organizations and on which he based his iron law [of oligarchy]."[8]

Although Lipset, Trow, and Coleman do not say so explicitly, one might well conclude that not only was sociability reinforced by the craft nature of the job and democracy in the union protected by sociability, but that the strength of the union itself and thereby the workers' ability to act collectively against their employers was increased by their socializing with each other. It is also likely that, within the context of a larger community (e.g., a city), wider solidarities with other workers could be established and strengthened through shared leisure-time pursuits. Thus solidarity need not be limited to a single craft but could embrace all crafts in a common sense of self-esteem or even all workers in a sense of common interest. It is argued here that, in one community at least, leisure-time institutions were not a mere appendage to the lives of skilled craft workers, but served rather to maintain a particular way of life.

Meriden was a moderate-sized industrial city with a population in 1900 of 24,296. Its main product was silverplate and silverware, both flatware (knives, forks, etc.) and holloware (bowls, teapots, etc.). This industry, which had developed early in the nineteenth century, demanded a high degree of skill of its workers. Such crafts as grinding, buffing, polishing, and chasing (i.e. ornamentation with small steel tools and a hammer to raise and indent the surface) were all part of the manufacturing process. All the crafts required an apprenticeship of several years, and few who had not completed an apprenticeship could find work. In many cases, sons followed fathers in their craft for several generations.[9] Observers of the Meriden work force repeatedly noted its high degree of skill. One visitor to a plant of the Meriden Britannia Company in 1887 reported that "the workmen appeared to be of a higher grade than those in most of our large factories." In 1899, Samuel Dodd, president of the International Silver Company, when asked what proportion of his men were skilled, replied: "I should say 90 percent."[10]

The most detailed investigation of Meriden was that carried out for the United States Immigration Commission in 1909. In the report that resulted, Meriden was referred to as "Representative Community B."[11] Again and again the report referred to the high level of skill of Meriden's workers. The following extract is typical:

> Over one-third of the city's industrial output consists of plated silverware and britannia ware. In those industries men of the highest skill are employed, and the average wages paid are the highest paid in any skilled industrial employment in the United States.... The various occupations in almost all industries in the community require men of experience and skill, and those who apply for work having no trade stand little chance of finding employment.... For example, in the silverware industry a man who applies for work, applies for employment in a certain occupation, as buffer, polisher, and engraver. If he has not completed his apprenticeship he is seldom given employment. The same conditions are found in the majority of industries in the community.[12]

The demand for craft labor and the high wage rates in Meriden proved attractive to those who acquired training in metal production and finishing in their native countries. Such immigrants came, in particular, from the British Isles and from Germany. Similarly, French Canadians, many of whom migrated to Meriden not directly from Canada but from other cities in New England, concentrated in one trade, burnishing, and passed their skill down from father to son.[13]

And just as Meriden was noted for the skill of its workers, so, by the 1890s, was it for its workers' strong unionism. The continuous existence of labor organizations in Meriden began in 1886 when a Knights of Labor assembly was organized in South Meriden (presumably for the workers at the Meriden Cutlery plant) in addition to the Mechanics Assembly in Meriden proper. Membership grew rapidly, and in September of that year at least one plant closed down for the Knights of Labor picnic on the first Tuesday in September, when 600 people went on an excursion to Mystic Island.[14]

By 1887 the city directory listed no less than six assemblies: the original Mechanics Assembly; the Cutlers and Grinders Assembly in South Meriden; a Metal Workers Assembly; a Brass Molders Assembly; a Metal Burnishers Assembly; and a Buffers and Polishers Assembly. There was, in addition, a Central Trades and Labor Union affiliated with the Knights.[15] With the nationwide decline of the Knights, some of these organizations died out, but others persisted to become the backbone of Meriden's labor strength in the 1890s. By the time the United States Immigration Commission surveyed Meriden in 1909, 24.8 percent of adult male wage earners were union members. The figures for native-born and foreign-born were not much different. In the survey households, 23.2 percent of the foreign-born were reported to be union members, 29.1 percent of the native-born of foreign fathers, and 30.0 percent of the native-born of native fathers.[16] The unions had no trouble assimilating the highly skilled immigrants who came to Meriden.

The power of organized labor in Meriden was given special recognition during Meriden's centennial celebration in 1906. A day was set aside to honor the workers of Meriden and their unions, and it was called "Labor Day." There was a parade, featuring floats from the various unions, followed by a picnic that featured addresses by the mayor, the president of the State Federation of Labor, etc.[17] The souvenir of the event boasted:

> Meriden has for over twenty years been considered one of the strongest labor union cities in Connecticut, and the organizations were never on a more solid basis or more widely distributed among the workingmen of various crafts than at the present time.[18]

But unions were not the only significant working-class organizations in Meriden, or indeed in other American cities. Fraternal societies had generally preceded unions, had far greater membership, and had sometimes a greater influence on the day-to-day life of workers. The earliest American fraternal societies were copies of British friendly societies. In fact, they were more than just copies, for they were actual branches of

British societies, formed by immigrant English artisans. The first such branch, of the Independent Order of Odd Fellows, Manchester Unity, was instituted in Baltimore in 1819.[19] By 1842, with membership close to 30,000, the American Odd Fellows felt strong enough to secede from the parent organization.[20] Numerous other organizations followed, and in spite of occasional lean periods during depressions or as the result of attacks on secret societies, membership generally grew steadily.

The attraction of the societies lay, on the surface, in their provision of sick benefits to workers for whom sickness could mean financial ruin and of funeral benefits to those for whom a pauper's funeral was the ultimate indignity. But the societies offered more than just benefits, coupled with the conviviality of the lodge room and the mysteries of a secret ritual. They fit the needs of workers at various levels. A travelling worker, seeking employment, was provided with a warm welcome:

> In a strange place he is no longer a stranger. Employment is produced, for with friends it is easily had; or otherwise, his purse is replenished, and he is aided on his way, and from place to place he has a like passport, until employment is found. If he is sick and unable to go to his brethren, they go to him; he is tenderly nursed . . . should death be his lot, his remains are decently buried, and his brothers at home, and through them his relatives, are informed of his fate.[21]

The society could act as employment bureau or as wefare organization. It could provide an instant network of friends to one far from home and it could give the member self-esteem through admittance to a secret society. No single explanation can account for the popularity of these organizations. They flourished because they meshed so well with working-class society.

By the end of the nineteenth century there were thousands of fraternal societies: they ranged from large orders, each of which had several hundred affiliated lodges, to small local societies; from temperance societies to societies that ran a bar; from nativist societies to socialist societies; from athletic societies to musical societies. One of the largest groups served was immigrants, and although these sometimes joined foreign-language lodges affiliated to such orders as the Odd Fellows, they tended more often to form their own ethnic societies.

To both immigrant and native, the fraternal society offered the possibility of establishing one's own "village" within the city. It could be an ethnic village, a class village, a village limited to a particular trade or particular religion. But whatever the group, the artificial village could offer an island of acquaintanceship in a sea of anonymity. This was particularly attractive to first-generation immigrants to industrial America, whether native or foreign, and to those who, remaining in one place, found their small town life swamped by industrial growth.

In Meriden, the fraternal societies found a particularly fertile field. Thirty-two percent of the city's population in 1890 was foreign-born.[22] And its skilled craft workers, scattered among the city's many plants, but provided with a sense of common interest and common status by virtue of their shared knowledge of a craft, required an institution where they could relax at lunchtime or after work, where they could meet with other, similar workers, and where they could perhaps share information on employment opportunities or on threats to the union.

For Meriden, the period between 1890 and 1905 might be called the golden age of the working-class community. The skill of the city's artisans, the strength of their unions, and the sociability typified by the fraternal societies they joined in droves, all reinforced one another to build a proud and vibrant culture. By 1900, Meriden had some 78 fraternal benefit societies. Out of 64 societies for which an analysis could be made, 53 could be identified as working-class.[23] In 1900 the city had 3.3 fraternal societies for each 1,000 inhabitants, and they came in every form. They included: nine Odd Fellows' organizations and the same number of Foresters' lodges; three lodges of the Knights of Columbus; two of the Knights of Pythias; and a host of other societies of every conceivable type, ranging from the Young Men's Total Abstinence and Benefit Society to the Windhorst Benevolent Society of German Roman Catholics, and from the Union des Ouvriers Canadiens to the Wilcox Silver Plate Sick and Funeral Aid Society.

New Britain presents in many ways the obverse of Meriden. Of similar size, with a population in 1900 of 25,998, it too was dominated by a single industry, in this case the hardware industry. But, whereas Meriden's silver industry required a high degree of skill of its workers, New Britain's hardware companies such as Russell & Erwin or the Stanley Works had an almost insatiable demand for unskilled labor, mainly from eastern Europe. The United States Immigration Commission reported on New Britain as "Representative Community C," and described its labor market as follows:

> The introduction of machinery, with its attendant opportunity to make use of low-priced labor, has made the employment of the immigrant not only possible but highly profitable.... In the case of all the races the opportunity for steady employment offered by the factories was the principal cause for their coming. The factories have desired immigrant labor and have gone in search of it.... Most of the immigrants have entered the lower, more unskilled occupations where the lowest wages were paid.[24]

The report noted that wages were "not sufficient to tempt the American workman."[25]

As one might expect this workforce of unskilled and semi-skilled workers, mainly immigrants, was unable to sustain any significant unionism. The United States Immigration Commission reported:

> The trade unions have little hold there; those listed are chiefly concerned with men who work outside of the factories, and it is within the factories that the majority of the city's working population is found. The factories do not welcome the labor unions; all of the more important industrial plants are "open shops," in which unions exert little influence. The attitude of the races employed in the factories appears to be largely one of indifference toward the labor unions.[26]

In the survey households, only 2.9 percent of wage-earning adult males reported that they belonged to a union, as compared to 24.8 percent in Meriden. This 2.9 percent was made up of 1.3 percent among the native-born of native fathers, 5.9 percent among the native-born of foreign fathers, and 2.8 percent among the foreign born.[27] Union membership was minuscule.

Fraternal society membership was considerably larger. In 1890, New Britain had 37 fraternal societies listed in the city directory, or 2.2 for every thousand inhabitants, and in 1891 some 18.5 percent of the town's inhabitants were fraternal society members.[28] But this not inconsiderable membership cannot be attributed to any thriving artisanal culture in New Britain. Instead, it is apparently the result of the influx of immigrants. The number of foreign-born was 5,753 or 34.8 percent in 1890, and 18,030 or 41.1 percent in 1910.[29]

After 1890 it was the "new immigrants" who flocked to New Britain—Jews, Italians, Lithuanians, and above all, Poles. Later, when the Polish tide had become a flood, a Polish neighborhood with its own main street, Broad Street, was established on the north side of town. The neighborhood survives to this day.

Polish immigration reached its peak during the decade from 1895 to 1905.[30] And the newly arrived immigrants did not take long to establish their own fraternal societies to provide themselves with a place for relaxation and a source of support in times of need.[31] Yet the existence of these societies was not enough to counteract the general weakness of working-class organizations in New Britain. They did not fit into a web of solidarity as in Meriden. Indeed, they may have reinforced schisms in the working class, because they solidified splits between skilled and unskilled, and between native and old immigrants on the one hand and new immigrants and the various other ethnicities on the other.

The existence of ethnic fraternal societies did not necessarily mean that the working class of a particular community was divided and incapable of united action. In Meriden, and in New Britain before the arrival of the "new immigrant," ethnic lodges were integrated with nonethnic lodges. German or French-Canadian branches of the Odd Fellows and Foresters existed right alongside the non-ethnic branches. And even if there were also societies that were exclusive to one ethnic group, the members of such a lodge were likely to be Odd Fellows or Foresters in addition. Thus workers could maintain pride in their ethnic origin and yet be aware of their common interests with Yankee workers or those of British ancestry.[32] The societies of the Polish or Lithuanian immigrants to New Britain, however, were not branches of trans-ethnic organizations. If they were branches of anything, they were of national Polish or Lithuanian societies, so that the allegiance to the ethnic group was reinforced without any counterbalancing tie to class.

Thus, in Meriden, there was a correspondence between high fraternal society membership and a high degree of organization and militancy in the workforce. In New Britain, fraternal society membership was substantially lower and more split along ethnic lines, and unionism was almost non-existent. If we were to extrapolate, we might expect to find this correlation between strong fraternal societies and strong unionism on a more general basis. Unfortunately, for Connecticut at least, reliable figures on union membership in each town or city are not available. However, we can examine part of the argument using a much larger sample of communities. The large number of such societies in Connecticut and their popularity among workers was sufficient to attract the interest of the state Bureau of Labor Statistics. The bureau conducted a major investigation of these organizations in 1891, surveying every corner of the state.[33] This study can be used to verify our earlier hypotheses—that communities with a highly skilled workforce and communities with a large immigrant population should have a high membership in fraternal societies.

For this purpose, a statistical analysis of factors predicting the size of membership in fraternal societies was carried out. Because the bureau study itself does not offer much information on factors that would predict high or low membership in fraternal societies, a number of variables were taken from the federal census. The analysis was carried out at the town level. The dependent variable was the proportion of each town's population that belonged to fraternal societies (unions that offered benefits were excluded).[34] The survey provided the membership in fraternal societies for 92 Connecticut towns; the population of each town was obtained from the 1890 census. It should be remembered that a "town" in Connecticut is a geographic entity, a subdivision of a county.

To test the hypothesis that communities with large immigrant populations would have more fraternal societies, because of the wish to create a kind of ethnic village, several variables to indicate both immigrants and native-born of foreign parents were taken from the 1890 census. These figures were, however, available in some cases only for cities rather than towns. Therefore in these cases, the population of the city, rather than the town, was used in calculating the proportion of immigrants in the population. The information was available for 63 communities.

A variable to indicate the proportion of skilled workers in each town was also required, to test the hypothesis that societies would be more prevalent in communities with a higher proportion of skilled workers. The 1890 census did not offer any indicator of the proportion of skilled workers by cities and towns. The 1900 census did, however, in the form of the total wage bill for male wage-earners and the average number of wage-earners. These figures were available for 58 cities and towns in Connecticut, as were similar figures for female wage-earners. Thus an average wage could be calculated for males, females, or both and this was used as a substitute for the relative skill of the workforce.[35]

The method of analysis selected was least squares regression: there were sufficient cases (55 towns had no missing data in any variable), the data was interval in nature, and a multivariate model could be developed. Sample variance was not a problem as numbers came not from a sample but from various censuses (the 1891 survey was a census of societies). First bivariate models were developed, and subsequently the independent variables that performed best were entered into various multivariate models.

None of the bivariate equations succeeded in predicting the proportion of each town's population in fraternal societies very well. Among the variables indicating the proportion of immigrants in the population, the best predictor was the proportion of foreign-born males plus native males of foreign-born parents which explained 19.2 percent of the variance (i.e., the R^2 was 0.192) in the population belonging to fraternal societies. Among the indicators of average wage (and so skill) the best predictor was the average wage of all adult workers, male and female, which explained 15.5 percent of the variance.

The development of the multivariate models is summarized in table 2.1. The variables that were added in the refining of the model were a dummy variable for population size, distinguishing between towns with a population of under 10,000 and those with a population of 10,000 or greater, and an interaction term between the dummy for population and the wage variable. The dummy for town size was introduced because it was believed that there might be a tendency for smaller communities to have a smaller proportion of their population as members of fraternal societies: they might not need smaller networks of sociability than the community as a whole. The actual size of a town's population was also tested as predictor, but it did not perform well.

The final model for all the towns, using all four independent variables, had an R^2 of 38.1. That almost 40 percent of the variance in fraternal society membership can be explained by the number of immigrant males and sons of immigrants, by the average wage for adults, by population

Table 2.1 Summary of Equations

Number of Cases	Coefficients: Foreign-Born	Wage	Interaction	Dummy	R^2
All Towns					
63	.489*				.192
58		.000523*			.155
55	.547*	.000621*			.335
55	.459*#	.439*#			.335
55	.477*	.000533*		.0403	.378
55	.460*	.000495*	.000221	.0638	.381
Large Towns					
21	.546*	.000853*			.549
21	.573*	.000636*		.0456	.610
21	.558*	.000547*	.000132	.0126	.612
Small Towns					
34	.441*	.000471*			.193

*Coefficient is more than twice its standard error.

#Coefficients from a standardized regression.

size, and by an interaction term between population size and average wage is satisfactory. The original hypothesis—that society membership increases with the skill level of the community and with the number of immigrants—would seem to be confirmed. A standardized regression run on the two main variables alone indicated that both wage rate and the immigrant male and son of immigrant variable had roughly equal strengths as predictors. The beta weight for wage rate was 0.439 while that for the immigrant variable was 0.459.

Analysis of the residuals from the previous equations indicated that they were larger for the smaller communities (i.e., the equations were performing better for the larger communities). It was therefore decided to carry out the analysis for large communities only. Various splits between small and large were tried. The most satisfactory turned out to be limiting the analysis to towns with a population greater than 7,000. The results of limiting the cases to larger communities were gratifying.

Each of the models showed a major increase in explanatory power. Inclusion of the interaction term, however, made little difference in predictive power. Without the interaction term R^2 was 61.0 percent; with it R^2 was 61.2 percent.

Also displayed in table 2.1 are the results of the runs for the smaller towns (those with a population of under 7,000) alone. Neither the dummy variable nor the interaction term could be used as all these towns had the same value for the dummy. The best model for these communities, with two independent variables, explained only 19.2 percent of the variance. Finally it should be noted that the variables for foreign-born and average wage, shown in table 2.1, met the test of significance at the .05 level throughout, and that their coefficients were relatively stable.

Thus for the larger towns, those with a population greater than 7,000, the final two equations show great predictive power, explaining over 60 percent of the variance. It seems safe to conclude that in these communities average wage and the number of immigrants have a strong effect on the proportion of the population joining fraternal societies. As for the small towns, it may well be that there is no consistent pattern at all; such random factors as a group of hard-working society officers may matter more in a community where one successful society could make a dramatic difference in fraternal society membership. In addition, no particular immigrant group may have reached the critical mass necessary for forming a society. In the larger communities, however, the skill of the workforce (in the form of wage level) and immigrant population size had a strong impact on the number in the population that belonged to fraternal societies.

The statistical analysis confirms, then, that fraternal societies were stronger in communities where a large immigrant population coincided with a highly skilled workforce. In Meriden, where both factors had a strong impact, the fraternal societies were notable for both their strength and their diversity. And, as we have seen, unionism was equally strong and appears to have been reinforced by the solidarities developed in the fraternal societies. Native and immigrant, Catholic and Protestant, were able to act together in defense of their way of life. But that way of life was not permanent. The Meriden of 1940 would in many ways have been unrecognizable to someone accustomed to the rich working-class culture of 1890 or 1900. There had been no fundamental change in the kinds of manufacturing or in the methods of production. But, in 1940, Meriden was virtually an open-shop city. Unions had been driven from the city's manufacturing enterprises in the silver industry and had been unable to regain a foothold during the Congress of Industrial Organizations' (CIO) organizing drive of the 1930s, even while unions made significant gains in Connecticut cities with no history of labor strength. Meriden's fraternal societies were in similar disarray. Their peak strength had been reached in 1900, when Meriden had roughly 3.3 fraternal societies for every 1,000 inhabitants. By 1920, a slight decline had reduced that number to 3.0. Thereafter their decline was precipitous: to 1.8 societies per thousand inhabitants in 1930, and to 1.6 in 1940.[36] In 20 years they had apparently lost almost half their number, and the actual drop may have been even greater. Such societies tend to persist on paper long after they have been sapped of all vitality.

The explanation for the change in Meriden's working-class culture, namely the transformation of Meriden into a city with a disorganized labor force and weak fraternal societies, is to be found in an altered relationship between workers and employers. The story of management attacks on the autonomy and skill of craft workers is by now somewhat familiar. The struggle in Meriden, however, was distinguished both by the fact that the actual work performed by the craft workers remained essentially unchanged and by the bitterness of the contest between management and workers.

The potential for a decisive change in the relationship between Meriden's workers and employers existed from 1898. In that year, the balance of power between the two was significantly altered with the formation of the International Silver Company, merging the Meriden Britannia Company and a number of other leading firms in the industry. This merger gave Meriden's main employer far greater resources in dealing with recalcitrant employees. Now, if there were trouble, the new trust, which controlled 55 to 60 percent of the silverplate market, could switch production elsewhere—to Bridgeport, Waterbury, or even to Canada.

Emboldened by their new strength, the employers of Meriden began to whittle away at the autonomy of their skilled workers. These workers had been accustomed to a situation in which they had a great deal of control over the methods of work, over the hours of labor, and even (through their union) over hiring and firing. But the corporations now began a campaign to assert the "rights" of management, or rather to establish management control of workers.

Over the next 20 years, in a process that Harry Braverman calls the "separation of hand and brain,"[37] the craft workers of Meriden were turned from artisans who exercised considerable control over production into skilled workers, who although they continued to employ many of the same handicraft techniques as before, had lost control of production to corporate management.[38] This transformation was not complete until 1919, and may be divided into two main stages. First, management asserted control over hiring and firing, placing restrictions on the power of the unions. Second, management asserted control over the organization of production. Both stages in the aggrandizement of management control were hotly contested by the workers.

The preliminary skirmish occurred in 1903. In August, 50 buffers at

Factory H, International Silver Company, walked off the job because a fellow employee had refused to join the union. The local newspaper reported: "The entire factory is unionized almost to a man."[39] The Polishers and Buffers Union had been attempting for some time to get the worker concerned to join, but he repeatedly refused. "The by-laws of the union do not allow of the men working with a non-union man. . . . "[40] When the men complained to the superintendent of the plant, he immediately laid off the worker in question. However, three days later the man was ordered to return to work by the president of the division, and the union men walked out.[41] Nine days later they returned to work without securing the agreement of the corporation to fire the non-union worker. The latter was kept on and, according to the superintendent, "would not be discharged because he did not belong to the union."[42]

Having won the first victory and secured control over hiring , International Silver went one step further two months later. Once again, the battlefield was the buffing shop at Factory H. In October 1903, the company discharged a union man. The union charged the man was fired for being too forceful in presenting the union point of view and ten rag-wheel buffers walked out.[43] The plant manager's reply was that "he had a right to discharge him if he saw fit."[44] The reaction of the union was to call out on strike, on November 10, the other workers and apprentices who belonged to the Metal Polishers and Buffers. The company, however, was able to resume production by importing about a hundred strikebreakers, many of them apparently from another company factory in Bridgeport, which was non-union.[45] In spite of community support for the strikers, evidenced by the refusal of many store owners to sell provisions to the strikebreakers, International refused to submit the matter to arbitration. The company president declared: "We reserve the right to hire and discharge our own employes without submitting such questions to outside parties."[46]

The various craft unions at International Silver, all affiliated to the parent Metal and Brass Workers Union, now made a fateful decision. They decided not to join the metal polishers in a general strike.[47] The strikers stayed out for several more months, but they had little power left to enforce their terms. The company was able to continue using the strikebreakers and in any case, with all its plants running, it had sufficient flexibility to transfer production elsewhere, even within Meriden. On April 5, 1904, the union called off the strike. International Silver agreed to put the men back to work at Factory H and at other company plants "as fast as they were needed."[48] However, from now on, Factory H was to be an open shop; the company promised not to discriminate against union members in hiring, but this can have been little consolation to the union members who had traditionally been able to enforce a union shop.[49]

The decisive battle in the second stage of the extension of management rights—the control over production—opened in 1915. In October of that year the silver workers at International Silver went on strike. On the surface, wages and hours of work were the issues precipitating the strike—the workers demanded a 50 hour week, time and a half for overtime, a 20 percent wage increase, a minimum of $8.00 a week for women, and the recognition of lathe work by a women as a "trade."[50] However the strike was in fact precipitated by International's use of scientific management techniques. The owner of a small local cut glass concern wrote an article for the local paper that attempted to give the worker's point of view. He blamed the strike on the speed-up caused by the introduction of "efficiency experts":

> The screws were put on here, there and everywhere. Everything was sacrificed to speed. Foremen were removed and so-called speed-producers replaced them. A system of espionage was introduced. All this was given a name—it was called modern methods. The workmen say it should be called school-room methods.
>
> The personal touch under which these factories prospered ceased to exist. A sheet of paper and many tags took the place of personal touch.[51]

The company clearly intended to end the traditional autonomy of the artisan. In Meriden no new machinery was introduced and no radical change in production methods suggested. Instead, the company set out to study the technique of the craft worker and to apply that study to the setting of production goals. The company planned to make the pace of work a matter for management control and management decision. Scientific management offered an opportunity to break the workers' control of their jobs, to replace the independent-minded artisanal worker with obedient skilled workers who would take their cues from management.

The silver workers were well aware that they faced a decisive challenge to their traditional way of life. With 1915 a recession year, they knew they had to defend themselves with far greater unity than before. So, to supersede their old craft unions, they decided to form an industrial union. This they termed "one big union" in the language of the Industrial Workers of the World (IWW).[52]

On October 4, when the company rejected the demands of the workers, about 3,500 employees of International Silver walked out. The silver workers were joined by the members of the Flint Glass Workers Union and, two days later, by the machinists at International Silver.[53] By November, four International plants outside Meriden had joined the strike.[54] However, this left the factories in Bridgeport, Derby, Lyons, New York, and Toronto still in operation. The parent union was unwilling to call a general strike at all the company's factories: "Officers of the local union say that so long as they are assured that work from the Meriden factories is not being shipped to factories outside the city, a general strike will not be advisable."[55]

The community rallied round the strikers. Meat markets offered price cuts for them, one of the local movie theaters was used without charge for union meetings, liquor dealers gave "supplies" for benefit picnics.[56] Not all such donations may have been voluntary; at one strike meeting "the names of merchants who are believed to be unfair to the strikers were read."[57] But many of the donations of time and money clearly were given willingly. A benefit picnic held in mid-October raised some $3,000. A barber gave free haircuts and shaves to strikers (for one day only). And an all-star baseball team, including at least three professional players, played a benefit game against a local team on behalf of the strikers. Two of the all-stars hailed from Meriden and presumably still felt ties to the workers of that city.[58]

The fraternal societies, in particular, extended a hand to the strikers. In Wallingford, Court Samuel Simpson of the Foresters donated one day's proceeds from its bazaar, and the Young Men's Total Abstinence and Benefit Society turned over half the profits from a minstrel show dance. In Meriden, the Moose organized another benefit minstrel show and set up a special relief committee to help out those members who were on strike. Later, when the strike began to falter, the names of scabs were circulated in fraternal organizations.[59]

Yet in spite of all the outside support, the company proved stronger than the strikers. In December 1915, a Bridgeport paper reported: "The conditions in Meriden are deplorable, according to persons interested in the strikers. Six thousand persons are affected by the strike and in many homes, not only will there be an absence of what other Christmases have brought, but suffering and hunger will be visitors."[60] In January 1916, the company obtained an injunction to restrict picketing.[61] Craft workers were being replaced with out-of-town scabs and unskilled workers were being driven back by hunger. Early in January, the company began advertising for skilled male workers in the various crafts and for female burnishers and packers.[62] By the end of the month, mention of the strike had disappeared from the columns of the local newspaper.

The strike was effectively over. Craft workers had left town to find work in other silver plants and the unskilled were back at work. But the strike was not officially declared off until January 2, 1919—three and a half years after it had begun. On that day, a meeting of three hundred strikers accepted the company's terms which amounted to total victory for the corporation—a ten-hour day and no discrimination against former employees. The company had set up a "service reward system." This allowed "all who work full time that their departments work each week, five per cent extra as a service reward, and in addition to this weekly service reward, we have an annual service reward, as explained in our booklet on service reward system."[63] This system was clearly designed to ensure an obedient labor force. In addition, the company announced its plan to establish a system of welfare capitalism: "Believing that a closer relationship between employers and employees is desirable, we have had in process for some time the formation and construction of a mutual welfare plan which we hope will be in operation during the year 1919."[64]

Meriden's silver unions were smashed. Also destroyed was the old artisanal culture which was dependent on the pride and independence of the worker. The fraternal societies of Meriden had not received a death blow, but they had entered a period of long and lingering decline. The memory of the strike was strong enough to inhibit union organizing for over 50 years and the workers entered on a period in which the institutions of company paternalism supplanted not only their old unions but also, in large part, their independent leisure-time institutions. Once the workers' craft autonomy had been undermined, then the fraternal societies no longer had the same function to perform. Instead of being a central part of a lifestyle in which they had extended work-based solidarities beyond the workplace, they were now adjuncts to a worker's life. As mere places of recreation without any centrality, they had to compete with all the other entertainments offered by twentieth-century mass culture. During the union upsurge of the 1930s the CIO unions were unable to gain a foothold in Meriden. In New Britain, however, they swept all before them. But this new unionism was very different from the old: it did not depend on the solidarity and sociability of craft workers.

NOTES

1. *Meriden Journal*, September, 5, 1892.

2. *New Britain Record*, September 2, 1895.

3. The precentage is obtained by subtracting from the total membership in benefit societies that in trade unions offering benefits. The resulting number is then divided by the population of the town from the 1890 census. The report is published as: "Fraternal Mutual Benefit Societies," State of Connecticut Bureau of Labor Statistics (hereafter Conn. BLS), *Seventh Annual Report* (Hartford, 1892), vol. 1, pp. 61–770; and vol. 2, pp. 771–1510.

4. Review of Alan Dawley, *Class and Community*, in *New York Times Book Review*, June 12, 1977. Similar criticisms might be made of the work of David Montgomery, which tends to see the workplace as an arena in which workers and employers struggle for control uninfluenced by relationships formed and maintained off the job. One pioneering interpretation of class behavior in terms of "daily class experience" both on and off the job is John Alt, "Beyond Class: The Decline of Industrial Labor and Leisure," *Telos*, no. 28 (Summer 1976), pp. 55–80.

5. The work of David Brody might be offered as an example of this tendency.

6. Seymour Martin Lipset, Martin A. Trow, and James S. Coleman, *Union Democracy: The Internal Politics of the International Typographical Union* (Glencoe, Ill., 1956).

7. Ibid., pp. 106–159.

8. Ibid., p. 105.

9. U.S. Immigration Commission, *Immigrants in Industries: Reports* (Washington, D.C., 1907–10), part 21: "Diversified Industries," vol. 1, pp. 158–159.

10. "A Chapter in the History of American Silver-Plated Ware," *Jeweler's Weekly*, July 27, 1887, p. 84; U.S. Industrial Commission, *Reports*, vol. 1, p. 1057.

11. U.S. Immigration Commission, *Immigrants*, part 21, vol. 1, pp. 123–207.

12. Ibid., pp. 157–159.

13. Ibid., pp. 131–132, 158.

14. *Meriden Republican*, January 30, 1886; September 7, 1886.

15. *Meriden Directory: 1887*, p. 275.

16. U.S. Immigration Commission, *Immigrants*, part 21, vol. 1, pp. 156–157.

17. *Centennial of Meriden, June 10–16, 1906: Report of the Proceedings* (Meriden, 1906), pp. 163–167.

18. Ibid., pp. 169–170.

19. Albert C. Stevens, *The Cyclopaedia of Fraternities*, 2nd. ed. (New York, 1907), pp. 256–257. One American society, the Improved Order of Red Men, later claimed to have an ancestry that was older than the first U.S. Odd Fellows lodge. It asserted that it was directly descended from the Sons of Liberty, of the American Revolution, through the St. Tamina or Tammany Societies. See Charles H. Litchman, ed., *Official History of the Improved Order of Red Men* (Boston, 1893), pp. 158–253. However, Litchman produced no firm evidence of the existence of the order prior to 1833 or 1834.

20. Stevens, *Cyclopaedia of Fraternities*, pp. 257–258.

21. C.N. Hickock, *Odd Fellowship: An Address Delivered at Bedford, Pa., April 26, 1859, The Fortieth Anniversary of the I.O. of O.F. in the United States* (New York, 1859), pp. 11–13.

22. U.S. Census Office, *Eleventh Census (1890)*, vol 1: *Population*, part 1, pp. 81, 453.

23. Where possible, the occupations of the officers were confirmed in the City Directory. Any society, for which half or more of the officers had working-class occupations, was counted as a predominantly working-class society.

24. United States Immigration Commission, *Immigrants*, part 21, vol. 1, p. 257.

25. Ibid., p. 218.

26. Ibid., pp. 259–260.

27. Ibid., p. 260.

28. *New Britain Directory*, 1890; Conn. BLS', *Seventh Annual Report* (1892).

29. U.S. Census, 1890 and 1910.

30. U.S. Immigration Commission, *Immigrants*, part 21, vol. 1, p. 224.

31. Some of the Polish fraternal societies, religious and otherwise, are described in Daniel S. Buczek, *Immigrant Pastor: The Life of the Right Reverend Monsignor Lucyan Bojnowski of New Britain, Connecticut* (Waterbury, Conn., 1974), pp. 12–20. See also S.J. Grohoski, "The Triangle: Polish Colony [of New Britain]," part 2 (January 9, 1940), pp. 16–19, in U.S. Work Projects Administration

Connecticut Papers (Connecticut State Library), Box 129: Ethnic Groups Survey; and Stan Dabkowski, "Poles of New Britain: Polish Organizations of the Sacred Heart Church" (December 14, 1939), p. 5, in WPA Conn. Papers, Box 130: Ethnic Group Survey.

32. Oliver Carsten, "Work and the Lodge: Working-Class Sociability in Meriden and New Britain, Connecticut, 1850–1940," Ph.D. dissertation, The University of Michigan, 1981, pp. 112–117.

33. Conn. BLS, *Seventh Annual Report* (1892).

34. It might have been desirable to test the proportion of a town's adult population belonging to fraternal societies, or even the proportion of a town's adult male population as the dependent variable. However, the 1890 census does not provide any breakdown of Connecticut towns beyond total population.

35. There is by now an extensive historical literature on the study of occupation, with a special emphasis on social mobility. Most of this work has used manuscript census and other data at the individual or household level. At this disaggregated level, there is little information for the United States on income, as the income tax was first levied in 1913 (except for a brief period from 1864 to 1872). Several of these studies have looked at the relationship of *wealth* to occupation. See, for example, Michael B. Katz, "Occupational Classification in History," *Journal of Interdisciplinary History* 3:1 (Summer 1972), pp. 63–88; and Clyde Griffen, "Occupational Mobility in Nineteenth-Century America: Problems and Possibilities," *Journal of Social History* 5:3 (Spring 1972), pp. 310–330. Unfortunately, the relationship between skill and income or prevailing wage rates at the aggregate level is relatively unexplored.

36. *Meriden Directory*. The decline in fraternal society membership was national in scope, although Meriden's was particularly steep. It seems likely that elsewhere too the decline of fraternalism was tied to the destruction of the artisanal way of life. Another factor was the reduced volume of immigration after 1924.

37. Harry Braverman, *Labor and Monopoly Capital: The Degradation of Work in the Twentieth Century* (New York, 1974), p. 126.

38. This distinction between "artisans" and "skilled workers" is somewhat analogous to that made by Shorter and Tilly between the "craft survivors of industrialization," who maintained both skill and autonomy, and the "threatened crafts," whose prerogatives came under attack from management. See Edward Shorter and Charles Tilly, *Strikes in France, 1830–1968* (London, 1974), pp. 216–217. My "skilled workers" are comparable to the "threatened crafts" that lost the battle over control without being deskilled.

39. *Meriden Record*, August 22, 1903.

40. Ibid.

41. Ibid.

42. *Meriden Journal*, August 31, 1903.

43. *Meriden Journal*, November 2, 1903.

44. *Meriden Journal*, November 5, 1903.

45. *Meriden Journal*, November 10, 1903 and November 18, 1903.

46. *Meriden Journal*, November 17, 1903 and November 21, 1903.

47. *Meriden Record*, November 23, 1903.

48. *Meriden Record*, April 6, 1904.

49. *Meriden Journal*, March 30, 1904 and April 5, 1904; Conn. BLS, *Twentieth Annual Report* (1904), pp. 395–397.

50. *Meriden Record*, October 4, 1915

51. *Meriden Record*, October 29, 1915. The writer of the article, James D. Bergen, was the owner of the J.D. Bergen Company, one of the small cut glass concerns in Meriden. See Albert Christian Revi, *American Cut and Engraved Glass* (New York, 1965), p. 85.

52. *Meriden Record*, September 16, 1915 and September 20, 1915.

53. *Meriden Record*, October 5, 1915 and October 7, 1915.

54. *Meriden Record*, October 16, 1915 and November 5, 1915.

55. *Meriden Record*, October 20, 1915.

56. *Meriden Record*, October 9, 1915; October 12, 1915; October 14, 1915.

57. *Meriden Record*, October 14, 1915.

58. *Meriden Record*, October 18, 1915; October 22, 1915; October 25, 1915.

59. *Meriden Record*, October 19, 1915; October 23, 1915; November 19, 1915; January 12, 1916.

60. Quoted in *Meriden Record*, December 23, 1915.

61. *Meriden Record*, January 18, 1916.

62. *Meriden Record*, December 23, 1915 and January 4, 1916.

63. *Meriden Record*, January 3, 1919.

64. Ibid.

3

Migration, Class Formation, and Class Consciousness: The American Experience

John Cumbler

In contrast to their European counterparts, American historians have encountered considerable difficulty in defining precisely concepts of class and class consciousness. The presence of large numbers of immigrants from a variety of nations, language groupings, and religions has sensitized historians to its peculiar nature. These differentiations, which have characterized the American experience, have been particularly important in the daily lives of those who have occupied the lower levels on the ladder of social hierarchy. As Herbert Gutman has noted, "Just as in all modernizing countries, the United States faced the difficult task of industrialising whole cultures, but in this country the process was regularly repeated."[1] In America, those whole cultures were made up of people who spoke different languages, attended different churches, and understood different national symbols. These differences have led historians to evaluate ethnic and religious differences as being more significant than those of social class.[2] The concept of class itself as used by American labor historians has changed over time. Since the 1960s it has been influenced decisively by the monumental work of E.P. Thompson. In his preface to *The Making of the English Working Class*, Thompson argues for the primacy of agency in understanding class. "The working class did not rise like the sun at an appointed time. It was present at its own making," he says; "class happens when some men, as a result of common experiences (inherited or shared) feel and articulate the identity of their interests."[3] For Thompson, then, class is co-determined. It is determined not only by the social relations of production (which in the American literature is understood as a person's economic relationship to the means of production), but also by the collective consciousness of that relationship. Class is used to focus on a potentially organized or an organized interest group. Although Thompson argues for a co-determinist analysis of class, American historians have tended to focus on the concept of agency of the working class in its own making. Developing the idea of agency, they have looked on the culture, values, and social composition of groups of workers. The role of the worker in the social relations of production has receded before the wave of ethnic culture. Although the significance of culture, agency, and ethnicity in understanding the world of the American worker cannot be denied, I believe a more illuminating approach to the question of class will come through a structural analysis, such as I construct in this essay. This approach will, I believe, reveal the primacy of "class" in understanding the American working-class experience.

During the period of intensive industrialization, the American economy looked to a worldwide surplus-labor market and attracted workers with a wide variety of historical experiences, resources, skills, and world views. Those world views were rooted within the historical-material experiences the workers brought to the New World. The American economy had differential labor needs historically, as well as between and within trades. Because of these differential needs, immigrants faced not one labor market, but multiple labor markets. The selectivity of employers and the economy was reinforced by the selections, in terms of both destinations and skill levels of migrants.[4] In the American workforce, therefore, class position took social, cultural, and sexual forms which affected the nature and the expression of class, but which did not alter the basic nature of class formation. Although this author accepts the emphasis that E.P. Thompson and others have placed on human agency and on the importance of historical experience, culture, and social networks in affecting human consciousness, I reject the tendency to see class as "self-determined" or the tendency to see culture and ethnicity as more important than social class in the historical experience of the American worker. I argue that class experiences may take ethnic forms, or even be expressed in ethnic terms, but that this in no way negates the importance of that class experience. Much work has already been done on the role of immigration in shaping the peculiarity of the American experience. Gutman's work in particular has made a major contribution in our understanding of how immigrants with pre-industrial culture clashed with the values and culture of industrializing America. I will not try to duplicate his work; instead, I will focus on the process by which migration interacts with industrial change to produce and shape social class. In this essay I will address three general problems: the nature of the relationship between immigration and changing relations in production and how these processes colored the emerging social-class system; the interplay of labor markets and social and cultural dimensions of class; and the significance of this process on the development of class consciousness.

The American economy has found the sources of its labor the world over. Throughout its history black Africans, first as slaves and later as internal migrants, have been crucial for the production of food and goods. In the twentieth century, migrants from the Caribbean and Mexico have been significant in American production, while in the nineteenth century Asians represented an impressive percentage of our immigrant workforce. In earlier works, I have discussed their experiences at some length. Here, I will focus on white free labor, mostly either immigrant or within a generation or two of immigration from Europe.

An astonishing abundance of land, a shortage of native labor, and massive social, demographic, and agrarian upheavals in Western Europe set the stage for American economic development. The expansion of the agricultural hinterland created demand for skilled craftsmen and unskilled casual labor in the growing port cities and towns. These centers gathered the goods of the hinterland heading toward European markets, the finished supplies from Europe's workshops, and the massive influx of migrants hunting for opportunity in either the lands of the west or the cities of the coast. Many immigrants came already indentured, as unfree labor to be used to alleviate the crisis of labor shortage. Others, while looking for opportunity, contributed to the growth of the developing economy when their meager savings were absorbed into the cash-short American economy, as they bought land, supplies, and room and board before venturing into the worlds of artisan, merchant, or farmer. The small farm was the workplace. Yet in the port cities and the towns of that period, workshops that functioned as both retail stores and centers of production supplied much of the local needs for crafted and manufactured goods. The shops were small owner-run units with the total family involved in the productive system.[5]

The growth of trade and the constant influx of new immigrants from the British Isles and, to a lesser extent, from Germany and France increased the importance of these small artisan shops. The goods that gathered at the docks of American cities needed barrels to hold them, warehouses to store them, docks from which to load and unload, and ships to haul them. The population that grew around the port cities and inland towns expanded the demand for artisanal goods and for artisans and mechanics to make them.[6] The rapid increase of population in the British Isles, particularly after the 1780s, the reorganization of land use leading to such events as the Highland clearances and land enclosure, and the punitive poor laws, as well as the destruction of traditional handicraft artisan industries with the introduction of steam powered production, provided not only the western hinterland with farmers and farm help, but also the shops and factories of the towns and cities with artisans and laborers.[7]

Those arriving in America for the first time were as conditioned by who they were, who they knew, and what they did before they came as by the conditions of the American economy. Even before the massive development of American industry, immigrants faced not a single but a multiple labor market. For the poor male cottager and crofter without contacts to the rural hinterland, casual labor on the docks, the digging of canals and roads, and the hauling of materials defined his labor choices. For the female, domestic labor or help in a family shop confined her choices, and for the artisan with skills and experience it was the workshops of the cities and towns that offered opportunity. The world of work was selective, but the workers brought to this world traditions, customs, and language that made their new environment familiar to them.[8]

Because labor recruitment was selective, the cultural and social structures of the working population developed differently and jobs and job classifications were manifested in social and cultural life. Relatively unskilled peasant cottagers from western Ireland and the Scottish highlands were of little use to master craftsmen hiring journeymen to meet the growing demands for manufactured goods. The frailer frames and lower statures of displaced weavers, cabinet makers, or cordwainers made them less useful to the employers of casual labor looking for brawn.[9] The highlander and Irish peasant found work and housing crowded around the docks and canals. There, they looked to compatriots for information about jobs, for places to stay, for loans to get them through the hard times of the slack seasons, and for comrades to share experiences and memories. Selective recruitment directed immigrants with various skills and experiences into particular occupations. Contacts with relatives and friends, often made before migration, steered newcomers into occupations and neighborhoods already identified with particular regions and origins.[10]

Thus, in the early nineteenth-century city, social and ethnic divisions channeled workers into worlds separated by traditions, customs, and skills carried over from their past and reinforced by the experiences of their present life and work in ethnic groupings. In later years, with the coming of industrialization, these divisions would become more rigid and the system would reshape cities into highly segregated ethnic-class enclaves separated by rail lines, factories, and warehouses.[11] Although the artisan and mechanic of the pre-industrial city shared much of the same urban space with the laborer and the merchant, ethnic and occupational lines were already being drawn.

Migrants to the pre-industrial city not only felt more welcome in certain parts of the city and in certain jobs, they brought to the city customs, traditions, and ways of looking at and understanding the world that allowed them to integrate more easily into some neighborhoods than others. These world views, traditions, and customs also functioned as guides to behavior and values. They had their origins in the material experiences of the past, yet they affected those experiences by guiding behavior, which in turn created new experiences.[12]

For the peasants constantly struggling to survive amidst limited resources—inter-generational continuity, family-kin collective work experience, seasonal and daily variation in work patterns, control over part of production, and conflict with distant land owners—the values of collectivity, kin and family dependence, fatalism, and suspicion of outside authority were values of survival and strength. For artisans, craft pride, skilled knowledge, the labor theory of value, and concepts of craft loyalty and solidarity with the ideals of independency and mobility were the central values of their world. Both artisans and cottagers adapted to what they were most familiar with, and employers looked for those attributes that were most easily adapted to their needs. Those entering the job market selected and were selected into particular societal stratas.[13] They gave to these strata certain cultural and social characteristics, which were themselves modified by the new world.[14]. This process, begun in the early nineteenth century, was exacerbated greatly by industrialization, the signs of which were just beginning to show by the century's third decade.

The influx of immigrants, the settlement of the hinterland, the expanded demands for agricultural surplus, and the intervention of wars (1812, 1845, and 1861) pushed the material capacity of the mercantile society to its limits. Agricultural demand for greater materials and implements, and the growing domestic market for textiles, shoes, wagons, trunks, boxes, canal and rail equipment, mining and building tools, and so on, led both master craftsmen and merchants to look for means for increasing production and cutting costs. For those with the resources to capitalize on the increased demand, reorganization of the means of production meant an increased role for themselves and greater profits.[15]

Those who came to work found it increasingly divided into smaller and fewer tasks. In certain industries, that meant tending machines powered by forces outside the control of the workers. By subdividing any given task into a series of tasks, the organizer of the means of production not only could increase the possibility of proficiency, but also could reduce the required skill level. This allowed the manufacturer to bring in unskilled workers, while confining the skilled worker to specific tasks requiring years of accumulated knowledge. This process brought the various labor markets together within the manufacturing process. It also increased the multiplicity of labor markets, for the manufacturers recruited skilled labor from a given pool, and looked to a different pool for unskilled labor. The skilled and unskilled now rubbed shoulders within the same areas of the cities, and even within the same manufacturing building.[16]

The multiple labor markets were reinforced by employer preferences, wage levels, worker inclinations, and social cultures. It was the journeyman who found himself pulled into a wage relationship with the controller of the means of production. Within the nineteenth-century American city, these journeymen artisans came to the factory gates with historic bonds of religion, common experiences, and language to the other craftsmen and skilled workmen they would meet inside. Patterns of recruitment that passed by word of mouth from neighbor to neighbor, from kin to kin, kept the skilled jobs within specific groups that shared common traditions, ideas, and culture. The self-images of most of these workers were rooted in the labor theory of value, which held that work, particularly that of skilled craftsmen, gave an object its value, and in the belief in their centrality to the production of wealth. These beliefs encompassed both a sense of collective support, exemplified in traditions of "pitching in" to help fellow craftsmen finish work, or aiding the families of craftsmen injured or killed, and a belief in individualism expressed in pride of craftsmanship, artistry, and knowledge of the trade. These workers' concepts of themselves were rooted in their experiences and in their mythologies brought to the factories from the small artisan shops. They had been raised in a world imbued with the image of Benjamin Franklin, the printer turned statesman, the son of a chandler who took control of his own life because of his skill as a printer—a craftsman. Equality meant equality among producers, all with equal access to the means of production, at least at a mythical level. Access was access by skill.[17]

With the expansion of mechanized production in American, especially in textiles, mining, iron, iron molding, machinery, boots, shoes, and clothing, skilled craftsmen from Europe joined the native-born in the American labor market. The patterns of local recruitment were replicated on an international scale. With shortges of skilled labor, manufacturers sought out skilled craftsmen from areas where contacts already existed. Cotton brokers involved in investments in textile companies, informally and formally looked to English contacts to recommend workers for American factories. Before the domination of large-scale capital-intensive corporations, the social distance between manufacturer and skilled worker was small enough so that personal contact established linkages and later became avenues for the flow of workers. A skilled English spinner recruited to oversee a spinning room would have contacts back in England that would be used to funnel workers to American mills. In times of recession in the English mills, friends, family members, or friends of friends would pass along information about jobs in American. Subsequently, English and Lancashire Irish (Irish with several years in the English mills) moved to specific jobs and towns. Trade unions in Lancashire sponsored emigrating mill workers who moved into homes of friends and relatives in America, and who found skilled work in areas for which they had already been trained.[18]

Differential patterns of development in Europe along with worldwide cyclical investment patterns meant uneven rates of industrialization and an uneven surplus of skilled craftsmen.[19] Economic recession in Germany, expanding populations, and the failure of revolutionary movements with heavy involvement of craftsmen meant a flood of craft workers of specific trades into America. Brewery workers, furniture workers, jewelers, Jewish German tailors, and cigar workers came with skills and familiarity with certain trades that gave them special entry into the job markets. Shortages of skilled master artisans and the relatively low capitalization of the trade at the time of entry gave German skilled workers public identification with certain trades. Lines of communication back to the homeland, stem-migration patterns of movement, and public identification with particular trades steered German migrants into specific trades.[20]

The traditions, cultures, and world views that these skilled workers brought to their trades helped formulate their responses to the changing structures of employment as they resisted what they felt were manufacturers' actions undercutting traditional rights and forms. Resistance to employers took many forms; strikes and early trade-union action by skilled craft workers predominated the early stages of industrial development. Calling on the shared traditions and language of the craft, skilled workers took job action against the introduction of less-skilled or less-trained workmen, attacked shoddy work, and struggled for the maintenance of artistry, pride in product, and dignity in skill. These skilled workers attacked reductions in piece rates in terms of its threat to their independence and equality.[21] Despite the language which the craftsmen took into the factories, increasingly with industrialization the probability of independence and equality declined. By 1860, most skilled craftsmen not only worked for someone else, but had little chance of achieving the status of master craftsmen. Factory reorganization, divisions of labor, and the introduction of steam- and water-powered machinery, which required capital intensity out of the reach of craftsmen, meant for all but a very few dependence on a wage paid by someone else, who owned the equipment and machinery needed for production. Even the very few who still did maintain independence and self-employment by 1860 played a marginal role in the economy, and their independence was often bought by lower standards than those enjoyed by the paid craftsmen. Although the craftsmen continued to use the language of independence ("we will not be slaves," "Liberty and Equality") in their struggles with manufacturers, by 1860 in most trades these slogans were the heritage of a lost world. Most labor issues involved not liberty and equality, but maintenance, wages, hours, and control over the work process. It was a struggle for control in a world where ownership already had been conceded; inevitably with loss of ownership went loss of independence and equality.[22]

Not all trades fell at once into the line of march of the industrial capitalists. Although in textiles the processes of subdivision and steam or water power for mechanized production were already well underway by the 1830s, in other trades the process of proletarianization occurred less dramatically and concretely. Craftsmen in garment trades continued to own the means of production—scissors, even sewing machines—long after they lost control over production. Despite their ownership of the means of production, these craft workers could not use their tools and maintain their livelihood outside their subordination to capitalists who controlled the production process by market control, efficiencies of scale, and subdivision of labor. Furniture makers, bakers, and other craftsmen involved in the manufacturing of consumer goods continued to maintain small shops and to keep alive the ideal of the independent master even as late as the 1890s. However, increasingly after 1860, capital sought out ever wider areas for investment, resulting in the larger master-craftsmen or merchant buyers reorganizing the production process to extract greater surpluses. The greater capitalization of the production process meant less opportunity for the craftsmen to become their own bosses and more subordination to the capitalists. Greater productivity also meant less opportunity for those producing on a small scale. As markets were saturated with ever-increasing goods, smaller producers went under and manufacturers increasingly looked for new means by which to increase their productivity and cut costs. The most obvious means for cutting costs were cutting the wages of the skilled craftsmen or increasing the number of low-paid unskilled laborers. Manufacturers tried both. Craftsmen fought the cutting of wages, and they resisted the introduction of machinery that would increase production and replace skilled workers with machine operatives. They used the language of craftsmen (concepts of dignity and labor theory of value) to attack the manufacturers' cost-cutting procedures, but they used a language inherited from the world of the artisan to combat the world of the manufacturer.

Just as the craftsmen called upon the traditions and language of a lost world for a common language of resistance, so too did the manufacturers call on the language of a lost world to co-opt that resistance. The manufacturers also talked of the world of independent producers, where workers and owners were all producers struggling against the profits of the banks and brokers and, in an earlier period, slave powers of the South. The craft worker recruited from a privileged community, paid a wage substantially higher than the semi-skilled operative, divided sexually and ethnically from those recruited to tend machines and sweep and haul, had historic ties with the master craftsmen. The manufacturer, ascribing to himself the role of master craftsman, called upon that common heritage as well as ethnic links to defuse the protests of the craftsmen. Demands by the craftsmen, reflecting an increasing conciousness of themselves in a subject position and a collective identity (demands for shorter hours, reflecting a new conciousness of the loss of ownership and control over the means of production) were countered by the manufacturers with demands for elimination of slave labor, control over speculation, public morality, and individual opportunity to move up within a system of private ownership and control over the means of production. Individualism of the artisan was tied to the ideal of independence and equality. The ideology of the new industrial period transformed the meaning of individualism into upward mobility without independence or equality.[23] The conflict over the control of the means of production also became a conflict over language. Both craftsman and manufacturer looked to a common culture to understand their world, but that new world forced both groups to develop different understandings and interpretations of that culture.

The skilled worker was not the only one affected by the process of mechanization, division of labor, and the factory system. In order to increase surplus value, manufacturers divided the production process into smaller units and utilized unskilled labor to perform those parts of the production process that did not require long periods of acquired skills. Even under the old artisanal production process, master craftsmen utilized their wives, children, and apprentices to help with production. In shoemaking, wives and children stitched uppers, prepared the workshops, and finished the shoes. In hand weaving, women were initially spinners; with the introduction of machine spinning, women and children were used by the hand loom weavers to set up machines, wind the warp, and draw in the thread through the hettle. Specific tasks and wages were associated with sex and age, with unskilled work going generally to women and children. When manufacturers introduced factory production—first the putting out system and then mechanized centralized production—they extended the artisans' labor divisions into greater and more rigid job classifications. Initially with the putting out system, women and less-skilled workers in the countryside were given specific tasks, but with the introduction of machinery, women and children were funneled into large rooms to tend machines at low wages. The sexual division of labor was most prominent in the textile mills of Lowell, Massachusetts, where skilled male textile workers recruited from Lancashire, England, lived and worked separately from the large number of New England farm girls who were recruited to work the looms.[24]

The persistent search by manufacturers for labor for the unskilled or semi-skilled machine-tending jobs led to recruitment of unskilled peasant and agricultural laborers, from Ireland and Germany in particular. The population increase, land reorganization, and crop failures, especially the Irish potato crop in the late 1840s, led to massive migration to the United States, where immigrants with few skills were recruited into expanding industries along specific ethnic lines. Earlier-arriving Irish weavers and spinners from Northern Ireland, and later from Lancashire, settled in areas around the textile mills, where they gave cities such as Philadelphia an Irish flavor. Later, Irish immigrants without skills, escaping the ravages of famine, gathered in the areas of the city already identified with the Irish and were recruited into the unskilled operative work of the expanding factory system. Manufacturers had a demand for unskilled and skilled labor, but they looked to different communities and groups for their different labor demands. Because workers were recruited not generally, but specifically, skills and trades took on social characteristics beyond the skill levels themselves.

The social composition of the various skill levels and the trades depended on a variety of factors. The speed of mechanization and relative labor needs in terms of skilled versus unskilled workers, the demographic and political pressures of European countries (which provided a major source for American industry) and the patterns of investment in manufacturing in Europe and America (which caused a collapse of traditional artisan economies and generated a surplus of artisan workers, many of whom fled to the United States, establishing communities from which skilled workers were recruited) all contributed to the social characteristics of the labor market. Employer biases about which social groups were adept at what jobs and workers' familial, friend, and kin ties, reinforced the social and ethnic characteristics emerging around specific jobs and skill levels.

These social and ethnic characteristics in turn affected the process of class formation and development of class consciousness. As Herbert Gutman has shown, the process was not confined to a single generation or even to a single period.[25] Persistent labor shortages and demands by expanding American industry led American capitalism on an every-expanding search for labor. Although Germany and the British Isles, traditionally areas of labor recruitment, continued to send workers to mines and mills, the population surpluses of southern and eastern Europe added even greater numbers to the flow of workers to the factories of America. By the end of the century almost four times as many immigrants arrived from eastern and southern Europe as from Germany, the British Isles, and Scandinavia.

Just as the juxtaposition of the development of the initial factory system and the massive migration of Irish and German peasants, farm laborers, and craftsmen gave an ethnic flavor to the emerging class system prior to 1880, so did the migration of later immigrants coinciding with the emergence of large-scale heavy industry, give that workforce an ethnic dimension. Established German, Irish, English, and native-born workers were recruited to fill jobs as skilled workers, while unskilled immigrants from eastern and southern Europe were recruited for the heavy loading and hauling work in the expanding mills. Italians and Polish and Russian Jews flocked to the expanding clothing trades to stitch pre-cut cloth with sewing machines in New York, Boston, Philadelphia, Rochester, and Chicago. Poles, Lithuanians, Ukrainians, and other Slavic groups found their way into the unskilled, easily learned, or assembly-line jobs of the steel or heavy industry in South Chicago, Gary, Pittsburgh, Akron, Detroit, or Flint.[26]

The multiple labor market was reinforced and indeed maintained through the process by which migrants moved from their community of origin to a community of destination. Given that the community of origin could no longer support an individual, family, or group of families for any variety of reasons, including the massive repression visited on the Jewish communities of eastern Europe, the migrants looked to areas where they had contacts for their new locations. This was done partly because those areas where there were familiar faces also provided familiar traditions, customs, and languages. Also, the process of survival meant locating oneself where one knew about or easily could discover information concerning jobs and housing. The very process of moving meant a loss—a loss of friends, community, and the familiar. Migrants tried as much as possible to reduce these losses, by moving to places where there was the greatest possibility of maintaining contacts with the familiar. Rather than maximizing the benefits in a move, the migrants tried to minimize the costs. This process of stem-migration located the migrants into communities and jobs already colonized by those from the source community. Immigrants with few skills and with limited knowledge of these new areas in turn learned about jobs from others with limited skills. This led to concentrations of particular groups in particular skill areas and, in particular, in industries and even in rooms of large manufacturing plants. Limited information also steered migrants into particular cities or areas of new cities, not only because they desired to live among their compatriots, but also because many migrants already had arranged housing either with or near their friends or relatives before they left. Connections well entrenched prior to migration placed migrants into particular cities and areas of cities. The industries located in those areas of the city or in those cities developed concentrations of immigrants from particular source areas.[27]

Concentrations of immigrants in particular areas meant that the expansion of a particular industry opened up new areas of employment, especially for the migrant communities located in the region. Thus, the expansion of the steel industry at the end of the nineteenth century opened up skilled jobs for the Irish. Job procurement was then possible not only in terms of individuals "trickling up" in a generally resistant labor market; at times of expansion and development migrant communities as a whole found new "higher" labor markets open to them, and in turn these openings became avenues for further advancement by the ethnic community. Thus, the multiple labor market functioned within the contraints of labor demand, labor supply, and the process of migration itself, which directed immigrants into particular labor market areas.

Because of the nature of the ethnic skill concentration in particular trades, due to stem-migration patterns, there emerged an ethnic-skill mix that was cross-sectional and led to an ethnic concentration in specific skill areas in some industries (as with the nineteenth-century Irish casual laborers in a variety of trades and English and Scottish concentrated in skilled sectors). In others, ethnic concentrations developed across skill lines and even between classes, as in the Jewish garment industry where Jewish manufacturers hired Jewish and Italian garment workers.

Even those ethnic migrants who arrived relatively late on the industrial scene, and who clustered within small neighborhoods for social, traditional, and practical bonds of mutual support, found a social hierarchy. Those who had arrived first and "learned the ropes" gained seniority within the community. They not only steered new immigrants into specific jobs, but their familiarity with the jobs and the labor sources made them important mediators both for the newly arrived migrants, and for the hiring companies and the larger political communities. On the job, they were appointed by owners or managers to low-level supervisory positions as gang leaders, section hands, or even foremen. In these roles the ethnic leaders supervised and integrated the newly arrived, and also maintained the roles of grievance advocates for the immigrants. Their roles as organizers and leaders of the ethnic workforce were dependent upon their ability to maintain loyalty and support from that community. Without support, the ethnic leader was less useful to either the capitalist or the local political community. To maintain support, however, the ethnic leaders had to address the interests and concerns of the ethnic community. Where the community was at work, those concerns were of a class nature. The ethnic leader was put under severe pressure to represent the ethnic workers' interests as workers, oftentimes in conflict with capital, and at the same time was often rewarded by employers and the local political community, through job advancement or political patronage, for holding the demands of the ethnic community within manageable bounds.[28]

The resulting contradictions help explain the complex and often contradictory behavior of the ethnic community and its leadership. As Daniel

Walkowitz and John Bodnar have shown, where these communities had particularly high concentrations in certain trades and particular skill levels, the ethnic bonds reinforced and solidified class actions. Ethnic leaders, feeling a unified voice below them demanding action on specific issues, were forced by the complex interactions and ties of kin and community into providing leadership. This in turn further mobilized the ethnic or migrant community for conflict and confrontation with the structure of authority both on the job and in the political world.

At other times, the rewards of political success that were offered to ethnic leaders for mobilizing ethnic blocks often led them away from the controversial class- and work-related issues, where it was most difficult to deliver results, to concerns of ethnic symbolic importance, such as the cultural or religious issues of prayers in school, Sunday drinking, general ethnic identity. These issues were salient in the ethnic community and at times overshadowed or even merged with class issues. Opposition to Sunday drinking laws also was opposition to middle-class Protestants trying to force their values and authority on ethnic working-class communities. The ethnic leader, by championing Sunday drinking, could champion a class issue and at the same time not be forced to confront a class issue which would challenge the system directly, such as housing reform, public housing, or minimum wages.[29] This contradictory pressure led to an ebb and flow in class identity and ethnicity. Although the nature of the relationship between ethnicity and class identity changed over time, contrary to the findings of Bodnar and Walkowitz, it is my thesis that particular historical convergences of a variety of factors could produce either orientation or a contradictory mix. That orientation in turn changed over time, but not necessarily in a linear fashion.

The Irish offer a classic example of this conflict. For the Irish peasant in the second half of the nineteenth century the links to America already were well established. Large numbers of Irish peasants had developed an intricate system of migration and communication well before the potato famine of the 1840s and 1850s. Although the famine increased the numbers and even the destinations of emigrants from Ireland, the cultural and social system of migration was well established. The Irish peasant population, especially in eastern counties, expected sons to travel to England to work harvests. While some returned to Ireland, many others stayed on in the textile regions of Lancashire to work in unskilled jobs, or on the docks of Liverpool or London, or in the foundries of Birmingham.

However, even these denizens of the growing industrial centers of Lancashire, Liverpool, or London were accustomed to returning home to Ireland during slack seasons, trade busts, or for social occasions at home. The constant movement back and forth between the cities of

England and the Irish countryside facilitated the movement of even more peasants into the urban areas. That movement kept alive issues of importance to the Irish within the new English-Irish working class, as can be seen by the common cause made between the Chartists and the Irish nationalists. Furthermore, it brought the new world of the English working class to those in the Irish countryside who were most receptive themselves to migration—particularly the young. Males were not the only ones subject to the new transnational labor market; large numbers of Irish women also crossed the Irish Sea to find work as domestics or factory "girls." Like their male counterparts, when they returned to Ireland they brought some of the new world into the traditional setting.[31] It was through these contacts that others moved to the new urban-industrial setting. These prodigal sons and daughters materially facilitated the migration process with information about jobs, housing, and transportation, and they were the mentors and guides in the new world. The potential migrants began learning before leaving home and were educated continually by the very process of migration.

The move from Ireland to England actually facilitated the move to America. Most of the first Irish to move across the Atlantic had moved already into the migratory stream to England or had heard about America through contacts with those from the English migratory system. Those who pioneered the migration process from Ireland to England to America sent back to Ireland new connections. They opened up America as a new source for the already-moving Irish population. Although those who remained home maintained traditional customs and cultural values, the new culture had penetrated already traditional Ireland through the chain migration system to those most likely to migrate—the young, especially those who may already have spent some time on the harvest or migration trail in England.[32]

These connections and contacts in turn became the links that tied the new migrant into a social system, a work group, a neighborhood and, ultimately, a class. Sometimes the contact was rooted firmly in the working class, as was the case with such individuals as: Ed Boyce, an activist in the local union movement, militant socialist president of the Western Federation of Miners, and socialist-populist member of the Colorado state legislature; United Mine Workers (UMW) organizer Mother Jones; J.P. MacDonnell, a journalist and trade union organizer; political radicals such as Frank Rooney, a radical and socialist Fenian; or just local laborers with experiences of low wages, bad housing, and insecure work. In such cases the new migrants' schooling in the new world would be in terms of both ethnic and class identity. The process of class formation overlapped the process of ethnic identity.[33] Where the contact was not deeply rooted in the community, for example a local priest or an ethnic small shopkeeper, the new migrants' integration into the working class would be more problematic. This situation would be exacerbated by the development within American capital and by the process by which older immigrant groups were placed in different sectors of the industry and came to identify their positions with ethnic privilege or actually to use their own ethnic organizations to keep the newer immigrant groups out of competition.

Where an ethnic group dominated an industry, such as the Jewish domination of the garment industry, ethnic language, shared foods, traditions, histories, folklore, and patterns of protest were welded into a powerful working-class culture, with the socialist Yiddish newspapers and radical Russian and eastern European parties and struggles serving as links with politics and activities back home. The union halls and socialist cafes were centers of politicization. For many American-born Jews, the glass tea cups with spoons of jam were associated not with Russian *shtetls*, but with hot and intense arguments over socialist doctrine and the conflicts between internationalism and Zionism, just as an earlier group of Irish immigrants argued about the link between Irish Fenianism and American radicalism. Trenton, New Jersey's Italian community, in a later period, deeply entrenched in the rubber and steel industry, came to see itself so totally indentified with Trenton's working class that when the Congress of Industrial Organizations (CIO) began organizing in the 1930s, the Italian Cultural Club announced not only its support, but that "Italians of Trenton" as a group were "wholeheartedly" behind the CIO.

Early immigrant groups brought with them trade-union traditions and working-class institutions that molded a clear and self-conscious working-class culture. Irish and English textile workers, for example, used traditional institutions from home such as Odd Fellows lodges, the Ancient Order of Foresters, co-ops, and English-molded trade unions to hold their community together and to maintain internal class discipline. These class institutions were schools for newly entering members of the social community. In times of strikes or other forms of class conflict, these institutions offered financial support. The Odd Fellows hall was opened for dances, rallies, and fund raisers. The Ancient Order of Hibernians, an Irish ethnic organization, expelled those who crossed picket lines or in any fashion helped the manufacturers against the workers. These ethnic institutions held the communities together, and where they were synonymous with class, cemented together a common social core within the working class. They had links to the earlier European traditions, but at the same time facilitated the integration of the new members of the working class from Europe and second-generation Americans into the common culture and values of the working class.[34] Although these institutions had a class base and acted as class institutions, ethnic allegiances could, in times of heavy migration of new ethnic groups and economic change, direct these institutions away from class unity and solidarity toward ethnic exclusiveness.[35]

The pressure on ethnic organizations to defend privilege and maintain ethnic identity was most acute in periods of economic insecurity and where the ethnic group already had an established foothold. In those communities, ethnic leaders within the political, industrial, or even trade union structures were besieged by their constituents with demands that were most difficult to realize. Ethnic solidarity and exclusivity functioned to deflect these demands. The psychological identity of an ethnic fellow in a position of authority who could selectively pass out dwindling rewards of the political-economic system cemented ethnic loyalties which acted to fragment class identity and common class action.

Ethnic organizations varied greatly according to the social traditions of the groups before migration, the structure of the industry when they arrived, and the length of time in the new community. In general, though, supra-local ethnic organizations that were national or city-wide were dominated by middle- or lower-middle-class ethnic leaders, particularly those dependent on the ethnic community for their livelihood—politicans, doctors, lawyers, and small ethnic shopkeepers. The smaller local and neighborhood ethnic organizations, such as athletic clubs, bars and taverns, and neighborhood clubs tended to be more working-class in orientation and leadership.[36] Typical of this pattern were the French Canadians in Fall River, Massachusetts, who established a series of ethnic clubs and lodges—the Ligue des Patriotes, the Grade Napoleon, and the Société de St. Jean Baptiste. These clubs provided French Canadian immigrants with community institutions that held them together and preserved ethnic beliefs and culture. Yet the culture of the French Canadian immigrants was rooted in a traditional peasant society. Fall River as an urban industrial community required adjustment and change. The institutions and clubs of the French Canadian immigrant community acted as agents of change within the traditional culture, while at the same time maintaining much of that culture's forms and symbols.

Within the framework of these organizations and the larger immigrant culture, the French Canadian community worked to protect itself and to resolve the contradictions manifested in the process of change. At the same time, the leaders of the institutions of the French Canadian church—Pierre Peloquin; Hugh Bubuque, a lawyer and lay leader in the French Canadian immigrant community; and Father Bedard, the local priest—tried to direct local interest away from class-based activity such as trade unions or strike actions into ethnic-centered action. Through the political organ, Le Club Politique, they led campaigns for nationalization of immigrants and for ethnic control over the local church, for maintenance of French-language parochial schools, for ethnic-bloc voting. French-Canadians were encouraged to vote Republican, in opposition to the

Democratic party, which was dominated by the Irish and English. Although these were concerns of the members of the ethnic community, the organizations were heavily dominated by those members with the greatest longevity in the community, and they, in turn, tended to be lower-middle class and upwardly mobile. Le Club Politique, for example, had no textile workers, the largest category of workers in the city, and most of the other clubs had only small working-class membership.

The working-class ethnics instead congregated around neighborhood bars, taverns, and social clubs, where working-class grievances were aired, though few of them managed to filter up into formal ethnic demands.[37] The political club of the French Canadian ethnic leaders had little working-class support and no working-class members. The club leaders' anti-union position, plus the club's identification with the pro-business Republican party, alienated it from the French Canadian working class which either did not vote or voted for the Democratic party, despite the party's strong identification with the Irish.[38]

Even for the Irish, who notoriously were the most politically minded of all American ethnic groups, contradictions between ethnicity and class caused ethnic machines much trouble. The Irish machine in industrial cities was dominated by middle-class members who were constantly waffling on labor issues in an attempt to hold the ethnic vote in line without letting the class issues dominate. Yet the avoidance of class issues threatened to undermine the position of machine leaders, as it did for the French Canadian ethnic leaders. Since many of the newest immigrants did not enjoy citizenship, the center of ethnic politics existed not in the poorest working-class districts, but rather in the zones of emergence, where the skilled working-class and lower-middle-class ethnics lived. Voter turnout was so small in the residential areas of the unskilled working class because of high geographic mobility and low levels of citizenship. Although these unskilled workers did play a crucial role in close elections that gave their ward bosses a certain level of power and visibility, their ability to affect the structure of the city-wide political process and machine was extremely limited. Thus, the working-class vote was defused.[39] For those in the zone of emergence, the skilled working class found its voting power mixed in with the lower-middle class, but even with this diffusion of working-class political "clout," the Democratic (or, in midwestern cities such as Cincinnati, Republican) machine had difficulty maintaining the structure of its support within ethnic communities.

The Irish machine dominated the Fall River Democratic party and focused strongly on ethnic issues within the community. The strong support for unionism and working-class issues by the Irish led the party to adopt a sympathetic but ambivalent attitude toward such issues as union recognition and union contracts on public works. On the one hand, local ward politicans supported strikes and refused to support bringing in police to break up strikes. In addition, the party "adopted" a local union leader to represent the district in the state legislature despite the fact that he was English. On the other hand, the machine's newspaper failed to support the pro-labor candidate in 1875 because of his labor stand, an action that infuriated English workers, who afterwards deserted the Democratic party. The Irish machine produced both pro-labor and anti-labor candidates who caused low turnouts in Irish working-class neighborhoods. The Irish machine was dominated during the 1880s by an Irish lawyer, John W. Cummings, who had a weak labor voting record. Yet the party rallied a significant proportion of the Irish vote on ethnic grounds and on the knowledge that the Republicans were no better. The pro-business orientation of the Republicans discouraged wide support from English textile workers, although the party did try to rally the English ethnic vote around the anti-Irish issue. In 1887, the Irish machine forced pro-labor Louis Lapham out of the party on ethnic grounds, and from that date until the end of the century, the party was the creature of the middle-class upwardly mobile Irish. In the 1890s, John Coughlin, a Fall River physician, took over the party and maintained "neutrality" in labor-capital conflicts, an orientation that contributed to the low voter turnout in the Irish community, and to even lower turnout rates among the English, the French Canadian, and later the Portuguese.[40]

Ethnic-class loyalties make an understanding of class consciousness in the American context problematic. The difficulty is complicated by our understanding of the notion of class consciousness, which itself has been clouded by the nature of the debate. What some historians see as class consciousness, others see as job consciousness or group consciousness, particularly those who reject a Marxist analysis.

The problem for historians and the solution to their dilemma is establishing a common understanding of class, let alone class consciousness. E.P. Thompson, working as a non-traditional Marxist, has argued for a non-structural definition of class. Rejecting the Marxist distinction between "a class *in* itself and *for* itself," Thompson argues that not only do productive relations not mechanically determine class consciousness, but that class itself cannot be defined solely in terms of production relations. Rather, Thompson posits that class is formed only when people, grouped within certain productive relationships, develop a consciousness of their common condition and interests.[41] However, we must be aware that the process of capitalist development in the United States increasingly reduced the ability of workers to control their own means of production. Where they did own the means of production, they could not use these means for their own survival without entering into subjected relations with others who controlled markets, materials, or production sites. The increasing mechanization and development of capitalist production brought more and more people into subjected relations with the owners or controllers of the means of production. These subjected people, because of the nature of their relationship to the means of production, made up a distinct class, a working class. Thompson is fully correct that those subjected classes affected and molded the conditions of their subjection and thus were not totally passive in the process of class formation. Although workers, to use Marx's concept from the "Eighteenth Brumaire" of Louis Napoleon in France, were agents of their own history, their dependent relationship within the capitalist structure constituted their class position.[42]

The development of American capitalism demanded more and more laborers as producers within a dependent system. It was to this expanding labor market that hundreds of thousands of European (and rural American) migrants came. They fitted into the system in a variety of ways and gave to their positions ethnic, regional, and sexual complexity. This complexity itself at times divided the American working class and led to conflicts between ethnic and class consciousness. Those who came to occupy positions of dependence within the class-stratified system made up a structurally defined working class, yet their position within that class did not inevitably lead to consciousness of their position, nor did it necessarily offer them a collective identity. Thompson reminds us that membership within a work group or strata does not automatically determine class consciousness. Yet he does somewhat slight the importance of the relationships between structural position in the economy and class. Consciousness, although not determined by productive relations, is not independent of them.[43] The historical reality of class experience, persistent confrontation of differential opportunities, economic subjection by others with entirely different world experiences, differential treatment before the legal and social structures of society—and the experience of collective work with limited returns—do not determine class consciousness. How individuals and groups of individuals have interpreted their experiences and past cannot be determined historically.

The differences and variety of the human experience create different historical-cultural world views; yet the commonality of those experiences also reinforces those aspects of the historical view that interpret the world on class terms. Although different immigrants may have identified their conditions in terms of ethnic, racial, or sex discrimination, the experience of reduced opportunity heightened their common sense of vulnerability and subjection. The struggles for security and stability within a system that rewarded selectively those with access to the economic and political resources of the system gave to other, unfocused grievances a class focus. The leaders' definition of issues of class conflict in ethnic terms have transformed the nature of class conflict within the structure. Because the nature of unequal rewarding in America historically has been class-based but ethnically expressed, ethnic terms have historical reality, but that reality also has economic and class bases. Struggle for greater rewards for Jews, Italians, Blacks, Irish, and others have also brought ethnic groups into struggle against the class interests of those who control the political and economic system. Where and when the struggle did not have ethnic outlets it emerged as a class conflict and generated a class analysis.

Historians of American society have emphasized the importance of social mobility and the economic "success" of the American system for social stability. We have been told that during key periods in our history, a segment of our workforce could expect to find job stability and security. The persistence of this opportunity gave to new members of the workforce the hope and belief that if not for them, at least for their children, skilled work, or even white collar jobs were available.[44] The belief in this opportunity and, to whatever degree its reality, has maintained within immigrant communities a counterweight to the views of radicals and socialists who argued for revolution and social upheaval. Precisely how to interpret the significance of this belief is still unresolved. Although large numbers of skilled workers did adopt a view that reform and simple trade unionism offered the working class the best vehicle for social improvement, it is unclear how deeply these views penetrated migrant communities. There still remains, from the point of view of "new" social historians, significant evidence that immigrants seemed to be either indifferent to social reform and political participation, or caught in the web of revolutionary rhetoric.

What was missing from the social compostion of the working class was a unified, class-based analysis through which was articulated a vision of a new society without class divisions and without equal rewards. What did not emerge in America was a broadly based socialist consciousness of a better world. By merely realizing this, however, have we as historians done much justice to the working-class experience, let alone gone beyond a circular argument about the nature of class consciousness reduced to a tautology? American workers have no class consciousness. How do we know? Because of the failure of a socialist movement. Why has the socialist movement failed? Because the American working class has no class consciousness.

The American working class, like all working classes, embodies a contradictory and often changing consciousness. American workers historically have demonstrated from their demands, for the ten-and then eight-hour day and free public schooling to demands for minimum wage bills and social welfare, indeed from demands for legalization of trade unions to Sam Gomper's famous demand for "more," a consciousness of class inequality of opportunity and the realization of collective class action. In the class demands for the benefits of the whole—such as the demand for the ten-hour day, elimination of debtors' prisons, or free public schools—we can see an emerging collective sense of class, and the embryonic development of a class conscious of itself and for itself. Nonetheless, that same class is fragmented into competing in hostile political and social factions over issues of temperance, religious training in the schools, and the division of political spoils. These differences divided Protestant from Catholic, Christian from Jew, ethnic from ethnic, and also divided worker from worker. These divisions led to a narrowing of class demands into the limited area of wage and job issues of trade unions, thus reducing in turn the possibility of greater class maturity and consciousness.[45] Collective struggle and class conflict were narrowed to avoid a larger social conflict that threatened inter-ethnic cooperation.

The immigrants who entered the labor force in the period after industrialization found a social system highly class-stratified, but with few institutional structures for expressing collective class demands. Although that stratification was blurred and its functions vague, nonetheless it was clearly unequal. Class antagonism and discontent found avenues in politically isolated ethnic radicalism, much of which was rooted in the politics of the nation of origin, or in generalized cynicism and alienation. Geographic mobility, plans to return home, lack of citizenship, and open hostility from the institutions of the skilled workforce all contributed to a failure of recent immigrants to develop and articulate a class-wide social movement that would have given their class hostility an institutional and social base.[46] The failure to develop that action was a failure to develop a form of class base to provide a recognizable class base and the articulation of class consciousness.

The depression of 1929 brought the economic collapse of the skilled workforce and the collapse of the political base of ethnic politics. In its place emerged political and social pressures for class-based politics and class-based trade unionism. In the demands of the discontented skilled and unskilled workers and ethnics of various nationaliities for social reform for the whole working class, we can see the development of a class-conscious working class making class demands for itself. Although in hindsight these demands fell far short of what could be called socialist demands, nonetheless for a short period they did represent an emerging consciousness of a class not only of its economic disadvantage, but of its collective improvement.

Traditional European immigrants were replaced after various restrictions of the 1920s with Black and inter-American migrants. Race and ethnic politics emerged again in the post-war period to vie for the loyalty of those who recently entered the industrial world. The class demands of the 1930s receded, but refused to die. Although the American working class is fragmented still and divided, it has refused to go away.

NOTES

I would like to thank Edward Countryman and William Lancaster at the Centre for the Study of Social History, University of Warwick, for help on this work.

1. Herbert Gutman, *Work, Culture and Society* (New York, 1977) p. 14.

2. See Paul Faler's comment on this trend in his *Mechanics and Manufacturers in the Early Industrial Revolution: Lynn, Massachusetts 1780–1860* (Albany, 1981).

3. E.P. Thompson, *The Making of the English Working Class* (New York, 1963) pp. 9–10.

4. See Charles Stephenson's introduction to his 1980 University of Wisconsin thesis, for a discussion of the process of migration and the literature on this subject.

5. See David Montgomery's "The Working Classes of the Pre-Industrial American City, 1780–1830," *Labor History* 9 (Winter, 1968) pp. 3–22, and "The Shuttle and the Cross: Weavers and Artisans in the Kensington Riots of 1844," *Journal of Social History*, vol. 5 (1972) pp. 411–446; Susan Hirsch, *Roots of the American Working Class: the Industrialization of Crafts in Newark, 1800–1860* (Philadelphia, 1978); Sam Bass Warner, *The Private City* (Philadelphia, 1968); Bruce Laurie, *The Working People of Philadelphia* (Philadelphia, 1980) for a discussion of the work process in the pre-industrial city.

6; See Allen Pred, *The Spatial Dynamics of U.S. Urban Industrial Growth 1800–1914* (Cambridge, 1966); Diana Lindstrom, *Economic Development in the Philadelphia Region 1810–1850* (New York, 1978); and Richard Wade, *The Urban Frontier* (Cambridge, 1958).

7. Sydney Pollard, "Industrialisation in the European Economy," *E.C.H.R.* (November 1973); L.M. Cullen, *Economic History of Modern Ireland* (Cork, 1976) p. 119; J. Sharpless and D. Lindstrom, "Urban Growth and Economic Structure in Antebellum America," *Research in Economic History* (1978); and Anthony Wallace, *Rockdale* (Boston, 1978).

8. See John Sharpless and John Rury, "The Political Economy of Women's Work," *Social Science History* vol. 4, (August 1980), pp. 317–346, for a discussion of the multiple labor market.

9. E.P. Thompson, *The Making of the English Working Class*, notes that the Irish migrants were preferred over English factory hands because of their strength, p. 310.

10. See Charlotte Erickson, *Invisible Immigrants* Part II, (Coral Gables, 1972) and Caroline Golab, *Immigrant Destinations* (Philadelphia, 1977) for a discussion of the process by which cultural and familial ties direct immigrants into specific neighborhoods, cities and occupations.

11. See Sam Bass Warner, *The Private City.*

12. Robert Berkhofer, "Space, Culture and the New Frontier," *Agricultural History* 38 (1964).

13. See David Montgomery, "The Working Class of the Pre-Industrial American City." Susan Hirsch, *Roots of the American Working Class*, and Bruce Laurie, *Working People of Philadelphia.*

14. Recent labor historiography has emphasized the relationship between culture and the self-determined nature of the immigrant consciousness, and de-

emphasized the role of economic structure in determining consciousness. This discussison has tended to revolve around such words as "voluntarism," "Agency," or "cultural Marxism" in the field of labor history. H. Gutman's *Work, Culture and Society* is probably the best known of this school. It, like many of the works which follow this tradition, takes its lead from E.P. Thompson who himself emphasizes the significance of agency in Marx's *Poverty of Philosophy*, p. 122.

15. See Stuart A. Marglin, "What the Bosses Do" in Andre Gorz, *The Division of Labour* (Brighton, 1976) for a discussion of the process by which capital came to reorganize production in order to increase their social role.

16. Although I am arguing here that the industrial city brought together unskilled day labor and skilled artisan labor within the factory structure I am not arguing that the pre-industrial city was more segregated than the industrial city. In terms of social and class structure the industrial city was far more rigidly segregated. See Sam Bass Warner, *The Private City*.

17. Benjamin Franklin, *The Autobiography of Benjamin Franklin* (London, 1817); see also David Montgomery, "The Working Classes of the Pre-Industrial American City;" Paul Faler, *Mechanics and Manufacturers in the Early Industrial Revolution*; Henry P. Rosemont, "Benjamin Franklin and the Philadelphia Typographical Strikers of 1786," *Labor History* 22 (1981) pp. 398–429; Bruce Laurie, *Working People of Philadelphia*; Susan Hirsch, *Roots of American Working Class*; and Bryan Palmer, *A Culture in Conflict* (Montreal, 1979).

18. John T. Cumbler, "Transatlantic Working-Class Institutions," *Journal of Historical Geography* 6 (1980) pp. 275–290; Thomas Dublin, *Women at Work* (New York, 1980); and Charlotte Erickson, *Invisible Immigrants*. For records of English trade unions supporting migrants see *Annual Reports of Operative Cotton Spinning Provincial Association Bolton, 1880–1900*; *Reports of the Amalgamated Association of Operative Cotton Spinners, 1880–1900*, Webb Collection, London School of Economics; and Rowland Berthoff, *British Immigrants in Industrial America, 1790–1950* (Cambrdge, 1953) and David Ward, *Cities and Immigrants: A Geography of Change in 19th Century America* (New York, 1971).

19. Francois Couzet, *Capital Formation in the Industrial Revolution* (London, 1971); See also E.P. Thompson, *The Making of the English Working Class*.

20. See Kathleen Neils Conzen, *Immigrant Milwaukee, 1836–1860, Accommodation and Community in a Frontier City* (Cambridge, 1976) for a discussion about the linkage between ethnicity and craft.

21. The piece rate itself was a carry-over from the old putting out system where merchants and master craftsmen subcontracted to smaller craftsmen to complete the product at home. See Paul Faler's *Mechanics and Manufacturers* and Alan Dawley, *Class and Community: The Industrial Revolution in Lynn, Massachusetts* (Cambridge, 1976) for a discussion of this process among shoe workers.

22. See Susan Hirsch, *Roots of the American Working Class* and Alan Dawley, *Class and Community*

23. See John T. Cumbler, *A Moral Response to Industrialism* (Albany, 1982) for a discussion about the emerging middle-class ideology within the context of industrialization. Also look at Bryan Palmer, *A Culture in Conflict* for a discussion about the tendency among skilled workers to be co-opted by traditional allegiances to the producer's ideology.

24. Thomas Dublin, *Women at Work*, and Philip Foner, *Women and the American*

Labor Movement (New York, 1980), both deal with the process by which women are segregated into specific work and work areas in the Lowell factories.

25. Gutman, *Work, Culture and Society.*

26. David Ward, *Cities and Immigrants*; Caroline Golab, *Immigrant Destinations*; Dean Esslinger, *Immigrants and the City, Ethnicity and Mobility in a 19th century Midwestern Community* (Port Washington, 1975); John Bodnar, *Immigration and Industrialization: Ethnicity in an American Mill Town, 1870–1940* (Pittsburgh, 1977); and Josef Barton, *Peasants and Strangers: Italians, Rumanians, and Slovaks in an American City, 1890–1959* (Cambridge, 1976); Michael J. Piore, *Birds of Passage: Migrant Labor and Industrial Societies* (New York, 1979).

27. The literature on the process known as stem migration is extensive. See Conrad Arensberg and Solon Kimball, *Family and Community in Ireland* (Cambridge, 1940) for a discussion of the movement of Irish migrants; Clifford Jansen, "Some Sociological Aspects of Migration" in *Migration*, J.A. Jackson, ed. (Cambridge, 1969); D.B. Grigg, "E.G. Ravenstein and Ravenstein's Laws of Migration," *Journal of Historical Geography*, 3, 1977; Charles Price, "The Study of Assimilation" in *Migration*, J.A. Jackson, ed.; Harold Runblom and Hans Norman, *From Sweden to America* (Minneapolis, 1976) have a discussion of the migration processes of Swedes. For a general review of the migration literature see J.J. Mangalam, *Human Migration: A Guide to Migration Literature in English 1955–1966* (Lexington, 1968). See also Charles Tilly and Edward Shorter, *Strikes in France* (London, 1974), and Gregory Kealey's discussion of the functioning of the Orange lodges in his 1977 Rochester dissertation, "The Working Class Response to Industrial Capitalism," (University of Rochester, 1977).

28. Although the literature on ethnic politics has been extensive as yet little coherence has come out of the problematic involved in understanding the relationship between political participation around ethnic lines and along class lines, and the convergence and divergence of these loyalties. Sam Hays in his work on political reformism has done much to move this discussion toward a class-ethnic view which sees the conflict in terms of a struggle for power. Samuel Hays, "The Politics of Reform in Municipal Government in the Progressive Era," *Pacific Northwest Quarterly* 60 (1964), pp. 157–169. See also John Bodnar's *Immigration and Industrialization*; Herbert Gans, *The Urban Villagers* (New York, 1962), and for a fairly detailed discussion of conflict between ethnic politics and class politics see James Green and Hugh Donahue, *Boston's Workers: A Labor History* (Boston, 1979) chapter 5.

29. See Michael Rogin, "Voluntarism: The Origins of a Political Doctrine" in David Brody ed., *The American Labor Movement* (New York, 1971); Zane Miller, *Boss Cox's Cincinnati* (New York, 1968); Victor Greene, *The Slavic Community on Strike: Immigrant Labor in Pennsylvania Anthracite* (Pittsburgh, 1968); Bruno Ramirez, *When Workers Organize: The Politics of Industrial Relations in the Progressive Era, 1898–1916* (Westport, Ct., 1978); James R. Green and Hugh C. Donahue, *Boston Workers: A Labor History* for a discussion of the process by which class issues can be diffused into social ethnic issues.

30. Daniel Walkowitz, *Worker City, Company Town* (Urbana, 1978); John Bodnar, *Immigration and Industrialization.*

31. Conrad Arensberg and Solon Kimball, *Family and Community in Ireland* (Cambridge, 1940).

32. John T. Cumbler, "Transatlantic Working-Class Institutions," *Journal of Historical Geography*.

33. See Ira Katznelson, *City Trenches* (New York, 1982).

34. Barbara Myerhoff, *Number Our Days* (New York, 1979); David Montgomery, *Beyond Equality* (New York, 1967) pp. 126–134.

35. John T. Cumbler, *Working Class Community in Industrial America* (Westport, Conn., 1979) chapter 11.

36. Ibid., chapters 4, 5, 8, 9.

37. Hugo A. Dubuque, *Guide Canadian-Francais de Fall River* (Fall River, 1889); Commonwealth of Massachusetts, Bureau of Statistics of Labor, *Census of Massachusetts* (1885). Although 38 percent of Fall River's male population found employment as textile operatives and over 40 percent in textile mills, only 11 percent of the Fall River Société of St. Jean Baptist, a major fraternal organization in the French Canadian community, who held positions within the society over the first decade of its existence, found employment in the textile mills. Although 92 percent of the French Canadian community was working class; only 22 percent of the Socíeté was working class. Although one would expect middle-class members of the community to dominate the organization, the overwhelming middle-class makeup of its activists indicates a huge class division within ethnic organizations designed to aid the ethnic community. What was true of the Socíeté of St. Jean Baptist was also true of the other ethnic organizations. Le ligue de Patriotes with over 200 members had only one working-class activist (out of a possible 33). L'Union Canadienne St Jean Baptist de Bowenville had no working-class activists. Only two of Fall River's French Canadian ethnic organizations showed any appreciable working-class membership. La Garde Napoleon had three working-class members who held any position within the organization (out of 12). Les Gardes Impériales was a drill company with two working-class drill instructors.

Although the occupations of the officers do not indicate the occupations of members, the heavy domination of these organizations by middle-class white collar leaders may indicate that the ethnic community was divided, with the small middle-class ethnic group dominating the formal ethnic organizations while the working-class ethnics looked to more informal institutional structures. This view is supported by the fact that especially the younger ethnic workers demonstrated strong class militance during strikes. Testimony of Rufus Wade, *United States Industrial Commission*, vol. 7, 56th Congress, 2nd sess. House Doc. no. 495 (Wash. D.C., 1901). Dean Esslinger, *Immigrants and the City*, also found ethnic organizations and fraternal associations vehicles for upward mobility particularly for middle-class migrants, p. 28.

38. See John T. Cumbler, "Continuity and Disruption: Working Class Community in Lynn and Fall River, Massachusetts 1880–1950," Ph.D., Diss., University of Michigan, 1974, p. 386 and Philip Silvia, "Spindle City: Labor, Politics and Religion in Fall River, Massachusetts, 1870–1905," Ph.D., Diss., Fordham University, 1973.

39. See Zane Miller, *Boss Cox's Cincinnati: Urban Politics in the Progressive Era* (New York, 1968); Sam Bass Warner, *Street Car Suburbs* (Cambridge, 1963); Steven Miller, "Boston's Irish Patronage Machine" (unpublished working paper); Ira Katznelson, *City Trenches*.

40. *Fall River Daily Herald*, August 7, 1884; *Fall River Globe*, December 10, 1904; Inaugural Address of John T. Coughlin, Fall River, Mass., January 2, 1905; Papers of the City of Fall River; see also Philip Silvia, "The Spindle City."

41. E.P. Thompson, *Poverty of Theory* (London, 1978) pp. 51, 298, 299. *The Making of the English Working Class*, p. 9. For a critical review of Thompson's work see Perry Anderson, *Arguments within English Marxism* (London, 1980) particularly pp. 31–58, and G.A. Cohen, *Karl Marx's Theory of History, A Defence* (Oxford, 1978) pp. 73–77.

42. Karl Marx, *The Eighteenth Brumaire of Louis Bonaparte* (New York, n.d.) p. 13.

43. G.A. Cohen, *Karl Marx's Theory of History, A Defence*. pp. 72–102.

44. Stephen Thernstorm, *The Other Bostonians* (Cambridge, 1973). See also Josef Barton, *Peasants and Strangers* (Cambridge, 1976).

45. Susan Hirsch, *Roots of the American Working Class*, pp. 130–135.

46. Charles Stephenson, "A Gathering of Strangers?" in Milton Cantor, ed., *American Workingclass Culture* (Westport, Conn., 1979).

4

Cash, Coffee-Breaks, Horseplay: *Eigensinn* and Politics among Factory Workers in Germany circa 1900

Alf Luedtke

The analysis of everyday life signifies the efforts to explore and to reconstruct the daily processes of production, reproduction, and transformation of social relations. My emphasis is on the mode of life, that is to say, those social practices by which modes of production become daily reality. The approach owes much to E.P. Thompson's classic, *The Making of the English Working Class*, in which the focus is on "class as a relationship, not as a thing."[1] Nevertheless, subsequent research inspired by this book has left important questions unanswered. First, does this kind of history represent anything more than a revival of simple historicism—now labeled reconstruction of experience? What, after all, dignifies those very moments of experience[2] that foster objections against demands from authority or stimulate the struggle for transforming class and power relations? The second question is whether the analysis of daily life necessarily excludes politics? This, however, may be turned around: what, after all, are politics in the context of actual daily practices?[3]

To pose the issue in this way is to question the conventional bipolar model that situates politics in what Thompson calls the field-of-force of domination. It seems to me that, even when it is focused on experiences, this model of politics fails to transcend the conventional historian's perspective, which is, after all, the perspective of the victor. Clearly, the new attention to popular movements and their socio-cultural practices overcomes traditional boundaries. These studies attempt to explore the realms of what appears to be peculiar and sometimes bizarre utterances, or in other cases the silent behaviour of those who have become objects of the research. Ironically enough, however, simultaneous hindsight is applied, at least when what are termed the political qualities are to be considered (in Thompson's case, for example).[4]

The point is not that contexts are to be depicted, that the interrelationships and ambiguities of pre-existing as well as of newly constituted social practices should be explained and understood. Instead, the enterprise goes wrong in its implicit assumption that the investigator and his objects are meeting on equal terms, as if the logic of the subject under study would be derived from a universal and ahistorical political rationality. The impact of the investigator's interests, of his codes of perception and interpretation, is not considered. Above all, there is neglect of the structure of the very scenario, which is nothing but an imposition by the active researcher trying to interrogate passive objects. Even more favored are the results, as we latecomers assess them. Either acceptance of domination or resistance to it is stressed instead of the potentialities which were at stake in a given situation.

I would like to start with this very last point, that is to say, try to use our limited sources for a more participatory observation. But, to be sure, going near and looking closely, even if possible, is no definite solution: it does not make those under study, in this case factory workers in the late nineteenth century, familiar to us.[5] But I hope to show in this paper that the reconstruction of work processes and of cash-earnings, of legal and illegal breaks, of articulation of needs, anxieties, and longings in physically violent horseplay should enable a specific understanding of particular workers' lives and politics. Notions and characteristics of the context can be derived from contemporary reports given by outsiders, or perhaps even by participant observers, as well as from memoirs of those involved, but also from evidence which was produced (almost) without any intention of fostering good (or bad) remembrance, such as wage-lists or factory regulations. In the latter case more than economic reconnaissance is possible. Irregularities of the work process, as far as they become visible in machine accounts or wage-lists, may be analyzed as specific methods of reappropriation or self-will of those on the scene.

Thus, abstract labels come into question. One understands that industrial work is more than "real subsumption of labor under capital," that it is not understood by referring to seemingly mechanical work and time discipline. Therefore, certainly analytical as well as interpretive understanding is useful—after all, it will be the chief viable path for historical reconstruction. But we have to be aware that these efforts to open any possible window on the reasons and motives of those involved still constitute the interrogation of objects. Even decoding does not span the gulf between us. Instead, the use of our limited sources for a second look, for the historian's participatory observation, perhaps enables us to accept that the others may seem even more like strangers when we try to understand them.

MACHINE CONSTRUCTION CIRCA 1900

The place is a machine construction factory in Chemnitz-Saxony, the year is 1890. One department of this factory manufactures machine tools, the other builds spinning machines. After having overcome the slump of 1886–87, the economic cycle is still on the upward swing, and both departments are busy filling their orders.

Paul Göhre was a young Protestant minister who lived and labored for six weeks with the workers of the machine tool department. Apparently he revealed casually, or at least did not consciously disguise his profession. He stayed as a "participant observer" with the roughly 120 smiths, drillers, filers, and especially turners, who worked together in one workshop. Their work day began at 6:00 AM and ended 12 hours later; almost 11 of these hours were scheduled as actual work time.[6] Within this twelve hour period *one* twenty-minute coffee break and a one-hour lunch break were allowed.

One year later, Göhre published a book containing his observations and impressions, and summed up his carefully detailed account of the work day as follows:

> It is no trifle to stay for eleven hours together with 120 men in one hot room which is filled with oily, greasy fumes, the workers' exhalation, and with coal and metal dust. Factory work is exhausting not primarily because of the heavy work-load and the toilsome motions of arms and hands which are required; more important is this living together, breathing together, sweating together of so many people, the permanent squeaking and droning noise, the continuous standing hour after hour almost on the same spot.[7]

Certainly this is a very different picture than the one given by photographs taken in the factories of the time, which show almost nothing of those daily experiences Göhre described. Instead, factory photographs are staged, reflecting the photographer's image of what factory work should look like—the activity of attentive, concentrated, and clean workers in a well organized workshop, no breaks or interruptions, and no exhaustion at all. But even if one relies on reports of the kind Göhre offered, one still must, of course, deduce the strange and mixed feelings that presumably disturbed this young theologian who, after all, not only was a newcomer to the shop, but also an invader coming from the higher-level world of academia and, even worse (concerning the anticipated feelings of his temporary workmates) from the pulpit. Not less important, one has to consider that Göhre voluntarily exposed himself to the demands and the toil of factory work, while most of his mates had no choice. In order to sustain themselves and their families, industrialized wage work was a sheer necessity of their daily life. To be sure, those divergent class positions and experiences would structure the perceptions of the familiar and the alien in the factories. What Göhre assessed as utterly depressing or coarse might be part of the workers' most common daily routines; workers would neither worry about them nor mention them at all.

Göhre's recollections, however, are very illuminating, for in order to accomplish his self-imposed mission to not confront workers' "atheism" but to raise their interest in religion, he chose not to rush in as a "visitor," but to undertake an ethnographic journey into the unknown territory, as it were, of the factories. The detailed descriptions of earnings, diets, behaviour, recruitment, and especially the work process itself, give abundant proof of this.

Göhre was hired as a handyman with the drillers and, particularly, the turners. They operated lathes and machines that were driven by steam-engines via transmission belts and clutches. In terms of workers' control, their work process differed from that of other groups within the shop.[8] The casters, moulders, and smiths prepared and produced the basic parts and operated tools as well as the finished pieces almost completely by hand. They thereby translated a given construction scheme according to their immediate, but experienced, assessment of the work process into the guiding of helpers and the handling of both tools *and* finished pieces. The same applied to the fitters and mechanics, who assembled the manufactured parts and finished the products. The drillers' task was the opposite. They usually worked according to a routinized, repetitious job, and had almost no opportunity to operate the tools themselves or to guide the final piece independently, according to their assessment of how best to perform any given task.

The turners, however, had to perform a kind of semi-manual labor. Their task was to give each piece its precise shape; therefore, they had to cut notches and to turn threads or screw-joints. To be sure, they did not operate their tools directly by hand, but, similar to the almost artisan-like work of the moulders or fitters, they prepared and adjusted the machine, and during the turning of the piece which was to be worked, they intervened, sometimes by hand, especially to file the piece to its final polish. The preparation of the lathe was relatively time-consuming. In order to achieve the optimal speed during the turning process, the gears had to be adjusted and calculated (using fractional arithmetic) and each time composed anew. The slug then had to be centered; sometimes it became necessary to put it onto the lathe and trim some splinters by hand-filing. After having started the lathe (or more precisely, after connecting it to the transmission-shaft of the workshop), the turner had to switch to a mostly passive watchfulness, simultaneously having an eye on the transmission belt and the clutch, the speed of the lathe, and the part of the lathe that carried the cutting or turning tool. The turners had to employ and develop skills involving manual dexterity, knowledge of the good and bad points of the worked metals, experience with the speeds and gears of the transmission belts, and of "their," that is, the factory's lathe or even two or three lathes that they had to operate. Sometimes they had to be able to read a blueprint and to translate its figures and symbols into the mechanics of the lathe. Clearly, their task was multifaceted, requiring not only experience but a kind of continuous activity (or, at least attentiveness). Of course, these skills and qualifications mostly were acquired on the job—contrary to some of the other groups in the workshop, particularly the smiths (most of them had served the legally recognized three years of apprenticeship). As for the turners, former wood-turners were often recruited. Such was the case of Moritz Theodor Wilhelm Bromme, for example, whose autobiography parallels Göhre's report of the shop floor, but gives a true participant's account of what it was like to work as a turner.[9] Bromme worked from 1898 until the early part of the twentieth century in a machine construction factory in Gera, about 100 kilometers west of Chemnitz.

Turners perceived themselves to be *the* crucial group within the workforce able to carry out the supervisor's admonition "to be productive."[10] This overwhelming acceptance of the productivity goal of the factory system and of those who mainly profited from its operation was not achieved simply by physical enforcement or by some simple manipulation of these workers. There are two additional factors one must consider. First, one must analyze the control of the work process (or lack of it) and the related self-esteem. Second, it is necessary to consider whether this self-perception might rely on a material equivalent and expression.

From the very beginning of machine production in the 1830s in Germany,[11] and until at least 1910–14, the turners ranked among the best paid machine construction workers in the country.[12] They, together with the miners, were at the top of the wage scale in the late 1870s, and ranked with the iron and steel workers after 1908. The figures Göhre gave as weekly earnings, from 1890, show turners earning 20 to 30 Deutschmarks weekly *if* they were mostly or completely paid in piece rates.[13] (We will see later that the assumption that piece-work was the common wage and payment system after the 1870s is faulty.) It should be noted that wage rates did not strictly favor the craftsmen-like workers against the unskilled ones. Instead, Göhre points out that the smiths or mechanics, most of them being formally trained, got 15 to 20 Deutschmarks per week, while fitters, who likewise were formally trained, got 22 to 28—these being paid time wages. Simultaneously, workers who were trained on the job got remarkably higher wages, like drillers (30 Deutschmarks) or planers and turners (between 20 and 30)—all of these being paid piece rates. Handymen and day laborers, like Göhre himself, were of course at the bottom of the scale. However, they could come close to the smiths or mechanics, earning up to 15 Deutschmarks.

Concerning the degree of control they had in the work process, the self-esteem and the status given them by the fellow workers, as well as in wage rates, the turners were typical of the top layers of machine construction workers. They belonged to the minority of factory workers who were relatively "well off," materially *and* symbolically. At least in these terms they were members of Hobsbawm's labor aristocrats.[14]

While these characteristics are more or less common for almost all machine construction workers, the status of the turners also depended on a peculiarity of their work process. In their branch, they were the only ones who operated machines and still performed a relatively individualized (or at least self-controlled) labor. The organization of their work at the same time stimulated and enforced competition with fellow turners at surrounding lathes, and also made possible the confirmation of one's calculative abilities and manual dexterity. In contrast to "traditional" artisanal workers such as smiths or moulders, the turners could demonstrate to themselves and to others their skill and experience even while controlling "modern" machinery.

What I have done so far is to give a relatively static view of what it would have been like to work as a turner or, more generally, as a machine construction worker in a late nineteenth-century factory. To expand the scope I will add some aspects of the life cycle, at this point avoiding, however, the complex intertwinings of work and non-work, of the productive and reproductive spheres. In other words, the life-course of males and females, the problem of domestic settings, of family structures and relationships are only mentioned here, but not elaborated.

Those machines construction workers who had been born after about 1855 might well have experienced a relative security of employment in this "leading sector" of the industrial economy. They could have experienced an increase in real wages, which would have been quite unexpected, including a precipitous jump of more than 25 percent between 1872 and 1874, followed by a stagnation that lasted until the mid–1880s and a moderate increase after that (this being the general trend for the Reich).[15] This increase in money earnings was accompanied only by a comparatively slight increase in the cost of living, at least until about 1900. In general these trends may not have caused, but surely allowed for a considerable degree of movement among employers.

Hermann Enters, not a turner but a journeyman mechanic who served a regular apprenticeship in the region's domestic metalwork industry in the Wupper Valley, discussed in his memoirs frequent changes of workplaces during the boom phase of the early 1870s, when he was in his early twenties and unmarried.[16] He worked at the famous Krupp works, as well as at smaller factories in Barmen, looking for a combination of high wages and satisfying work. With Krupp, he got piece-work, but had to do only a very limited number of tasks connected with the turning of gun barrels, and had been rigidly controlled. In Barmen he got a time wage, a lower amount of cash, but he could work completely independently as a repair mechanic. He switched back and forth twice, finding no solution to his dilemma.

To be sure, in some parts of the machine construction sector, workers also could have experienced devaluation of skills at the same time that they experienced control over the work process. At least in the relatively standardized production of bicycles and sewing-machines, the range of different tasks was limited, offering no prospects for further training on the job. This may have been the reason for the comparatively high turnover rate in these factories.[17] From the mid–1880s on, more than 70 percent—in 1890 even 86.3 percent—of the workers of the sewing-machine fatory of Thomas Calsow in Bielefeld/Westphalia left within the first 12 months after entrance, including almost all of those under age 25.

But even more important than the mobility of workers who stayed (or tried to stay) in the same line of work is the fact that not all of the machine construction workers or turners had or looked for a permanent career in those occupations. Bromme, who had had half a dozen jobs before he got on-the-job training as a wood-turner, perhaps is not typical; but at least his case indicates that different patterns might have existed, and that even a relative permanence of occupation was not a general feature with the workers in this sector. In contrast, for example, records from the mechanical workshops of the Gutehoffnungshütte, GHH, Oberhausen Rhineland, show that in the early 1870s more than 30 percent of their workforce consisted of fathers and sons, uncles and nephews.[18] In any case, the assumption of any typical life-course and accompanying experiences or of a lifelong or even inherited career as a skilled machine construction worker, seems to be dubious.

UNCERTAINTIES OF THE WORK EXPERIENCE

The long-term figures, as well as the more qualitative accounts of machine construction workers, especially of the turners, stress the relative *homogeneity* of the group's experience and of their daily practices. They also assume a basically *steady* development geared towards a better standard of living, more generally toward socio-economic improvement in terms of a more respectable daily reproduction. And equally, the notion of labor aristocracy, already mentioned—although reluctantly even if it is used analytically—seems to be fostered by this implicit meaning.

It is important, if perhaps only secondarily so, that machine construction workers were not simply conservative reformists. It is true that they, or their trade union representatives, did not strive for big strikes and did not participate very actively in the pre-war *Massenstreik* debate by the organized labor movement, but they never became "traitors" to the workers' struggles before 1914 or to the mass movements that became visible in the strikes of 1917 (and more so in the subsequent two years). Instead the turners, at least in Berlin, triggered off-shop-floor activity that combined their immediate interest in high wages and improved working conditions with their disapproval of the government's war policies since the very first days of World War I.[19] What is important in this circumstance is that the accounts of their resistance against both labor leaders and the state still suggests the picture of a homogeneous group, perceiving and acting according to a *consistent* set of standards and preferences. These were the men who one of their most active fellow workers and comrades, Richar Müller, characterized in 1924 as stressing "cool and matter-of-fact calculations of success and failure," bound for systematically organized political movements."[20]

All of these divergent, partly contradictory assessments of the political attitudes and actions of machine construction workers, and especially of turners, insist to a significant degree on their *consistency* and *homogeneity*. This implication is as strong as to seem to be unquestioned. Accordingly, occupational structures, qualification levels, or migration rates—in other words, formal characteristics—are accentuated, and the different groups that might be examined on this level are taken as entities. We never are able to unfold mulitfaceted, even contradictory, experiences and practices. We should take a second look.

Let us still consider the turners. Contemporary observations such as Göhre's, and more recent writings as well, somehow assume implicitly or explicitly that since the early 1870s the work and wage systems generally were based on piece-work. But some brief remarks in Bromme's memoirs may raise some doubts. He recalls shifting several times between piece- and time-work.[21] Bromme concedes that he preferred piece-work and requested this type of work from the master; instead of coming home with 13 to 15 Deutschmarks on Saturday night, he could expect 20 or more Marks each week. Of course, it is obvious that Bromme was harnessed by a "cash nexus," by the daily necessity of assuring his and his family's survival. By "speeding up" at the lathe he matched the capitalists' (as well as their middle-men's) interests. More important, here is the *simultaneity* of both systems of work payment. According to Bromme's report, the proportions of which products were paid according to which system could be switched back and forth based on the calculations of the managers and masters.

At least in part, their calculations were determined by disciplinary reason—to punish or, as in the case of Bromme, to stimulate individual workers, thereby also enforcing internal splits and fissions between workmates. But cost calculations were ultimately decisive; the objects or series of objects that had to be shaped and finished varied considerably. There were worked bolts, screws, handles, pipes, cranks or shafts—the rhythms and time sequences of the work process changed with the kind, size, and number of the pieces. To optimize profits, it made sense to work on a time wage, especially if complicated shapes on only a small number of pieces had to be done.[22]

Since the evidence is very scattered, one has to rely for a more detailed picture on the wage records of the above-mentioned mechanical workshops of the GHH (Oberhausen Rhineland).[23] Although these lists refer to a period 30 years earlier, the structure of work organization and work processes in machine construction, at least in the construction of machine tools and driving machines, did not begin to change essentially until about 1910, and they still apply to the period around 1890–1900. These lists start with September 1869 and exist for a period of less than three years, ending in April 1872, but they offer a detailed account of the wage structure affecting some 200 workers. Since deductions for punishment and the factory's compulsory health insurance were given, we can calculate the actual amount of cash the workers received evey second Friday. Figure 4.1 and figure 4.2 show in detail wage calculations from this factory for six men. Except for one (Altekamp), all of these six workers experienced within 12 weeks increases in total wages of 50 percent or more, in one case (Menzen, September 1–15) of about 80 percent, and in one other (Dickmann, the same period) of almost 70 percent. But all of them faced tremendous decreases as well, leaving them less than half, and perhaps only one-fourth (Dickmann, the very next period, September 15–30) of what they had received previously.

At the beginning of this period three of the workers, the turners Altekamp, Schlagermann, and Melis, were relatively close in terms of their wage, all of them earning between 11 and 14 Talers, while two others of the quoted sample found themselves significantly below. The turners Dickmann and Menzen received between 7 and 8 Talers. Finally, the handyman Wewel was far below all of these turners; he got slightly more than 3 Talers. While two weeks later, at the next payday, the discrepancies had increased, after another two weeks (September 15) just the reverse could be observed. In the middle of September the wages of all five turners can almost be depicted as a cluster, the distances having become relatively narrow, not more than about one Taler between each of them. Again, only one pay day later the picture had changed completely. The wages of one of the turners (Dickmann) had dropped to less than a quater of what he had earned two weeks before. Simulta-

Figure 4.1 Variation of Wages

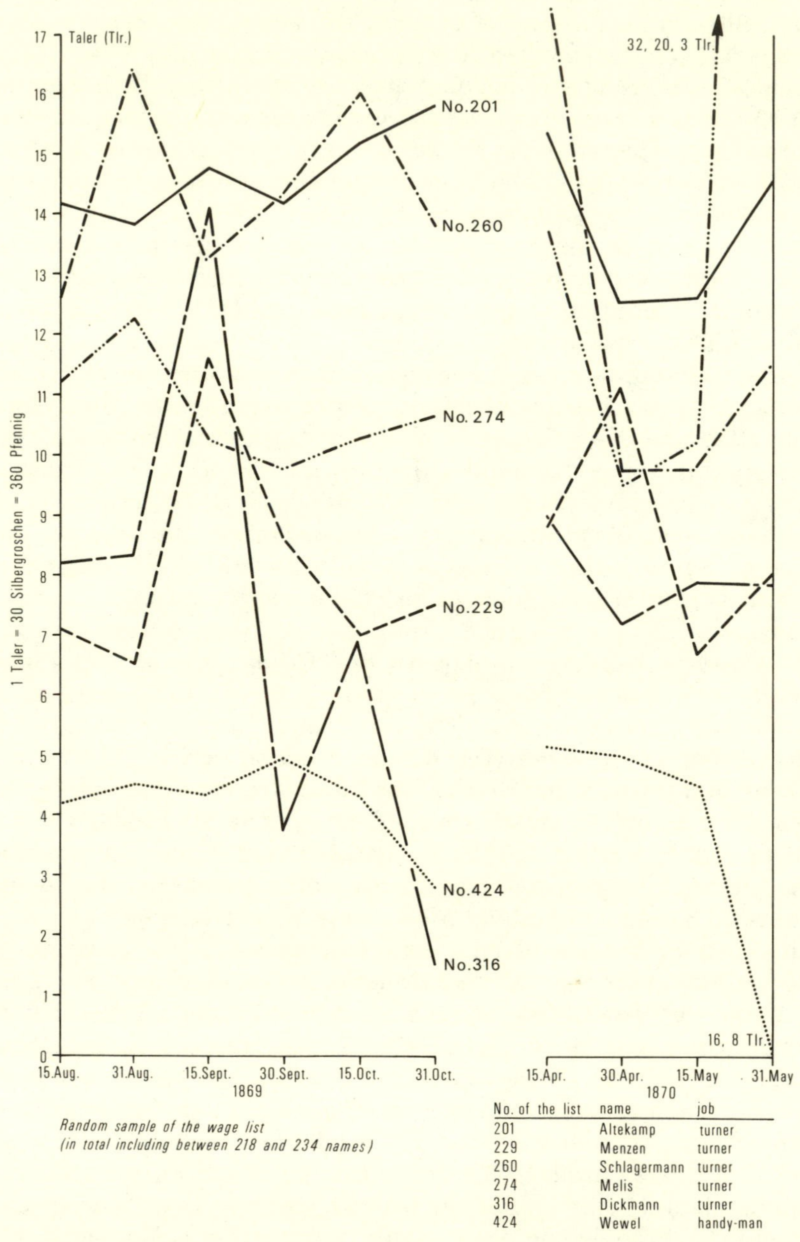

No. of the list	name	job
201	Altekamp	turner
229	Menzen	turner
260	Schlagermann	turner
274	Melis	turner
316	Dickmann	turner
424	Wewel	handy-man

Figure 4.2 Piece- and Time-Wages: Simultaneity and Proportions

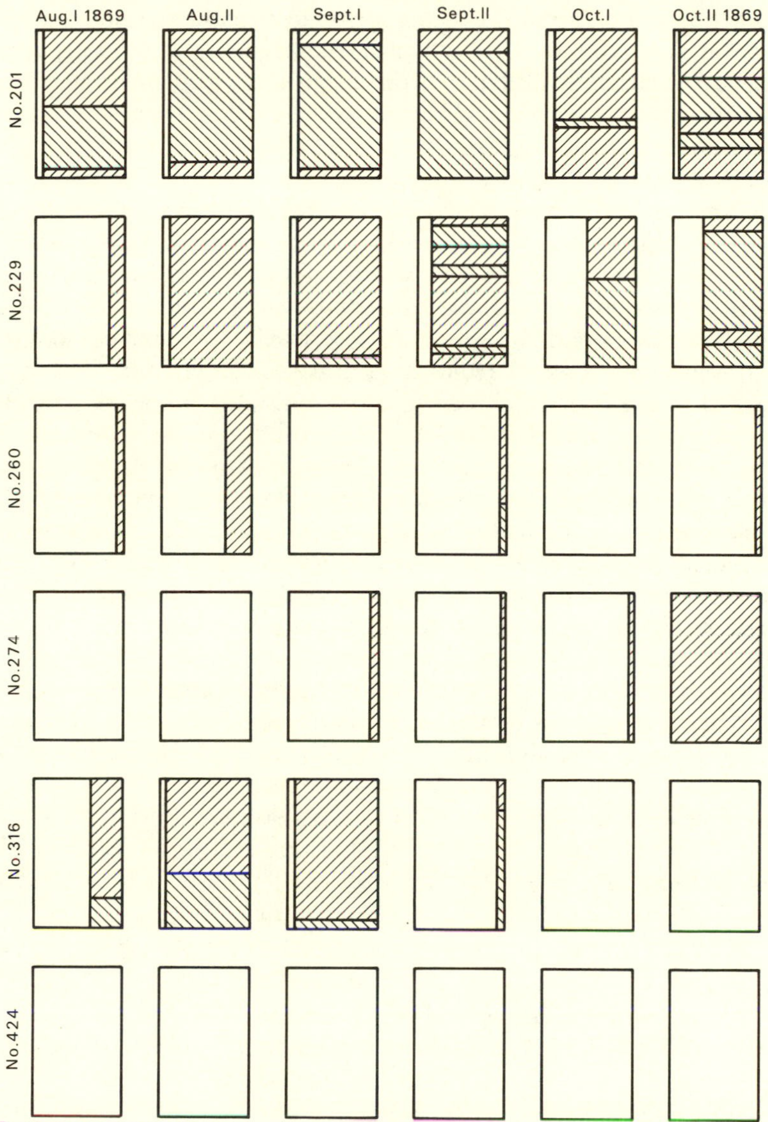

The blank spaces represent the proportion of wage which was earned on an hourly basis (time-wage) the cross-hatched spaces represent the proportion which was earned on a piece-wage basis. The sub-segments of the piece-wage spaces stand for the different 'piece-numbers' worked by each worker; their size indicates the relative amount which they contributed to the piece-wage of the worker.

neously, Altekamp and Schlagermann, on the one hand, and Melis and Menzen on the other, found themselves almost on the same respective levels but the distance between the pairs now was more than 5 Talers.

In October, Altekamp and Schlagermann remained relatively close and stayed on a high level, only Schlagermann being faced with a small decrease. But Menzel fell back to the level he was at in the beginning of August. To pursue one individual's experiences, Dickmann for example could double his wage from the end of September until the middle of October. But at the end of October he was much worse off than in the weeks before. Because he had fallen ill he only got wages for two days, amounting to 1.2 Talers. And since the factory's compulsory insurance did not pay for the first seven days of illness—and after that only up to one-tenth of the previous wages—he and his relatives (assuming that he was contributing to their support) must have had a hard time in the second half of October and also in November. The actual amount of cash Dickmann received during his illness was less than half of the wage the handyman Wewel got. But while Wewel routinely had to expect a wage ranging from 2 to 4 Tales, Dickmann was afflicited by a drastic downswing hitting from one pay day to the very next. This example shows that the inclusion of the periods in which workers were out of work for several days because of being injured or ill is important, and makes clear that these mostly unintended interruptions contributed remarkably to the degree of uncertainty workers experienced and had to bear daily.

There is still more to this wage book. The list enumerates each piece-work by giving the production order's number. As those who worked to fill the order can be identified by these numbers, it is possible to trace these numbers to the order books and identify the pieces (screws, pipes, cranks, etcetera), and thus, it becomes possible to reconstruct the work units and their products on a detailed daily basis. It becomes fairly clear that the composition and the structure of the work units changed. Tasks that only one man had to fulfill were followed by others involving three, nine, or even 15 workers—one man's piece being, for instance, a complicated shaft (worked in time- or in piece-work), the 15 workers' piece an order that implied the turning of threads of equal size or caliber for the parts of a machine or a series of machine tools (usually this type of order was given as piece-work to the turners). The variations both in the turners' work process and in the system of payment had futher implications. The often incalculable shifts affected daily relationships with workmates, as well as the actual amount of cash that was to be expected on pay day.

A preliminary conclusion from this attempt to read wage lists should emphasize the variations not only of tasks but also among the forms and degree of cooperation with fellow workers. Yet it was not only the pieces that had to be worked and the work units themselves varied.[24] Simultaneously two different wage forms were used and, most important, the actual amount of cash one could expect displayed extreme differences and quick changes, partly due to the permanent and ubiquitous danger of injuries.

These daily or at least weekly variations strongly influenced the experiences of those concerned. They interfered with and even contradicted the imposed demands of the factories' time and work discipline. The variations also generated a certain sense of isolation, even between those working next to each other at the lathe or drilling machine. Since the actual wage was not made public by the superiors—at pay day the workers gathered, but everyone got his wage in a covered box—the knowledge of those individual variations required discussion, which was not possible without mutual trust. But this mutuality was simultaneously underminded. For speaking frankly to the mate working next to oneself could trigger his efforts to get a better deal for himself which could be to the detriment of the man who spoke first (as Bromme reports repeatedly). In the end, cautiously keeping some distance from one's co-workers and hesitating to become too close to them could pay off better. Even a collective action might be penetrated by a sense of ongoing intimate hostility among all the participants.

These ups and downs in cash amounts drastically limited one's ability to buy bread, beer, milk, or cheese—to afford the daily necessities, not to mention saving a *Notgroschen* or "emergency dime." Thus, the "cash nexus" remained extremely fragile. Ironically enough, a process that was supposedly part of the capitalization of social relationships in general was in fact severely hindered—namely, to make everyone a participant in the consumer market in the long run. Or, put another way, these incalculable variations of cash flow could stimulate the creativity of those concerned. How could they make their own the desired or even desperately needed goods? How could they appropriate their share by the means available to them?

These experiences of unevenness of variation and of incalculability must have directly affected the ability to plan for even the immediate future. Perhaps our analytical notion of life-course has to be adjusted. Perhaps the expectations of future earnings, including the recognition of old-age poverty, of relatively or even absolutely decreasing cash income after 45 years of age, were less important than people today assume. If this were so, it might have been because the middle-aged and older workers experienced relatively higher cash earnings in the 1890s and after 1900 than they could have expected on the basis of prior extrapolations from the earnings their fathers, uncles, or other "older workers" had received during their working lives. This experience on the job and that in the consumer market may be seen to have shaped the workers' families' *perception of time*, a conceptualization that imposed on them a special mode of understanding throughout their lives.

THE CONCEPT OF *EIGENSINN*

Uncertainties, inconsistencies, and discontinuities in the tasks and wages moulded workers' experience in general, and those of machine-construction workers and turners specifically. While it is important to stress this in criticizing straightforward notions of "unilinear" experiences and attitudes of workers, still it does not give a complete picture. As mentioned above, workers not only operated their tools and machines, not only cooperated sometimes in different ways, but also lived together for many hours. These aspects of cohabitation, of cooperating with and having physical contact with each other, were a reaction in certain ways to these uncertainties.

Let us begin again with a quotation from the "participant observer" Göhre: "The cooperation at work led to continuous and frequent contact and immediate exchange. These were especially lively between workers of the same age, between immediate colleagues and people of the same work-group, and under the same foreman. Almost unintentionally these contacts became close and intimate. Every occasion to chat or engage in conversation was used."[25] Göhre recalled that the topics included news of new workmates and events within the factory, on other floors or in other shops, plans for the coming weekend and, most important, the well-being of their children. From time to time, as Göhre put it, "serious" issues also were raised, including "religious, economic, [and] political topics as well as matters of education."

It seems, however, that the non-verbal exchanges and physical contacts were most important. Göhre noted:

More than anything else these people teased one another, scuffled and tussled—indulged in horseplay, where and whenever it seemed possible. People looked for friends, and acquaintances; clay was thrown at someone who passed by, the slip-knot of his apron was untied from behind, the plank of a seat was pulled away while a fellow-worker took a break, someone's way was blocked unexpectedly or they "pulled someone's leg." But, to be sure, especially favored among older workers at the end of the week was another form of horse-play: "beard-polish." Shaving was a once-a-week affair, a common practice among workers, and was performed usually Saturday night or Sunday morning. By the end of the week, the worker whose beard had grown in would grab the head of a chap with more tender cheeks, lips, and chin, and would rub his face against the youth's face, a process which of course had a quite painful result. Before the victim realized just what had happened to him, the wrong-doer had already disappeared. Even less pleasant was another practical joke, which I—fortunately enough—had to experience only once. A worker is leaning against a post, taking

> a break, for no particular reason two of his co-workers recognize him, a look of understanding passes between them—and one of them approaches the leaning one from behind, claps him tight with his arms while the other takes the face of the immobilized victim in his black, dirty hands and slowly pulls his moustache to either side, pressing his thumbs against the face of the harassed workmate. This joke is, as I can testify, very painful. . . . Among those who knew one [an]other nobody was excepted. Even age made no difference.[26]

This gives a very vivid account of intense and continual non-verbal social exchange between those who worked and at least partly lived together.

These brief interludes of interaction were carried out especially by means of body contact, including physical violence. The struggle for control of one's own body, which was simultaneously the demonstration of manual dexterity and physical skill as well as the cultivation and preservation of social relationships, required obvious physical force, at least between males in this period of industrial capitalism in the late nineteenth century. Of course, in these interactions the participants also expressed and reaffirmed the social hierarchy and displayed "typical" male behavior.[27] Basically at stake, however, was reciprocal appreciation, recognition, and encouragement—next time the victim was likely to be one of the other "players." Everybody on the shop floor knew that the victimization was general and not individual. Simultaneously these interactions can be read as reconfirmation of experiences that all participants shared—being bound tight, fixed on the spot, being marked and made dirty—in other words, being exposed to external manipulations whose authors, at least temporarily, were beyond control of the victims. Therefore, violent physicality in this context might have been one moment of the endeavour "to-be-let-alone" *and* "to-be-with-oneself-and-the-others." To put it differently, these interactions and expressions were not meant primarily as direct resistance to demands "from above"; instead, they expressed a space of their own—*Eigensinn*[28] (self-will or self-reliance).

However, this form of social intercourse did not occur in the officially conceded breaks. Rather, the workers expropriated bits of the time formally designated as working time. They made it their own by frequently neglecting or breaking the imposed time schedule. Their chatting with each other, their walking around and, not the least, their repeated horseplay—these were illegal breaks.

In contrast, the legal breaks were used intensively for physical replenishment.[29] During breakfast and lunch breaks Göhre observed a certain wordless camaraderie. The rustling of a newspaper page being turned, or the passing on of a newspaper section complemented the sounds of eating. The workers, as Göhre reports, sat "relaxed and silent beside one another."[30] These breaks very literally consisted of reproductive activity, the laborious replenishment of one's own strength for the following hours at the workbench, at the drilling and milling machines, and at the lathes. More theoretically, these breaks were *reproductive* work; they fit the demands of the factory system. Breakfast and lunch breaks were scheduled as well as used for physical recuperation; they were directly tied to the needs of survival. Of course, they also contained short moments of being together.

Illegal breaks were different. Here workers broke with the demands and constraints of the factory system as well as with the toil of labor and reproduction. Their activities were not at all generally influenced by any intention of being resistant; nevertheless, their breaking with time schedules or disciplinary regulations partly affected the factories' work process or order. Certainly, resistance was at stake with the silent reappropriation of some minutes by starting late in the morning, by cleaning the machines while they were still running, washing themselves, and leaving the workplace a little earlier than was allowed by the factory regulations. Quiet and primarily individualistic withdrawal, and also literal disappearance happened even more frequently. Workers took a nap before they got a new order or a missing part, or even more frequently one or another disappeared to use—without any hurry—the lavatory. These reappropriations and withdrawals interfered, of course, with the owners' and supervisors' efforts to devote the entire operational time to the production of commodities, not to waste a second. The ever-more detailed new editions of the factory regulations mirror how far the workers' silent transgressions were perceived as resistance.

Eigensinn was something else again. *Eigensinn* was expressed and reaffirmed by walking around and talking, by momentarily slipping away or day-dreaming, but primarily by reciprocal body contact and horseplay—in short it was "being-with-oneself" and "being-with-the-others." Thereby workers neglected, but mostly did not directly interfere with the ongoing work process or with the factory's regularity as it was conceived by management.

Illegal breaks, to be sure, were multifaceted and ambivalent situations. Resistance could be and was practiced then, sometimes even displayed. But simultaneously, and even more intensely, these were moments of actively taking distance not only from capital's domination at the workplace, but also from fighting or resisting the restrictions of one's own needs and interests—immediate joyful "depense"[31] (expenditure of time on the spot) without any calculation of effects or outcomes. The workers then were with themselves by actively neglecting the consequences of their social intercourse, at least for some minutes, or perhaps only seconds.

They interacted on their own terms, albeit temporarily. Although body contact seems to be the most common language of this social intercourse, *Eigensinn* also was expressed verbally, sometimes even conspicuously, in speech. The workmates who time and again tried "to-be-with-themselves" called each other by their first names and addressed each other by the familiar, almost familial, "du." By so doing they signaled mutual respect and, even more, brotherhood. Also articulated was the distinctiveness of one's own peer group and the otherness of the rest demarcated; all of "them" were addressed by the distant, formal "Sie."[32] While other workers with whom one did not have permanent or frequent contact mostly did not seem to care, or were used to it and practiced the same thing, the masters and supervisors (but not the foremen) demanded the more formal usage. They heard an appropriate submissiveness and distance; for the workers, the familiar hierarchy of school, church, and military service[33] was invoked.

Eigensinn happened in isolated, though in constantly repeated, reappropriated moments, in which the workers created, articulated, expressed, and fulfilled needs. In the factory, these needs were blocked or suppressed by the disciplining regularities of work orders, factory regulations and organization, by the constant danger of being under the surveillance[34] of supervisors, masters, and foremen and, above all, being encircled by a tall concrete factory wall. The meaning and the function of the moments of *Eigensinn* were at least twofold—workers could be alone as well as with the others. By interacting on their own terms they could keep at a distance the constraints of the factory as well as those of the struggle for survival. Simultaneously, capabilities for individual or collective action on the shop floor could be developed. This was the case when masters or foremen put forth the usage of "du," offending the workers especially by the implied connotation of the father-child relationship (children were generally addressed as "du").[35] Workers answered or shouted back "du" instead of the expected "sie" or sometimes did not hear at all. This was also the case when workers, who usually seemed to be acting separately and fought on an individualistic basis, quickly found a collective basis, when they forced management to allow cleaning of the lathes during the work time, as occurred in Bromme's factory.[36]

Thus, the boundaries between *Eigensinn* and calculated resistance remained blurred and fluid. *Eigensinn* was different from pursuing one's interests; it was not identical to strategically optimizing the effectiveness of behaviour. In order to keep or even to improve one's wage it might have been wise to act collectively—for example, to combine demonstrative obedience and silent sabotage at the workplace or to go on strike. Instead, *Eigensinn* practices circumvented, even neglected, any calculation of risk-taking. *Eigensinn* could be part of those collective efforts. But simultaneously and primarily *Eigensinn* expressed needs of both the group and the individuals; it articulated longings and desires as well as anxieties. Therefore, *Eigensinn* activities constituted a distinct experience of autonomy as well as of collectivity, perhaps even of homogeneity. In its double meaning *Eigensinn* signified and expressed the peculiarities of workers' politics—"being-with-oneself" *and* "being-with-the-others."

Now it is necessary to add another facet, but one that does not fit easily into the basically harmonious and joyful picture that Göhre's recollections suggest. Handwritten accounts of several retired *Arbeiterveteranen* workers from the Gutehoffnungshütte (taken in 1939 at the suggestion of a manager of the company) not only reported anecdotes on horseplay, but also complained about the frequent theft of tools in the mechanical workshops.[37] At that time in the mid–1880s the tools were owned by the workers.

Horseplay or evoking of power and of social distinctions by "du" expressed needs and simultaneously reappropriated time or space, for some moments at least. These practices were a mixture of claims against the supervisors' demands maintaining customary rights and of striving for the humanity of the individual and his comrades. More importantly, they did not seriously hurt those comrades. Stealing others' tools was the contrary. The tools that the workers owned were not significant to them in the sense of bourgeois property. Instead, they were meaningful as basic means in the daily struggle for survival. At the same time tools symbolized one's dexterity and skill. They had become part of the owner's products and stood for his productive labour as well as for their products. By using his tools he could remember those products which, by now, had been appropriated by the factory's bosses or anonymous buyers. In many respects the victim could not do without his tools.

Leaving aside the possibility that the differences between the shop floors of GHH and the factories at Chemnitz or Gera may have been because of the regional aspects of the workers' lives or different characteristics of the production processes, this stealing suggests that daily practices included many divergent, even contradictory aspects. *Eigensinn* or "self-will" was and remained ambivalent. Distancing oneself from demands of the supervisors and from the constraints of the work process without directly fighting them could imply not only individualistic, but even hostile neglect of one's own workmates.

EIGENSINN AND PRIVATE POLITICS

I have discussed above in some detail the turners' work processes, payment systems and variations of actual wages, and especially their horseplay and *Eigensinn*. These illustrations should show how the mode of production was becoming real for the people concerned. After all, economic cycles and factory regulations exist only on the paper of analysts or supervisors, and behind the backs of the people.

No societal process becomes part of daily interaction and (re)production unless it is experienced in terms which are meaningful (i.e., as an opportunity for a wage increase). In theoretical terms, the mode of production and the mode of domination are reconstituted by the perceptions and interpretations, and the actions and expressions of those concerned,[38] in this case by the practices of male machine construction workers. Or to put the theoretical point a bit differently, the reciprocity of objective and subjective moments makes possible societal reproduction as well as societal transformation. To grasp the fullness of this vital point requires a perspective that does not measure significance and meaning against socio-economic position, or vice versa. Only from such a perspective can one begin to discern contradictions in society, and with them the potential for alternatives to become reality. To give proper attention to the ambiguities of forms of domination and societal intercourse it is necessary *not* to reduce them to their apparently most elementary degree. Only by investigating the complexities and the intertwinings of their contradictory moments can the meanings as well as the functions of daily practices be unfolded and no longer count as mere peripheral phenomena. Attempts to fragment historical and societal processes into separate dimensions cannot do justice to the interrelatedness of concrete situations; they only obscure the synchronism[39] that inevitably characterizes practice—the acceptance of constraints, as well as disobedience to them, and a very distinct and distanced *Eigensinn*.

This brief discussion should indicate that I am aware of some of the problems which are assembled under the somewhat awkward notion of culturalism. There is, however, a second and equally serious point. The question of politics figures even more prominently in the examination of everyday life. To use one of the terms in use on this battlefield, what about romanticism? Isn't this search for *Eigensinn* just another example of the attempt to escape from the hard political questions, from the seemingly ubiquitous relationships of domination and resistance?

"Politics" traditionally refers to the formulation, achievement, and sustained organization of collective interests. Generally this is considered political, especially when it capitalizes on and solidifies, or when it confronts, prevailing norms, societal patterns of distribution, or patterns of state domination. Any other forms of expression that do not meet these criteria generally are said to be private. In contrast, I would like to argue for a perspective that views the articulation and assertion of individual needs as political behaviour, particularly for those directly concerned.

The point, then, is to expand the focus on the political beyond strategic and calculated action. In the perspective of strategic calculation, most of the ensemble constituted by emotional expressions and symbolic meanings is split off. However, it is precisely these that create from ideal types individuals and groups who not only respond but act, sometimes determinedly and consistently, sometimes contradictorily and even inconsistently.

To put this more concretely, these turners and other machine construction workers participated only reluctantly in the "free" (socialist) *Deutsche Metallarbeiterverband* (DMV), the metal workers' trade union which was founded in 1891, a year after the repressive anti-socialist law of 1878 had expired. Except of those workers in big cities such as Berlin, on the average, three out of four workers stayed outside this effort to organize socio-economic interest, and the membership rate in the Sozialdemokratischen Parte: Deutchlands (SPD) was even considerably lower, as figures from Berlin show.[40] To be precise, from the late 1890s, most machine construction workers joined the DMV, but most of them also let it go after one or two years (i.e., they never showed up again, never paid any fee after the first months and thereby accepted that they would be scratched from the union's list).[41] In other words, participation in the organizations that claimed to be the only tool to satisfy the workers' economic and political interests remained very limited. (However, after 1900 the participation still added up to one of the highest rates of union membership, matched only by the dockers and the construction workers or those workers in artisanal trades, such as the glove-makers.) But spectacular collective action was not the machine construction workers' style. In contrast to the miners, construction workers, and even the much-less-organized textile workers, not to mention the printers or brewers, the machine construction workers almost never went on strike. However, this does not imply that these workers were inactive or apathetic.[42] They pursued direct interests, sometimes even militantly, on the shop-floor level (as illustrated above), they reappropriated time and material resources, such as metal chips or residues, and tools (as already mentioned). They also expressed their hopes and longings, anxieties and fears—they practiced *Eigensinn*. In any case, they participated actively in the distribution and in the redistribution of resources and of "life-chances" (Max Weber); that is, they behaved and acted politically.

Concerning what may be considered political in the daily life of "immediate producers" (Karl Marx), I believe we can make two points on the basis of this material:

1) Workers neither pursue individual wages and survival in a strictly instrumental sense, nor do they act politically in the sense of striving for a change in the mode of production.[43] This distinction follows an inappropriate one-dimensional model of politics, and it fails to grasp the ambiguities, intertwinings, and contradictions of interest and *Eigensinn*, as well as their synchronism. What is overlooked here, and elsewhere, is the mode of life of those concerned.

2) At least in more developed industrial capitalist societies, divergent, perhaps separate and even contradictory political arenas can be discerned. However, the politicizing of the private by interconnected assertions of interests, needs, and *Eigensinn* in face-to-face relations is misread if it is taken as "privitization of politics." The daily politics of the time do not show a tendency for depoliticizing. On the contrary, they reveal various forms of redistribution of material and emotional resources, as well as of life-time and life-chances. Such forms implicitly relativized the arena of formal politics, especially regulating and redistributing on the central or national level. In other words, state-centered politics were put into perspective by the self-willed politics of the so called dominated.

In the context of their daily politics, material interests and individual needs, social obligations and *Eigensinn* were not to be stripped apart or split up; they did not fall into neat boxes analysts are too easily prepared to use. "Material" and "symbolic capital" (Pierre Bourdieu)[44] were not directly interchangeable: the silver watch of one's late father was never pawned;[45] the humiliating "du" used by supervisors was not more easily accepted when real wages went up (which was the general trend from the 1870s to the 1890s and perhaps even into the early 1900s).

The ideal of "respectability" has to be reconsidered. This notion, shared by both men and women, was neither a pale reflection of petty-bourgeois dreams and idylls, not some distorted form of class-consciousness. Instead, it was a standard with different distinct notions and experiences. It nurtured the efforts of the workers to earn one's living,[46] but it never was or could be disconnected from daily uncertainties and insecurities, from anxieties or hopes and dreams for a better future. Thus, endeavours to survive by illegal means—the unlawful appropriation of food, coal, or wood—were not perceived primarily as disgraceful or non-respectable. (The common practice of pilfering as it is reported from the Hamburg docks indicates this clearly).[47] Success in terms of survival, of material and social improvement, fostered that demonstrative pride that became visible in encounters with neighbors and workmates, as well as with, as Marx put it, "commissioned and noncommissioned officers" in the workshops or in the streets or in the inns.

These daily politics were in no way fixated on resistance, on any determined stance against demands, constraints, or open repression. Simultaneously, again and again, a self-will or *Eigensinn* as tenacious as it was effortless, could be detected in associations with colleagues, friends, and relatives, most often in peer groups of sports or drinking buddies (for the men), in *Kaffee Klatsches* for the women. Always the point was the chance to be only with and for oneself. Interference by or threats from the rulers, or their agents, from policemen, superintendents, or foremen were then literally far away, and could—for a time—be forgotten.

In these efforts to ensure physical survival, as well as in the stabilization of one's own person and one's own worth, victory perpetually coexisted with defeat—at work, inside and outside of the family. From the permanent risks, however, resulted an attitude of skeptical caution, especially in the face of offers and unreasonable demands that exceeded immediate experience.

In terms of the politicization of private life, it must be recognized that interference from above was part of the private mode of life of the workers and their families. Rigorous enforcement of order in the factory, on the streets, or in schools and offices constituted the daily experiences of children, youngsters, and adults alike.[48] These experiences with the physical violence of the state and of private dominators were interconnected with a form of violence "from above" that masked itself in the way it worked—"*violence douce*."[49] Government policies that strove for physical as well as mental cleanliness or for education were enforced consistently by the police or by the threat of police intervention. Vagrants were chased and arrested; "mad" people were increasingly detained in special institutions;[50] compulsory education was enforced by the police, at least in the towns and cities. Of decisive importance was the simultaneous match of these standards of cleanliness and education to the immediate interests and needs of those concerned. To be clean and to become educated, after all, could open up a real prospect for a better life. If this were so, the question of whether a specific (perhaps "bourgeois") type of cleanliness or of education was pursued might rest for a while. In any case, the whole range of interferences should or could contribute to a politicizing of the private. Unknown to them, the administered, trained, or agitated people were drawn into the realm of formally organized pursuit of interest. Politicizing of the private actually functioned as politicizing from above. Contrary to any self-willed politicizing of those concerned, these processes could smooth the reconciliation of unsatisfied and antagonistic interests and needs. Those concerned responded on their own by erasing, in their terms, through refusals and in self-willed action any division between private and political.

But the significance of the politics of daily life should not blur problems yet unsolved. Parallel to the politicizing of the private, one can see the separation of broad and diffuse masses from the centralized politics of the dominating classes as well as of the offical opposition by the SPD. Preliminary evidence for this separation can be found, at least after 1906, in the less steady and slower increase in membership figures for the nationwide socialist organizations.[51] Even more important were unorganized movements such as those that surfaced in January 1906, in the midst of an SPD demonstration in Hamburg,[52] or in September 1910 in Berlin-Moabit.[53] The latter riots were triggered by rapidly increasing food prices. In both instances so-called "disorderly people," most being casual labourers and the unemployed, went from demonstrating to ransacking and plundering, in which not even "revolutionary discipline" was displayed. SPD and labor-union functionaries did not disagree with state authorities: in unison they harshly condemned such mob rioting.

The impression of an increasing separation between political arenas is enchance by the lack of any self-mobilization of the masses after 1890; demanding such new official politics as colonial imperialism or naval armament remained restricted to petty-bourgeois public opinion and organizations. It is very dubious whether industrial workers or proletarian masses in general participated in these efforts at all.

This separation between the political arenas becomes obvious in spectacular, though fatal, examples, two of which are of particular prominence and importance. First, there was the peaceful, sometimes even enthusiastic, march into the imperial war in August 1914 by masses of workers[54] who, until that very moment, had participated in strikes or at least seemed to be ready for some form of resistance to dominant policy patterns. Second, there was the acceptance of fascism in 1933 and thereafter by the large majority of the proletarian masses.[55]

For the workers, first of all, the separation of political arenas mirrored the practices and stereotyped expectations of their party leaders. The hierarchical organization of the internal party processes, and even more their public appearances, underline this. When the party mobilized its adherents, their demonstrations all too quickly paralleled military parades.[56] The use value of marching in a row and of keeping up with the front rank man seems to be overwhelmed by the surplus value of this military way of structuring and organizing huge masses. Such military practices infiltrated the very notion of alternative societal organizations developed by party functionaries, but even more by rank and file members in their daily practices. There was a military terminology congruent with this—the "revolutionary army" or the "battalions of the revolution" were kept "marching" in the written or spoken rhetoric of the party establishment.[57] Also, public speeches were conceived and performed as monologues. The speakers faced the crowd, but the crowd's role was to listen, not to argue. In the case of mass rallies, it is not clear whether the people in the back could even hear the speaker. The "happening" and the scenario, therefore, the being-together with comrades and sympathetic mates, may have become much more important and meaningful than understanding the text of the distant and distanced speaker.

More generally, such events may put into question the notion of "zig-zag-loyalty,"[58] which has been employed to describe the simultaneous giving of loyal support to the party of the proletariat as well as the nation-state, the Imperial Reich. In fact, the term "zig-zag-loyalty" was coined to grasp the double allegiance such as appeared in the display of portraits of Aupust Bebel and Ferdinand Lassalle alongside those of Field Marshall Helmut von Möltke and Chancellor Otto Bismarck, a feature that Bromme reported in his own parents' flat. Perhaps there was only a very limited sense of loyalty at all, one corresponding to a massive disinterestedness in any sort of formal and state-centered politics.

CONCLUSION

If one wishes to avoid simple moralization, the analytic differentiation between the political arenas is unavoidable. For investigative purposes, in societies of developed-industrial capitalism the distinction between private and *Eigensinn* politics on the one hand, and state-centered or formal politics on the other is in no way obsolete. But the analyst should be aware that the emphasis then is on the surmised function rather than on the perspective of those concerned. To be sure, the separation of political arenas was functional for the protection of existing positions and structures of domination. This applied not only to the dominators, and their shifting alliances,[59] but also to the leaders of opposition organizations, such as the SPD of 1914.

To understand the uses dominating groups made of the separation of the political arenas, we must consider their strategies, which included labor leaders. In this way, the current forms of hegemony in the society may be discerned more clearly. The latter concerns the process of unspoken permeation of society as a whole with cultural and ideological patterns, which cause dependence to appear as necessary or irrevocable. The bourgeois-classical education, as it was imitated by the educational efforts of the labor movement, contained within itself multifaceted tendencies of accommodation to the dominant culture.[60] To be more precise, included should be the broad spectrum of progressive advice and training for an improved home economy, especially for preserving food, for the well-being of clean and disciplined children and housewives alike, but also efforts for reducing work hours of young workers and female workers by law and administrative control. All of these incentives implicitly backed not only bourgeois but patriarchal structures. Nevertheless, they were stimulated by humanitarian motives that did not impinge on practice. Instructors behaved rudely and seemed to like authoritarian treatment of disciples. Above all, there remained or even developed a notion that was much closer to home for wage workers in daily (re)production—the demand for a just wage. The structure of wage work itself was no longer debatable!

But this is only one side of the coin. Demonstrative silence of the proletarian masses in state and organizational politics often corresponded to political sensibility and militancy, indeed to active self-will, in the factory or the office, in the tenement house and on the street. Even more, expressions and articulations of the dependent and dominated stated the mode in which they interconnected politics, private sphere, and *Eigensinn*. If one looks closely, what becomes visible is not separation, but a seamless simultaneity of private small joys in the daily practices. Involved was an alternative vision of what life should be like, for oneself and for all mankind. The fact that they ignored the arena of state and party politics does not mean that the dependent and dominated did not have any concept of alternative political organization for society; rather, such concepts remained close to peculiarly private and self-willed politics. More concretely, the answers of miners, and textile and metal workers to a questionnaire sent out in 1910 by a theologian who strove and agitated for social reform, Adolf Levenstein, are revealing. One of the questions asked about their hopes or wishes for the future. Many of the responding 5,040 workers expressed the wish to "eat as much as I want," to own a microscope, and at the same time to see the "godly spark" or, at least, the "prevention of war" spread throughout the world.[61]

The socialist political organizations of the time did not recognize this problem. At best, it became part of the technical or tactical question "how to approach people to make them party or union members?" It is typical, therefore, that a trade union's guideline for visits to the homes of possible candidates for membership emphasized the use of the "du"[62]—as if the term automatically would invoke the richness of experiences and connotations of those whom one tried to recruit, as if the simple use of this meaningful symbol would bridge the gap between their self-willed politics and the union's bureaucratic politics. The workers' organizations measured distinct and deviant needs only according to whether they would fit their notion of class consciousness, and would support organizational strength. They never took seriously the simultaneity of interests and *Eigensinn*, the peculiarity of workers' politics.

NOTES

This is the revised version of a paper which I presented to the Davis Center Seminar, Princeton University, April 2, 1982.

As is common with academic work, this paper owes much to discussions with other people. Here, I want to thank my colleagues at the Davis Center, especially Rhys Isaac. His stimulating remarks and, not the least, patient support in polishing the English-language version, helped me considerably. Of course, I still am responsible for all of the deficiencies and shortcomings.

I also would like to mention helpful suggestions and critiques by participants of seminars at the History Departments of the University of Michigan, Ann Arbor; The John Hopkins University, Baltimore; SUNY, Buffalo; North Carolina State University, Raleigh; Stanford University; University of Oregon, Eugene; New York University.

1. E.P. Thompson, *The Making of the English Working Class* (London, 1963), p. 11.

2. This is especially the point made by E. Genovese and E. Fox-Genovese (in their critique of social-anthropologically informed approaches), "The Political Crisis of Social History: a Marxian Perspective," in *Journal of Social History* 10 (1976/77), p. 205–20. Directly criticizing what he—in my opinion inappropriately—perceives as sheer "culturalism," R. Johnson has put forward a critique of Thompson's work along these lines: "Edward Thompson, Eugene Genovese, and Socialist-Humanist History," in *History Workshop Journal* No. 6 (1978), pp. 79–100 (cf. the clash at the History Workshop of Nov. 1979, see pp. 386–96, 396–406 in R. Samuel ed., *People's History and Socialist Theory* [London, 1981]).

3. Cf. for the German historiography which stresses everyday-life analysis the critique by G. Eley and K. Nield, "Why Does Social History Ignore Politics?" in *Social History* 5 (1980), pp. 249–71, especially 264ff. See also J. Kocka, "Klassen oder Kultur? Durchbrüche und Sackgassen in der Arbeitergeschichte,", in *Merkur* 36 (1982), pp. 955–65.

4. Or, to refer to a German case: When the "failure" of the revolutionary movements of 1918–20 is considered, this "either-or" characterizes even the writing of sensitive authors of the grassroot activities, such as E. Lucas; cf. E. Lucas, *Zwei Formen von Radikalismus in der deutschen Arbeiterbewegung* (Frankfurt, 1976).

5. The related problems are pinned down, or opened up in a stimulating article by K. Dwyer, "On the Dialogic of Field Work," in *Dialectical Anthropology* 2 (1977), pp. 143–51. I owe this reference to my colleague at the Davis Center, Elizabeth Traube (Chicago).

6. P. Göhre, *Drei Monate Fabrikarbeiter und Handwerksbursche* (Leipzig, 1891), p. 29.

7. Ibid., p. 74.

8. For the work process cf. D. Lande, "Arbeits- und Lohnverhältnisse in der Berliner Maschinenindustrie zu Geginn des 20. Jahrhunderts." In: *Auslese und Anpassung der Arbeiterschaft in der Elektroindustrie, Burchdruckerei, Feinmechanik und Maschinenindustrie,* (Schriften des Vereins f. Socialpolitik 134/2 (Leipzig 1910), pp. 306–498, 354ff. E. Barth, "Entwicklungslinien der deutschen Maschinenbauindustrie von 1870 bis 1914," (Berlin/DDR 1973), pp. 51f., 83ff., 91ff., 113ff. More generally focusing on distinctive features of turners' work: H. Popitz et al., *Technik und Industrie-arbeit* (Tübingen, 1957), p. 130ff. Göhre: ibid., pp. 45ff., esp. 50f.

The equipment of mid–19th century machine construction workshops is described by A. Schröter and W. Becker, *Die deutsche Maschinenbauindustrie in der Industriellen Revolution* (Berlin/DDR 1962), p. 85ff.; concerning the 1870s see W. Renzsch, *Handwerker und Lohnarbeiter in der frühen Arbeiterbewegung* (Göttingen, 1980), p. 147ff. E. Barth, *Entwicklungslinien der deutschen Maschinenbauindustrie von 1870–1914* (Berlin/DDR, 1973), esp. pp. 83ff., 91ff.

For the assessment of "control" of the work process cf. D. Montgomery, "Workers' Control of Machine Production in the 19th Century," in D. Montgomery, *Workers' Control in America* (London, 1979), pp. 9–31.

9. M.T.W. Bromme, *Lebensgeschichte eines modernen Fabrikarbeiters* (Frankfurt, 1971; reprint, 1st ed. 1905), p. 243.

10. Ibid.; R. Müller, *Vom Kaiserreich zur Republik* (Berlin, 1974; reprint, 1st ed. 1924), p. 13f.

11. A. Schröter and W. Becker, *Die deutsche Maschinen/bauindustrie*. pp. 76ff., 236ff.

12. A.V. Desai, *Real Wages in Germany 1891–1913* (Oxford, 1968), pp. 108–110.

13. Göhre, p. 13f.

14. E.J. Hobsbawm, "The Labour Aristocracy in Nineteenth Century Britain," in P.N. Stearns, D.J. Walkowitz eds., *Workers in the Industrial Revolution* (New Brunswick, N.J., 1974), p. 139. The discussion on (English) labour aristocracy has become vigorous again, loaded (perhaps overburdened) by the problem of "hegemony" (in the Gramscian meaning); cf. recently H.F. Moorhouse, "History, Sociology and the Quiescence of the British Working Class: A Reply to Reid," in *Social History* 4 (1979), pp. 481–90; and "Response" by Reid, pp. 491–93.

15. Cf. Desai.

16. H. Enters, *Die kleine mühselige Welt des jungen Hermann Enters. Erinnerungen eines Amerika-Auswanderers an das frühindustrielle Wuppertal*, 3d ed., (Wuppertal, 1979; 1st ed., 1970), p. 69ff.

17. K. Ditt, "Technologischer Wandel und Strukturveränderung der Fabrikarbeiterschaft in Bielefeld 1860–1914," in W. Conze, U. Engelhardt (eds.), *Arbeiter im IndustrialisierungspozeB* (Stuttgart, 1979), pp. 237–61, 255ff.

18. Historisches Archiv der Gutehoffnungshütte (H. A. GHH) 2121/3; 2121/5; 2121/7.

19. Cf. R. Müller, *Vom Kaiserreich zur Republik* (Berlin, 1924).

20. Ibid., p. 131.

21. Bromme, *Lebensgeschichte*, p. 251f.

22. The comparison of order books and wage lists of the GHH, 1870, supports this point.

23. H.A. GHH 2121/3; 2121/5; 2121/7.

24. Deviations of the workers' productivity during the work day as well as during the work week were measured (by taking the factories' output figures) in some textile mills in the early 1900s by Marie Bernays; but I should add that she was interested in contributing to the achievement, as she put it, of a more steady and regular flow of production, informed, as it were, by efforts in the manner of Taylor; cf. M. Bernays, *Untersuchunge über die Schwankungen der Arbeitsintensität während der Arbeitswoche und während der Arbeitstages. Ein Beitrag zur Psychophysik der Textilarbeit* (Leipzig, 1911).

25. Göhre, p. 76f.

26. Göhre, p. 77f.

27. For the general importance of this dimension cf. P. Willis, *Learning to Labour: How Working Class Kids Get Working Class Jobs*, 2 ed. (New York 1981), esp. p. 43ff.

28. The term which is introduced here is derived from a passage of "thick description," as it were, which the popular philosopher Charles Garve published in the 1790s. He was commenting on dependent peasants in Silesia, their gestures and behavior toward the lord. Part of this piece reads:

> Part or even a consequence of their [i.e., the peasants] being insidious is a certain "*Eigensinn*," which makes the peasant distinct when he is embarrassed or when some prejudice

has become deep-rooted in him.... As his body and his limbs get stiff the same happens apparently with his soul.

He, consequently, gets deaf to all propositions which are made to him.... Judges... know such persons whose stubborness is due either to their blindness or to determined malice. Sometimes entire communities are obsessed by such cheating spirit. They come close to mad people who are obsessed by an *ideam fixam* which cannot be removed either by evidence or by giving counter-reasons.... Nothing else raises stronger antipathies against peasants. What, after all, is more difficult for the superior to stand than if those who are subject to him do not listen to him? What may infuriate a sensible person more when even that utmost explicitness and clarity, with all its power of truth, does not move the slightest the mind of those whom he wants to lead back to duty and order?" (Cf. Charles Garve, "Über den Charakter gegen die Regierung, in Ders.: *Popularphilosophische Schriften*, Bd. 2, [Stuttgart, K. Wölfel, 1974), pp. 799–1026, 859f.)

But one should also keep in mind that the term in German is colloquially used to describe (and implicitly criticize) childish behaviour, which, at least for "reasonable" adults, by this very term is labeled as "irrational." See for the use in the late eighteenth and during the nineteenth century also Ad. Freiherr von Knigge, *Über den Umgang mit Menschen*, 14th ed. (Hannover, 1865, first ed., 1788), p. 86ff. Knigge employs the term to characterize a kind of behaviour which nowadays is usually perceived as "stubborn." I owe this reference to Arnd Bohm.

I hope that it becomes clear that I try to use the notion in a somewhat different way, especially not negating the legitimacy of *Eigensinn*.

29. Cf. Alf Luedtke, "Arbeitsbeginn, Arbeitspausen, Arbeitsende," in G. Huck, ed., *Sozialgeschichte der Freizeit* (Wuppertal, 1980), pp. 95–122.

30. Göhre, p. 29ff.

31. G. Bataille, "Der Begriff der Verausgabung," in G. Bataille, *Das theoretische Werk*, vol. I (München, 1975), pp. 9–31.

32. Göhre, pp. 79, 81. C.f. the recollection of Wenzel Holek, a Bohemian digger and brickmaker: the use of "Sie" was fined in the local (socialist) workers' association; W. Holek, *Lebensgang eines deutsch-tschechischen Handarbeiters* (Jena, 1909), p. 215.

33. For the latter see the precise account the agrarian labourer Franz Rehbein gave of his military service in the 1880s. F. Rehbein, *Das Leben eines Landarbeiters* (Jena, 1911), pp. 153–93.

34. For this aspect cf. Luedtke, "Arbeitsbeginn ... " and especially M. Perrot, "The Three Ages of Industrial Discipline in 19th Century France," in J. M. Merriman, ed., *Consciousness and Class Experience in 19th Century Europe* (New York, London, 1979), pp. 149–68. Perrot "spells out" M. Foucault's thesis on "discipline" as the core mechanism of "modern" efforts "pour surveiller et punir"; see M. Foucault, *Surveiller et punir* (Paris, 1975). For the stages of management's efforts to increase control over the actual work process cf. R. Edwards, *Contested Terrain: The Transformation of the Workplace in the 20th Century* (New York, 1979).

35. Cf. some evidence from the late 1860s given by U. Englehardt, *Nur vereinigt sind wir stark*, Vol. I (Stuttgart, 1977), p. 93f.

36. Bromme, *Lebengeschichte*, p. 290f.

37. H.A. GHH 40016/9 (esp. Fischedick).

38. Cf. L. Hack, et al., "Klassenlage und Interessenorientierung," in *Zeitschrift für Soziologie* I (1972), pp. 15–30, 24f.

39. The notion of "synchronism" refers to Ernst Bloch's—the Marxist philosopher—concept of the "Gleichzeitigkeit des Ungleichzeitigken" (perhaps: synchronism of asynchroneities), involving the different, but parallel use of old and new symbols and sets of meanings which informed people's (political) orientation in the 1920s/30s, at least in Germany. According to Bloch's view this was exploited by Nazi ideology and activism but not recognized at all by Marxist analysts or (SPD or KPD) "left" political leaders; cf. E. Bloch, *Erbschaft dieser Zeit*, 2d ed. (1st 1932/36) (Franfurt, 1962).

40. See the figures given by D. Fricke: *Die deutsche Arbeiterbewegung 1869–1914* (Berlin/DDR 1976), pp. 718f., 731.

The participation in the "yellow" "Gewerksverein" and in the Christian trade union is only to be mentioned at this point. Apparently the "yellow" organization had at least some attraction for the group which is under consideration here from the 1860s until the early 1890s. More in detail: U. Engelhardt: *Nur vereinigt* . . . , vol. 2, ch. 14, p. 967ff. The "yellow" organizations were revitalized by some leading figures of the big corporations around 1905/06. But these "Werkvereine" (trade associations) remained, even though dropping by far, below 5 percent of the socialist trade union's membership until 1914; see K.-J. Mattheier: *Die Gelben, Nationale Arbeiter zwischen Wirtschaftsfrieden und Streik* (Düsseldorf 1973). In comparison with the rapid increase of the socialist union's membership until 1905/06, and a more moderate increase thereafter, the Christian union movement decreased in the last years before 1914 (not only in relative but also in absolute numbers); cf. M. Schneider: *Die christlichen Gewerkschaften 1894–1933* (Bonn, 1982) esp. p. 767ff. But, of course, variations according to regional circumstances and branches have to be taken into consideration; see Schneider, pp. 221ff., 290ff.

41. K. Schönhoven, *Expansion und Konzentration. Studien zur Entwicklung der Freien Gewerkschaften im Wilhelminischen Deutschland 1890–1914* (Stuttgart, 1980), pp. 143ff., 190ff.

42. See D. Geary, "Identifying Militarism: the Assessment of Working-class Attitudes towards State and Society," in R.J. Evans, ed., *The German Working Class 1888–1933* (London/Totowa, N.J., 1982), pp. 220–46, 233ff.; E. Lucas, *Zwei Formen* . . . ,p. 147.

43. Concerning the political struggle under the conditions of the Kaiserreich's "Half-absolutist pseudo-constitutionalism" see H.-U. Wehler, *Das deutsche Kaiserreich 1871–1918* 2 ed. (Göttingen, 1975), p. 63.

44. Cf. P. Bourdieu, *Entwurf einer Theorie der Praxis* (*auf der ethnologischen Grundlage der kabylischen Gesellschaft*) (Frankfurt, 1976 [1972]), p. 335ff.

45. Of course, this point would need more elaboration and further evidence, but cf. H. Schomerus, *Die Arbeiter der Maschinenfabrik Esslingen* (Stuttgart, 1977), p. 244.

46. Even the labor aristocrats had to rely on extra earnings to feed their families. A statistic of Chemnitz indicates that in 1900, 58, or 8 percent, of the "skilled metal workers" could not feed a household of two adults and three children (the figures for construction workers and for textile workers were 81, 6 percent). Not only unpaid domestic labour, but also women's wage work and wage work for children, as soon as possible, remained a basic economic need for sustaining one family; cf. H, Rosenbaum, *Formen der Familie* (Frankfurt,

1982), p. 399 (and further evidence there); cf. also K. Tenfelde, "Arbeiterhaushalt und Arbeiterbewegung 1850–1914," in *Sozialwissenschaftliche Informationcen f. Unterricht u. Studium* (SOWI) 6 (1977), p. 106ff. It should be mentioned, however, that the males themselves tried to get extra earnings. At least Göhre points out that one of his workmates made wood-cuttings on Sunday mornings and sold them by sending his children to local fairs, and played the fiddle at local dances; somebody else, a former tailor, tailored late at night, a driller worked as coachman on Sunday afternoons, worked as a smith, and as a waiter almost every night in a workers' pub—and all of them tried to get overtime. But only a few usually got a chance depending upon the masters' mood and interests; see Göhre, Drei Monate, p. 15.

More generally, the complex problem of family income and especially of old-age poverty has been depicted and analyzed in a study which relies on material of the Ruhr region; see H. Reif, "Soziale Lage und Erfahrungen des alternden Fabrikarbeiters in der Schwerindustrie des westlichen Ruhrgebiets während der Hochindustrialisierung," in *Archiv für Sozialgeschicte* 23 (1982), pp. 1–94.

47. M. Grüttner, "Working-class Crime and the Labour Movement; Pilfering in the Hamburg Docks, 1888–1923," in R. J. Evans, ed., *The German Working Class*, pp. 54–79.

48. For the public practices, especially the "chasing of socialists," see K. Saul, *Staat, Industrie, Arbeiterbegung im Kaiserreich* (Düsseldorf, 1974).

49. Cf. P. Bourdieu, *Theorie der Praxis*, p. 364ff.

50. D. Blasius, "Bürgerliche Gesellschaft und bürgerliche Angste: Die Irren in der Geschichte des 19. Jahrunderts," in *SOWI* 8 (1979), pp. 88–94.

51. Cf. not only the nationwide figures (see D. Fricke and K. Schönhoven) but also case studies, such as M. Nolan, *Social Democracy and Society: Working-class Radicalism in Düsseldorf 1890–1920* (Cambridge, 1981), pp. 182ff., 232ff. (focusing on the years after 1907).

52. R. J. Evans,"'Red Wednesday' in Hamburg: Social Democrats, Police and Lumpenproletariat in the Suffrage Disturbance of 17 January 1906," in *Social History* 4 (1979), pp. 1–31.

53. H. Bleiber, "Die Moabiter Unruhen 1910," in *Zeitschrift für Geschichtswissenschaft* 3 (1955), pp. 173–211.

54. The present state of insight, still being rather preliminary, is discussed by F. Boll, *Frieden ohne Revolution? Friedensstrategien der deutschen Sozialdemokratie vom Erfurter Programm 1891 bis zur Revolution 1918* (Bonn, 1980), p. 110ff.

55. Of course this is a multifaceted problem. But one should draw upon E. Fromm, *Arbeiter und Angestellte am Vorabend des Dritten Reiches*, ed. W. BonB. (Stuttgart, 1980); *Deutschlandberichte der Sozialdemokratischen Partei Deutschlands (SOPADE), 1934–1940* (Frankfurt, 1979).

56. Cf. the proud notation the social-democrat Düsseldorf "Volkszeitung" gave of the May day parade of 1903: "Many a bourgeois made a bewildered face as he saw the lively Reds parade by like a brigade of soldiers," quoted by M. Nolan, *Social Democracy*, p. 138. The reporter of the May day parade in Solingen, 1903, wrote of the development of the proletarian movement towards a "proletarian army" which had been made visible by the parade; cf. P. Friedemann, "Feste und Feiern im rheinischwestfälischen Industriegebiet 1890–1914," in G. Huck, ed., *Sozialgeschichte der Freizeit* (Wuppertal, 1980), pp. 161–85, 167.

57. Cf. for instance J. Dietzgen's article "Dass der Sozialist kein Monarchist sein kann," *Der Volksstaat* (Aug. 13, 1873), quoted by C. Stephan, "*Genossen, wir dürfen uns nicht von der Geduld hinreifen lassen*!" (Frankfurt, 1977), pp. 282–93, 290f. A systematic content analysis by W. Liebknecht of even more of Bebel's speeches—and of those of other leaders or speakers—is not yet finished.

58. H. Bausinger, "Verbürgerlichung—Folgen eines Interpretaments," in G. Wiegelmann, ed., *Kultureller Wandell im 19. Jahrhundert* (Göttingen, 1973), pp. 24–49. In a different but parallel way my skepticism concerning the "loyalty" thesis applies to the widely debated notion of "negative integration," as it was set forth by G. Roth and D. Groh; instead, I tend to stress active non-integration, or better: *Eigensinn* (see D. Groh, *Negative Integration und revolut. Attentismus* (Frankfurt, 1973).

59. See for this D. Abraham, "Corporatist Compromise and the Re-Emergence of the Labor/Capital-Conflict in Weimar Germany," in *Political Power and Social Theory* 2 (1981), pp. 59–109 (which includes an analysis of the Kaiserreich patterns).

60. Cf. the material (on Austrian workers) which is discussed by D. Langewiesche, *Zur Freizeit des Arbeiters* (Stuttgart, 1979). For German workers, see M. Nolan, *Social Democracy*, pp. 126–45; D. Langewiesche, and K. Schönhoven, "Arbeiterbibliotheken und Arbeiterlektüre im Wilhelminischen Deutschland," in *Archiv für Sozialgeschichte* 16 (1976), pp. 135–204; H. Lüdtke, "Von der 'literarischen Suppenküche' zur Bildungsanstalt der Nation," in *Buch und Bibliothek* 3 (1979), pp. 409–26.

61. A. Levenstein, *Die Arbeiterfrage* (München, 1912), (the reference is to the sections which give the quotations of the replies of machine construction workers).

62. K. Schönhoven, *Expansion*, p. 212f.; the guideline was published in 1908.

5

The Formation of the Rural Proletariat in the South African Countryside: The Class Struggle and the 1913 Natives' Land Act

Martin Murray

> From a comparatively free husbandman the Native has been converted into a modern wage-slave, with only his labour-power to sell. . . . This is the change in South Africa, the transformation of the Native farmer into a landless proletarian.[1]

> Economically, the closing of native areas to Europeans [with the 1913 Natives' Land Act] will be a gain to the country, as it will mean the adopting of Europeans of a more efficient system of agriculture, a great need in South Africa to-day. We are suffering from the somewhat inevitable necessity of having to use untrained semi-savage labour in agriculture, and thus in comparison with other countries not working on this basis, and where intensive production and the maximum efficiency are applied, we get an inferior average yield, and are able to place scarcely 10 percent of South African land under cultivation.[2]

INTRODUCTION

Capitalist Accumulation in South African Agriculture

During the "phase of transition" (ca. 1890–1920), the hybrid forms of production that surfaced in the South African countryside represented a *transitional conjuncture* increasingly subjected to the laws of motion of commodity production and circulation but not completely under the sway of capitalist accumulation proper. These "primitive" (i.e., "germinal") forms of capital did not exhaust the complex range of heterogeneous class forces in the countryside, but represented the dynamic vehicle in the process of establishing the essential preconditions for the accumulation of capital proper in the countryside.

In a nutshell, European embryonic capitalist farmers constituted the principal active agents in the historical process of capitalist development in agriculture. They increasingly engaged in the production of commodities and, as a direct consequence, became more and more dependent on exchange and markets for their own reproduction and survival. As "personifications" of distinctly petty-bourgeois forms of capital, embryonic capitalist farmers maintained both relations of economic ownership and of effective possession of means of production. Moreover, they depended on a combination of family (i.e., self-organized household) laboring-time, and appropriated surplus product in the form of commodities (i.e., tangible objects exchanged on the market). In short, these emergent capitalist farmers were not, by any stretch of the imagination, merely subsistence units, "manufacturing" items chiefly for self-survival with an occasional foray into the impersonal commodities markets. On the contrary, embryonic capitalist farmers in the South African countryside had become increasingly dependent on the exchange of surplus product on the market and were thereby compelled by economic necessity to compete as petty capitals with other petty capitals and with larger capitals in order to ensure their own reproduction and survival.[3]

These germinal forms of capital depended almost exclusively on the appropriation of surplus labor of subordinate wage-laborers and rent-paying squatters. Agrarian class relations thus rested on the combination of capitalist and non-capitalist forms of exploitation. The accumulation of capital remained indeed "primitive"—not only in the sense of being historically prior (i.e., "transitional" in V. I. Lenin's terms),[4] but also in the sense of depending upon distinctly "labor-squeezing" methods of surplus extraction.

Finally, these germinal forms of capital did not spring *de novo* from the gradual class differentiation of small-scale owner-occupiers, but instead emerged "from above," (i.e., from the collapse of *rentier* landlordism). This non-capitalist form of production was characterized by large-scale landed estates where the principal propertied classes (i.e., European landlords) derived their income from the exploitation of landless rent-paying squatters. With all the endless variety of forms characteristic of a transitional epoch, the economic organization of embryonic capitalist farming accounted, strictly speaking, to two principal "systems" in the most varied combinations: the "labor-service (or labor-tenant) system"; and the "capitalist system." The former consisted chiefly in the landed property of European landowners being cultivated with the implements of the resident squatters. The form of payment did not alter the essential nature of this system (whether remuneration assumed the form of money, as in the case of job-hire, or in surplus product, as in the case of share-cropping or "farming-on-the-halves," or in land or grounds, as in the case of labor-service in the narrow sense of the term). The "capitalist farming system" consisted of the hire of wage-laborers (annual, seasonal, day, and so forth) who tilled the land with the landowners' implements. These two "systems" were actually interwoven in the most heterogeneous and fantastic fashion where European landowners on their landed estates applied the two "systems" in various combinations to different farming operations. Lenin's words are appropriate here: "It is quite natural that the combination of such dissimilar and even opposite systems of economy leads in practice to a whole number of most profound and complicated conflicts and contradictions, and that the pressure of these contradictions results in a number of the farmers going bankrupt, etc. All these are phenomena characteristic of every transitional period."[5]

No precise statistics were officially recorded that would permit us to measure the relative incidence of these two "systems." It is just as unlikely that precise statistics could be reconstructed from available materials, since this procedure would have required a registration not only of all landed estates but also of all economic operations performed on all these estates. Approximate data are available in the shape of general descriptive accounts of diverse localities as to the predominance of one or another "system." This evidence must, unfortunately, suffice to reconstruct the patterns of agricultural production. In practice, the "labor service system" coalesced with the "capitalist system" to such an extent that it becomes nearly impossible to distinguish with complete accuracy one from the other. Lenin captures the essential feature of the "mixed congestion" of agrarian class relations in his description of the Russian countryside at the turn of the century: "Life creates forms that unite in themselves with remarkable gradualness systems of economy whose basic features constitute opposites. It becomes impossible to say where 'labor-service' ends and where 'capitalism' begins."[6]

The essential precondition for the development of capitalist production and accumulation was the fundamental transformation of rural production relations, namely the emergence of capitalist farmers in effective possession of concentrated means of production and wage-laborers sufficiently separated (i.e., "freed") from these means of production such that the exchange of their laboring capacity (labor-power) became an economic necessity for their reproduction and survival. The bourgeois production relations had only partially evolved during the "phase of transition" (ca. 1890–1920). Seen in broad terms, this *transitional conjuncture* was marked by ongoing and persistent structural crises of capital accumulation in the double sense: on the one hand, an overall slowing-down in investment and hence a stagnation in the rate of accumulation; and on the other, a "creative rupture" in the continuity of the reproduction of social-production relations resulting in their restructuring in new forms.[7]

One specific form of the accumulation crisis in South African agriculture during the phase of transition revolved around the inability of capitalist farmers (who had concentrated means of production in their hands) to harness sufficient supplies of labor-power and, hence, their class's inability to organize the capitalist labor-process directly under their sway. Seen from the point of view of embryonic capitalist farmers, this unreliability of sufficient supplies of requisite labor-power constituted the principal barrier to capitalist expansion in agriculture. Put specifically, restraints on the unimpeded growth of capital accumulation were associated with the hindrances in the sphere of circulation such that the "free" movement of labor-power as a commodity remained impeded. This structural obstacle resulted from the widespread existence of non-capitalist forms of production, thereby allowing African rural dwellers considerable leeway to choose their means of obtaining an income and hence remain somewhat immune from the unpredictable vagaries of the market pressures to exchange their labor-power.

The 1913 Natives' Land Act in South Africa

The agrarian class transformation "from above" in the South African countryside cannot be measured simply in terms of an aggregation of "single events" or discrete decisions of far-sighted state managers. Instead, the class transformation of agrarian relations must be understood as a historical process of economic, political, and ideological ruptures between old forms of production and circulation and new, capitalist, ones. To be specific, capitalist forms of production can be distinguished not in terms of a one-to-one correspondence with market relations, but as the ensemble of social-production relations in which capital has acquired a monopoly over the principal means of production (relations of economic ownership and relations of effective possession) and where concrete laboring-time (combined with means of production and raw materials) in a distinctly capitalist labor-process operates as the material source of exchange value.

As a "single event," the 1913 Natives' Land Act marked the close of an era and the beginning of another. Capitalist relations had already undergone considerable expansion "within the pores" of *rentier* landlordism. The statutes of the 1913 Natives' Land Act formally codified certain relations ("landed property" relations), thereby contributing to the relatively rapid breakdown of the structural constraints that had historically impeded the expansion of capitalist accumulation processes. The act itself represented a "compromised conflict" between competing capitalist interests (particularly, agrarian and mining interests) that coalesced around the conjoined desire to encourage, for whatever reason, the rapid development of agricultural production and circulation. This state policy did not derive from any one single source, but instead germinated in a long series of sometimes bitter and sometimes cordial confrontations among competing fractions of capital that finally produced a compromised consensus around this so-called territorial segregation policy. Capitalist state policies must always be understood as the specific products of the inherent contradictions of the capital-accumulation process itself. As such, the class capacity of the agrarian bourgeoisie (and its class allies in urban-industrialized production and circulation) to overcome through the 1913 Natives' Land Act the structural barriers to capitalist development in agriculture remained strictly conditioned by the contradictions of the accumulation process itself.[8]

THE 1913 NATIVES' LAND ACT

Combined and Uneven Capitalist Development

Combined and uneven capitalist development in South Africa manifested itself in the "separation" between "town" and "country," or, to put it in another way, between "industry" and "agriculture." To be specific, the diamond-mining and gold-mining branches of industry and their ancillary operations had experienced rapid amalgamation of numerous production units under increasingly unified economic ownership between the 1880s and the turn of the century. Mining magnates mobilized capital and requisite supplies from abroad, fashioned outlets (markets) for their commodities on a world scale, and continuously restructured the capitalist labor-process at the points of production as a means of minimizing costs and maximizing outputs. Seen in broad historical terms, mining capital at the end of the Anglo-Boer war had undergone tremendous concentration and centralization, was thoroughly incorporated into the capitalist world economy, and had consolidated its position on the political terrain as the "hegemonic fraction" of the reconstituted "power bloc" (i.e., the site of arbitration and confrontation between the various factions of capital).[9]

In contrast, agricultural capital languished in relative backwardness, obscured in the shadow of *rentier* landlordism in the countryside and confronted with numerous obstacles to uninterrupted expansion. Agricultural capital itself was divided into "many capitals," differentiated by scale of operations, relative fertility of the soil, access to inexpensive labor-power and markets, and so forth. Put directly, the principal barriers to capital accumulation in the field of agriculture remained the widespread existence of non-capitalist forms of production (characterized, chiefly, by European landlord/African squatter social-production relations).

The dictates of large-scale capital investment in mining required that sufficient quantities of unskilled labor-power be compelled or persuaded to submit to a relatively elaborate social division of labor, including technical differentiation of task and cooperation, and to an elaborate hierarchy of social control and supervision (unleashed through the "prison-like perfection" of the compound system). Equally important, because wage-laborers at the point of production were remunerated both in money wages and in kind, mining capital possessed considerable leeway in reducing their outlay for variable capital by purchasing relatively inexpensive agricultural foodstuffs. By 1913, the Witwatersrand had become a thriving metropolitan region. The population reached 518,930—or nearly one-seventh the total of British South Africa.[10] The cost of living (prices of foodstuffs and housing rentals) was an estimated 40 percent higher than in the United States and nearly 80 percent higher than in any European country.[11] In this same year, South Africa imported £7,485,281 of foodstuffs from abroad.[12] An objective foundation, thus, existed for a political alliance between large-scale industrial capital situated in the urban areas (and mining capital in particular) and agricultural capital over the political question of expanded state aid in hastening the process of capitalist development in agriculture as a means of cheapening the price of foodstuffs.

African Squatting: Class Obstacles to a Comprehensive Native Policy

The 1913 Natives' Land Act reflected the "conflicted compromise" between the politically hegemonic mining capital and emergent agricultural capital. Mining capital clearly benefitted from both the rapid growth of commercial agriculture and the setting aside of reserves for so-called "tribal" land tenure. Correlatively, agricultural capital directly benefitted from the 1913 Natives' Land Act through the statutory restrictions placed on squatting and "farming on the halves."

The *sine qua non* for the expansion of capitalist agriculture in the immediate post-Boer War period was the elimination of squatting relations which, in turn, entailed the erosion of European *rentier* landlordism and the restriction of African access to fertile landed property. The Milner "Reconstruction" Administration—closely associated with mining capital—operated on the premise that the consolidation of the four South African colonies under British imperial hegemony required, *inter alia*, the placement of European settlers (of British stock) on the land.[13] Lord Alfred Milner himself, in the words of Richard Keiser, "felt confident that Britain's resources of money and people were sufficient to consolidate their victory (after the Anglo-Boer War) by attracting British settlers to a prosperous South Africa, thereby outnumbering and Anglicizing the Africaners."[14]

The so-called "closer settlement"[15] schemes, however, came face to face with a particularly formidable barrier: namely, widespread African

Table 5.1 Estimates of Squatting Relations Compiled by the Department of Native Affairs, 1913

	Cape Province	Natal	Orange Free State	Transvaal	TOTAL
African Urban Residents	113,000	35,000			508,000
African Rural Residents					3,508,000
Africans in Locations or 'Reserves'	1,145,000	430,000			
'Squatters' on Crown Lands		57,000		65,000	
Employed 'In Service'	232,000	48,000			
'Squatters' on Land Occupied by Owners	22,000	261,000	73,000	142,000	
'Squatters' on Land Unoccupied by Owners	5,600	119,000	7,000	174,000	
TOTAL	1,519,000				

Source: Union of South Africa, Parliament, House of Assembly, Debates of the Third Session of the First Parliament, 1913 (Cape Town: Cape Times Limited, 1913), Statement of Minister of Native Affairs, J. W. Sauer, p. 2274. See also "Natives and Land," Farmers' Weekly, 10 January 1917, p. 1823.

squatting relations. As has already been seen, African squatters occupied fertile and easily accessible lands. For example, an estimated 180,427 African squatters in the Transvaal resided on approximately 30,840 square miles.[16] Estimated figures for the number of squatters throughout the union are provided in table 5.1. Correlatively, the continued class capacity of African squatters to move from place to place (whether European farmstead, vacant crown lands, the properties of large-scale land companies, and so forth) provided them with a decided advantage in the determination of both where and when to venture out to work and considerable choice over the terms of work.[17]

The secretary for native affairs, Godfrey Lagden, began to implement the existing 1895 anti-squatting legislation (the *Plakkers Wet*) in the Transvaal in a serious manner only in August, 1903.[18] The rigorous enforcement of this legislation entailed almost insurmountable difficulties. As Lagden wrote to Sir George Farrar, "The prevailing conditions have been the growth of many years and of very many systems [of landed property relations] and it would be most unwise if not stupid to attempt any sudden derangement or dislocation calculated to disturb the untutored mind which is apt to get in a panic if made to hurry too fast."[19]

Embryonic capitalist farmers were anxious to have the state administration enforce whatever "anti-squatting" regulations were in existence.[20] Nevertheless, the Milner administration exercised extreme caution in its dealings with rural Africans, fearing that any abrupt measures would simply fuel an already tense political situation. Godfrey Lagden, for example, instructed the Native Commissioners under his command to enforce the *Plakkers Wet* to *protect* the interests of rural Africans, (i.e., only in places "where there is a manifest abuse of farming Natives [i.e., 'Kaffir-farming'])."[21] By 1904, even a cursory review of the various reports of Native Commissioners in the Transvaal reveals that the rigorous implementation of anti-squatting legislation *per se* in isolation from a comprehensive "Native Policy" would only further exacerbate political tensions and increasingly complicate an already confusing state of affairs in the countryside. According to the Native Commissioner for the northwestern Transvaal, S. W. J. Scholefield, "The Squatters' Law can only, in my opinion, be considered in conjunction with the vexed question of land settlement and with the education of Natives. In fact, the whole question of Native policy is involved."[22] Lagden himself commented in early 1905 that "no effective administration of the Squatters' Law is possible until the law has been amended and that in view of impending constitutional changes it will be left to the new legislature to consider what form the amendments to the law shall take."[23]

European Debate over Proposed Territorial Segregation Legislation

Political organizations such as *Het Volk*, the Transvaal Agricultural Union, and so forth, vocally demanded more strongly-worded legislation in order to more effectively promote the interests of "progressive" European farmers. In 1908, the state administration in the Transvaal introduced the Native Occupation of Lands Bill, which "was based as far as possible upon certain principles recommended by the South African Native Affairs Commission."[24] The principal objectives of this bill centered on the reduction of the number of Africans that would be permitted to reside on any single private farmstead and the creation of special, demarcated African townships and village (rural) settlements.[25] Put concretely, those who advocated passage of the bill hoped to appease those embryonic capitalist farmers desiring the curtailment of Kaffir-farming. However, the bill alienated *rentier* interests, particularly those landlords grouped around such bodies as the Transvaal Landowners'

Association, who handsomely profited from leasing land to African squatters while simultaneously retaining mineral rights to any potentially profitable discoveries that might be unearthed on these properties at some future date. This proposed Native Occupation of Lands Bill also failed to satisfy the desires of emergent capitalist farmers. One European farmer from Mylstroom, for example, wrote to the minister of native affairs: "I am quite convinced . . . that the general dissatisfaction at present existing amongst our people [i.e., European farmers] will in no way be abated or diminished by [the passage of this Bill] as there is no provision made against natives squatting on Crown lands and the low annual rent of £1 per annum."[26] In the wake of the widespread political opposition to the bill from almost all quarters, the Native Occupation of Lands Bill died in the Transvaal Legislative Assembly.

In late 1910, the South African Parliament had appointed a special Select Committee—with the Minister of Native Affairs, the Cape Liberal Henry Burton, as chairman—to thoroughly investigate the perplexing question of African land settlement with particular reference to the so-called squatting problem.[27] This committee concluded its deliberations with the opinion that the combined anti-squatting legislative measures that had previously been enacted over the years in the Transvaal, Natal, and the Orange Free State were wholly unsatisfactory from the point of view of the future of European prosperity in South Africa. It recommended a uniform policy throughout the recently formed Union of South Africa for regulating the settlement of rural Africans on European-owned landed property and, where such settlement existed or was presently permitted, for ensuring means for proper control by the European owners of such property as well as by the state administration.[28] To achieve this desired end, the Committee recommended legislation "broadly on the lines of the resolutions arrived at by the *South African Native Affairs Commission* [1903–1905]."[29] The committee also published a preliminary draft bill that embodied its conclusions.[30] The fundamental principle of territorial segregation that was contained in it formed the essential ingredients of the 1913 Natives' Land Act.[31]

Provisions of the 1913 Natives' Land Act

Act No. 27 of 1913, the Natives' Land Act, effectively became law in the Union of South Africa on June 19 of that year. It was a complex and comprehensive measure, significant above all for its claim to officially declare and to implement the principle of territorial segregation (or separation) between European and native races living in South Africa.[32] In addition to this primary object, the act itself also contained secondary objectives: first, to check squatting on private farmsteads; second, to terminate any existing agreements in the Orange Free State whereby Africans might lease land on the "ploughing on the halves" (or "half-shares") principle; and third, to remove statutory restrictions on the number of families that might be permitted to reside on private farms as laborers in the Transvaal.[33] Seen in broad terms, the sweeping provisions of this 1913 Natives' Land Act, in Colin Bundy's words, "are virtually unparalleled in importance in twentieth-century South African history."[34] Its most far-reaching provisions stipulated that, except with the governor-general's formal approval, an African was deprived of the right to acquire from a person other than an African (or a non-African from an African) any land or interest in land, in any area outside existing areas of African occupation (the "reserves" and areas of African freehold occupation). Similarly, this legislative enactment prohibited any person other than an African from acquiring any land, or interest in land, within the existing areas of African occupation, now redefined as "Scheduled Native Areas," except with the same official approval.[35] These "Scheduled Native Areas" consisted of the existing African "reserves" and "locations" in the four provinces as well as land privately owned by Africans. The act only applied to landed relations in the rural areas; the questions of African tenure and occupation of land in the municipal townships surrounding the urban-industrial centers were to be considered elsewhere.[36]

All in all, this 1913 Natives' Land Act had tremendous consequences. In the initial phase, the area set aside for exclusive occupation by Africans constituted only 7.3 percent of the total land surface of the Union and was "thus patently inadequate to support them."[37] The so-called Scheduled African areas came to a total of 10.7 million morgen (one morgen = 2.116 acres). In addition to the initial 7.3 percent set aside, 5.7 percent of the total land area was legislated to constitute so-called "released" areas where Africans would be freed from the general prohibitions on buying land.[38]

A commission was appointed under the provisions of the act in order to find and purchase further land for African occupation to add (from the "released" areas) to what had already been set aside. Under the chairmanship of Sir William Beaumont, a former administrator of Natal and a Supreme Court judge, the Natives' Land Commission was charged with completing its investigations and presenting its reports and recommendations within two years.[39] In a nutshell, the 1913 Natives' Land Act demarcated only about 13 percent of the surface area of South Africa as "Native Reserves" and prohibited Africans from purchasing, leasing, or renting cultivatable lands in the remaining "European" areas.

THE IMPLEMENTATION OF THE 1913 NATIVES' LAND ACT

Restructuring Agrarian Production Relations From Above

For the most part, agrarian capital hailed the 1913 Natives' Land Act as a godsend. From their class perspective, European embryonic capitalist farmers intuitively recognized that drastic state action had been required in order to hasten the ongoing process of separation of the direct producers from effective possession of the materials and instruments of production. Put simply, African squatters had enjoyed in certain instances considerable leeway to pick and choose the terms of their employment because they had not been compelled by economic necessity to compete on the market in order to survive. With the enactment of the 1913 Natives' Land Act, embryonic capitalist farmers were overjoyed with the prospects for the days ahead.[40] The secretary for native affairs, Edward Dower, for example, spoke glowingly of the swift eradication of any quixotic or whimsical illusions about cooperative partnership on the land between European and Native: The effect of the Act is to put a stop, for the future, to all transactions involving *anything in the nature of partnership between European and native*, in respect of land or the fruits of land except with the special approval of the Governor-General.... All new contracts with natives must be contracts of service [i.e., wage-labour]."[41] High-ranking state officials regarded this Act as "broadly speaking... a *preliminary step* toward checking indiscriminate occupation of land."[42] At another place, the Secretary for Native Affairs referred to the Act as "*a first step* in the direction of territorial separation of black and white, Parliament having decided that an effort should be made to put a stop to the *many social and other evils* which result from too close contact between European and native."[43]

The fact that the 1913 Natives' Land Act was conceived as a provisional measure (subject to substantial revision when the results of the Native Lands Commission were analyzed) meant that it was bound to produce confusing and often contradictory interpretations. In petitioning the prime minister of South Africa, John L. Dube, the president of the South African Native National Congress, remarked that "it is true there seems to be a great deal of misunderstanding about [the act] even by those of the highest authority."[44] The state administration in fact published numerous memoranda advising magistrates, native commissioners, and so forth, in the proper interpretation of the provisions of the act. For example, E. L. Mathews explained the act in the following manner:

> The Squatters Laws are not repealed; in fact they are expressly kept alive by section *six*, but the provisions of the Act are super-imposed upon them, and in the event of a conflict the Act will prevail. One of the clauses of the Act relates to the Transvaal.... It is in the Transvaal where the squatting evil has existed to the greatest extent. On the other hand, it is impossible to dispossess these squatters, many of whom, or their progenitors, have been on the land from time immemorial.
>
> If, therefore, natives are farm labourers (i.e., when their occupation of land is due to agreements of service, the test of which is ninety days' service per year and the absence of any payment in money or in kind for the use of land) there

will be no limit to the number who may reside on the property. Where, on the other hand, the existing natives are no such farm labourers, they are saved from dispossession till Parliament acts upon the report of the [Beaumont] Commission, i.e., until other suitable land is found for them by the creation of additional native reserves.[45]

Further, the secretary for native affairs issued strict instructions concerning conceivable methods of implementing the act and outlined the stiff penalties for contravention of its statutes and evasion of its provisions.[46]

Pariahs in the Land of Their Birth:[47] The Assault on Squatting

The 1913 Natives' Land Act established statutory prohibitions against African land purchases in European demarcated areas and reinforced the prevailing proscriptions against squatting relations. These conjoined pressures accelerated the ongoing process of conversion of both landed property and labor-power into commodities. The agrarian class transformation that erupted with a quickened pace in the second decade of the twentieth century took place both through a distinctive political break—the direct intervention of the state administration against squatting relations—and through "a number of quite imperceptible transitions as labour tenancy itself was internally transformed."[48] The "Prussian path" to capitalist development in agriculture had thus triumphed in the South African countryside.

African professionals and intellectuals engaged in a spirited defense of what they regarded as Native rights, demanding a "redress of grievances"[49] and a return to the *status quo ante* on the land. John L. Dube reproached the state administration in disdainful terms: "We have seen our people driven from the places dear to them as the inheritance of generations, to become wanderers on the face of the earth."[50] Saul Msane revealed his utter amazement in his testimony before the Eastern Transvaal Native Lands Commission: "We were astonished that such a thing [i.e., the 1913 Natives' Land Act] should happen under the British flag."[51] One member of Parliament reported to the House of Assembly that "he held in his hand resolutions passed at a recent [African] congress in Johannesburg [concerning the 1913 Natives' Land Bill], and at that present moment numbers of intelligent and influential [African] men were going through the Union and scattering those by the thousand. The [African] people were stirred, and they were going to take a definite stand."[52]

African public protests escalated. The Natal Missionary Conference, for example, released a statement that strongly condemned the dissolutory effects of the 1913 Natives' Land Act: "Scarcely any legislation has ever been enacted which has affected the Native population with so much dismay."[53] In a similar vein, the *Christian Express* registered what its editors understood as "Native opinion": "Since the Land Act was passed, Native opinion has solidified in a manner and degree altogether new in South African experience. Until now, the Natives have been separated by tribal differences and jealousies."[54] Finally, Sol Plaatje summarily denounced the state administration: "By a stroke of the pen," he intoned, "this cruel law"—a "gross sacrilege"—"disturb[ed] such harmonious relations between these people of different races and colours."[55] In a peculiar sardonic style unparalleled in South Africa at the time, Plaatje faulted seemingly honest European members of Parliament for "play[ing] up to the desires of the racial extremists," noting that "nothing short of a declaration of war against [the native population] could have created a similar excitement [as the 1913 Natives' Land Act]."[56]

In relaying the prime minister's reply to the protest lodged by the South African Native National Congress, the secretary for native affairs, Edward Dower, admitted without even a hint of remorse that "it is inevitable that some hardship should arise in individual cases."[57] Numerous accounts directly contradicted this temperate appraisal of the overall impact of the 1913 Natives' Land Act. Again, Plaatje's eyewitness tale of widespread misery remains perhaps the most authoritative summary of the ignominious momentum put into motion by the act. At one place, Plaatje recounted the confession of a "well-known Dutchman": " 'The object of this law,' said the Burgher, 'is to goad the Natives into rebellion, so that the Government may legally confiscate what little ground was left to them, and hand over the dispossessed Kafirs and their families to work for the farmers, just for their food.' "[58] At another place, he described how these "unfortunate nomads of an ungrateful and inhospitable country" were summarily evicted from their homes in the Orange Free State, forced to wander from farm to farm, "trudging aimlessly from place to place in search of some [European] farmer who might give them a shelter."[59] "Evictions around here," he continued, "were numerous.... A pitiable spectacle, however, was the sight of those who had been evicted from the centre of the Orange 'Free' State. It was heartrending to hear them relate the circumstances of their expulsions, and how they had spent the winter months roaming from farm to farm with their famished stock, applying in vain for a resting place."[60]

Evidence concerning the inordinate hardships experienced by rural Africans in the wake of the 1913 Natives' Land Act can be adduced from a kaleidoscopic profusion of sources. Plaatje, for example, reported that the "Plague Act was raging with particular fury in the old Cape Districts of Fort Beauford, Grahamstown, Kingwilliamstown, and East London."[61] Nevertheless, the Report of the Native Lands Commission is perhaps the most recognizably authoritative and comprehensive account of changing rural class relations. In testimony after testimony presented to this [Beaumont] Commission in 1914, European farmers, state officials, and Africans reported massive evictions of squatters from European farmsteads. For example, a retired farmer from the Estcourt district, Natal, reported: "The Act will have the tendency of driving the natives off the farms. When I bought my farm there were 60 huts and I was obliged to turn 40 of them off."[62] A farmer and storekeeper at Marianhill, Natal, testified that: "A great many people are turning them off. The natives have been given notice because they will not agree to the terms. The idea is to turn them off and get them back again under the Act and thereby get more power over them."[63] Finally, Josiah Gumude (representative of the Pietermartizburg branch of the South African Native National Congress) declared that "there are some 40 cases of natives known to me personally in the neighborhood of Pietermartizburg who have been moved off private lands and are now wandering about not knowing where to settle."[64] Examples of widespread evictions from practically every rural district of South Africa could be repeated almost endlessly.[65]

THE CLASS STRUGGLE OF THE PRINCIPAL AGRARIAN SOCIAL CLASSES

Invisible and Individualized Forms of Class Struggle from Below

Open rebellion did not erupt in the countryside. However, Africans in the rural areas did engage in a wide variety of practices that, taken together, constituted invisible and individualized forms of class struggle. The character of this rural agitation is sometimes difficult to classify and nearly impossible to measure with any exactitude. Nevertheless, there is no doubt that these class activities clearly blocked the tranquil and uninterrupted expansion of capitalist relations into agricultural production and circulation. Whether Africans in isolated locales were conscious of the overall impact or not, numerous actions—registered in the aggregate—constituted a distinctive class barrier to the unimpeded and smooth transition to the class hegemony of agrarian capital in the countryside.

Extensive stock theft symbolized one way in which African rural dwellers attempted to recoup what they reasoned had been stolen from them. For example, W. Rose-Gordon, justice of the peace for the Province of Natal, testified that "there are so many thefts of stock that it is very difficult for a farmer to exist.... It is almost impossible for white men to live round a native location—if the natives have the slightest little grudge they make things impossible, and in self-defense they must be kept to their areas."[66] Similarly, Jacobus van der Walt, minister for labor affairs for Pretoria district (South), reported:

> There are thousands of natives in my constituency, they mostly come from locations in the bushveld. They live in the neighbourhood of the goldfields from 6 to 18 miles away.... They sow lands mostly on the half share system and pay £6 to £7, sometimes as much as £10 or more, and get up to a thousand or two thousand bags of mealies. The lands belong mostly to [absentee land] companies and rich people.... This area is not protected by the town police and the rural police are too few in number to look properly after these natives, and numerous cases of stock thefts and even murder take place.[67]

The gradual transformation of agrarian class relations from "farming on the halves" (where the mechanism of surplus appropriation took place through non-capitalist rent) to "labor–tenant" production relations coincided with the wholesale onslaught of embryonic capitalist farmers against the plethora of ancillary privileges that African direct producers had previously enjoyed as a consequence of their class bargain with the dominant agrarian propertied classes. Specifically, the development of labor-tenant production relations entailed the gradual reduction in the absolute size of garden plots and grazing grounds offered to African direct producers as a declining portion of the total wage package. This shrinkage of cultivatable plots and grazing rights contributed to the sharp increase of African stock thefts and frequent pilferage from the European "baas."[68] Frustrated embryonic capitalist farmers demanded harsh remedies to counteract the "direct action" of African direct producers who attempted to reclaim what they considered had been wrongfully stolen from them. "There is only one solution [to stock theft]," a farmer in the Orange Free State argued, "*viz.*, all natives, bag and baggage, to be segregated to those respective countries and to be allowed to return as labourers, and for the whites to hire their labour on the market. All town natives to be in their compounds at six o'clock p.m."[69]

Another invisible and individualized form of class struggle that emanated from below was the frequent outright refusal of evicted Africans to leave or to pay rent on land they considered their own by right of occupation. In its final report, the Beaumont Commission warned of "the difficulty of removing any considerable number of natives from land occupied by them." The report continued:

> Natives cling to the localities occupied by them with the greatest tenacity. The failure to enforce the *Plakkers Wet* in the Transvaal, the troubles arising out of the concentration of Natives in the Barkly West District, and the altogether unsuccessful attempt to move a small tribe (the Umnini tribe) from the locations in Natal are all experiences in proof of this fact, and many others might be

added. Everyone is agreed that any attempt to forcibly remove natives is inadvisable and sure to lead to trouble.[70]

In describing European efforts to enforce evictions of African squatters, one magistrate in Natal claimed that "there will be passive resistance. In a number of instances their huts have been burnt to get them to remove from land and as soon as the backs of the police are turned they rebuild."[71] An agent for the Natal Land and Colonisation Company described his company's attempts to bring certain plots of land into wattle cultivation:

[The Africans] won't work and they won't pay us their rents, and the owners want them ejected. If they are ejected they remain on the land. I call to mind one man who was kicked out three times. They are brought up for trespass and fined £5 or three months and they come out and go on living happily on the same land. They have no stock and in some instances have not even got a fowl. They live by stealing in many instances.[72]

In response to the question, "In your experience, is there any tendency on the part of the individual farmer to keep more boys on his farm than are actually necessary for his farming operations?" G. D. Wheelwright, the sub-native commissioner for the Barberton District, Transvaal, answered: "Natives will not move to another farm where the conditions are not so easy."[73] Finally, Hugh Griffiths, a sub-native commissioner in the Eastern Transvaal, testified that "the farmers have great difficulty in getting labour tenants, for the natives are not satisfied with the conditions. They would rather buy land and be free."[74]

Large numbers of rural Africans also migrated from place to place, frequently drifting to the towns or mining centers, in search of higher wage-paid employment and better working conditions than were available on European farmsteads in the agricultural districts. This largely invisible and individualized form of class struggle created serious labor shortages for European farmers in the countryside. For example, David Worth Hook, a sub-native commissioner in the Eastern Transvaal, remarked that "there is a tendency on the part of the natives living in rural places to gravitate to towns with their families. They are generally accommodated in locations near the town . . . where they pay . . . to the municipality for rent."[75] According to W. H. Beaumont, chairman of the Natives' Land Commission, "Farmers are chiefly interested in the supply of labour, which has been gradually drifting from the farms to the industrial centres and the towns."[76] Specifically, European farmers were particularly vexed over the migration of able-bodied young men from the rural areas:

It is a fact that the father of the Native family has lost hold on the young Native; employment on the farm does not satisfy the young Native any more, the wages and work offered are not sufficiently enticing; furthermore, life in a town, in a location or in a compound offers him, according to the stories of his friends, better employment, more excitement or pleasure. The consequence is that he leaves his father and his womenfolk on the farm to look after the cattle and other belongings. The farmer, deprived of the services of the children of the old man, does not wish him with the women to stay any longer on the farm, and gives him notice to quit. He with the women drift to some mining location, to the ruin of the young girls.[77]

Despite the battery of legislative devices designed to create a rural proletariat, European farmers continued to experience serious difficulties in harnessing sufficient quantities of labor: "We cannot get farm labourers now because the young men run off to Johannesburg and it is useless taking proceedings. They are asking higher wages now and are doing less work than they used to do."[78]

Correlatively, rural Africans still possessed a certain flexibility in their selection of the terms of agreement with European farmers. For example, in 1919 the magistrate for the Ladybrand District, the Orange Free State, complained about the problem of labor shortages, revealing the persistent variability of contractual arrangements outside the wage-form per se:

Farm labour is none too plentiful at present. The European is apparently too expensive a luxury and the native works just when he has to. A plentiful supply of native labour can be procured provided the farmer supplies grazing for stock and ground and facilities [i.e., farm implements?] for planting crops, but owing to closer settlement and reduction in the size of farms few owners can afford to give these privileges.[79]

Similarly, the magistrate at Bloemhof reported in 1919: "It is obvious that at the present time the agriculturalist [i.e., European progressive farmer] is obliged to require . . . a given quantity of work from his squatters for fear that they should leave him and "lonza" to the man possessing an abundance of land where, stock raising being the principal occupation, the cultivation of crops is a matter more or less of secondary consideration."[80]

While reliable evidence is somewhat sketchy and excessively impressionistic, it appears that frequent contravention of the statutes of the 1913 Natives' Land Act remained a fairly common practice, particularly in the most remote and outlying regions, for more than a decade. African direct producers also migrated from place to place in the rural areas in seach of unoccupied farmsteads where they could squat. As Johann Dicke put it: "This distribution scheme [i.e., the creation of small rural 'locations' as opposed to 'tribal' Reserves] was counteracted greatly by natives also *flocking on to unworked farms*, mostly held by powerful land companies, who charged rent and thereby got sufficient interest on their capital for dividends. This farming of natives was a standing complaint of farmers, for the natives preferred paying cash rent to working instead of rent."[81]

Put directly, labor-starved European farmers were desperate and reckless men, hoping against considerable odds to eke out a livelihood on the land under trying circumstances. Poor European farmers occasionally returned to modified "farming on the halves" production relations and hence willingly risked official castigation and punitive reprisals for evasion of anti-squatting laws. From the point of view of high-cost European landowners with limited access to labor-power and credit, modified sharecropping offered certain genuine and immediate benefits: sharecroppers provided the means of production, assumed more or less half the risk of crop failure, and undertook the greatest productive efforts.

Gradual Eradication of Squatting Relations From Above

The dominant European understanding of the character of the 1913 Natives' Land Act revolved around the ideological notion of the "principle of the separation of the races." In a particularly insightful fashion, John L. Dube demystified this prevailing conventional wisdom in his petition to the prime minister:

> But we do not see how it is possible for this [1913 Natives' Land Act] to effect any greater separation between the races than obtains now. It is evident that the *aim of this law is to compel service by taking away the means of independence and self-improvement.* This compulsory service at reduced wages and high rents will not be separation, *but an intermingling* of the most injurious character of both races. [Emphasis added.][82]

Whether he was fully aware of it or not, John Dube recognized that the combination of prohibitions against African land ownership in the most fertile areas of the South African countryside and the wholesale restrictions on African squatting relations contributed to the ongoing process of class polarization in agricultural production and circulation, *namely*, the creation of an agrarian capitalist class and a rural proletariat. The historical possibility of the consolidation of large-scale independent African petty commodity production in agriculture (the actual separation of the races) gave way to the stark reality of the dominance of wage-labor/capital production relations (the intermingling of the races).

The extent to which the provisions of the 1913 Natives' Land Act were actually applied to remove African squatters from choice lands remains a matter of considerable conjecture and historical debate. In one sense, the question of the extent of success or failure of the act is irrelevant.

The act was one prominent weapon in a heavily-laden arsenal of state repression. The state administration made selective use of the panoply of means at its disposal to accelerate the process of class transformation of the countryside from above. Specifically, embryonic capitalist farmers clamored for state support in the widespread effort to dislodge those African squatters whose conditions of existence posed a direct competitive threat to European commercial farming. For example, the resident magistrate for Kroonstad, one of the richest agricultural regions of the Orange Free State, reported:

The squatting families own heads of cattle ranging from sixty in the highest cases to ten on the lowest. Some own flocks of sheep and goats ranging from 250 to 20. *Their incomes are dependent to a great extent on the mealie harvest.* They are thrifty in their habits and *there is a distinct upward tendency in respect to the state of their material resources.* One instance was brought to my notice during the past season of the squatters on a farm receiving 800 bags of mealies as their share of the harvest. The approximate average income of a squatting family in an average year may be taken to be 150 bags of mealies per annum, apart from any increase in stock. [Emphasis added.][83]

Similarly, a Christian missionary in the Transvaal highveld testified before a special Select Committee on Natives Affairs in 1917:

Squatters paying half their produce . . . have looked upon it as an avenue of progress. . . . They are better off on the farms. . . . Some of them have wagons of their own and oxen, and some of them have been able to buy land in townships, or even small farms, that they have purchased with money they have saved through living as squatters on the farms. . . . The farm Natives have left tribal rule for many years. They have been allowed to squat on farms . . . paying a portion of their produce in lieu of rent, giving what service was required of them, and developing a certain amount of village social life, building little churches for worship and schools for the education of their children.[84]

Numerous witnesses testified before the Beaumont Commission that for the most part the wealthier and more successful African squatters were the first ejected from private European farmsteads. The resident magistrate from Winburg in the Orange Free State reported that "these natives are now receiving notice to leave, and in practically all cases they are natives who have large possessions."[85] In his chronicle of the plight of ejected squatters, Plaatje recounts the arduous journey of large numbers of African households fleeing with the stock and possessions across the borders:

Look at these exiles swarming towards the Basuto border, some of them with their belongings on their heads, driving their emaciated flocks attenuated by starvation and cold. . . . It was a distressing sight. We had never seen the likes of it since the outbreak of the Boer War, near the Transvaal border, immediately before the siege of Mafeking. Even the flight of 1899 had a buoyancy of its own, for the Boer War, *unlike the present stealthy war of extermination* [i.e., the law which caused this flight], was preceded by an ultimatum.[86]

This option, however, remained open for only a relatively small number of evicted squatters. Undoubtedly, pockets of squatting relations persisted for quite some time in certain districts of the countryside. However, the death blow had been effectively dealt to squatting in the richest and most fertile agricultural regions.

NOTES

1. Clements Kadalie, "The Aims and Motives of the I.C.U. [Industrial and Commercial Workers' Union]," 1925.

2. J. R. Sullivan, *The Native Policy of Sir Theophilus Shepstone* (Johannesburg, 1928), p. 131.

3. See Robert Sherry, "Comments on O'Connor's Review of *The Twisted Dream*: Independent Commodity Production versus Petty Bourgeois Production," *Monthly Review* 28, 1 (May 1976), pp. 52–60.

4. V. I. Lenin, *The Development of Capitalism in Russia. Volume III: Collected Works* (Moscow, 1972), p. 194.

5. Ibid., pp. 194–195.

6. Ibid., p. 197.

7. See Mike Davis, " 'Fordism' in Crisis: A Review of Michel Aglietta's Regulation et Crises: L'experience des Stats-Unis," *Review* II, 2 (Fall 1978), p. 212, for an elaboration of this point.

8. See Giovanni Arrighi, "Towards a Theory of Capitalist Crisis," *New Left Review* 111 (September-October 1978), pp. 3–24.

9. For a detailed discussion of the concept 'power bloc,' see Nicos Poulantzas, *Classes in Contemporary Capitalism* (London, 1975), pp. 93–108. In his words, "As far as the terrain of political domination is concerned, this is also occupied not by one single class or class faction, but by several dominant classes and factions. These classes and factions form a specific alliance on this terrain, the power bloc, generally functioning under the leadership of one of the dominant classes or factions, the hegemonic class or faction" (p. 93).

10. British Parliamentary Papers, Trade of South Africa, *Report of the Board of Trade on the Trade of the Union of South Africa for the Year 1913*, Cd. 7648 (London, 1914), Statement of Sir R. Sothern Holland, p. 5.

11. Ibid., p. 7.

12. Ibid., p. 24. It is also important to note that South Africa imported 43 percent of its total agricultural machinery imports from the United States (as opposed to 33 percent of the total from the United Kingdom). Similarly, 53.3 percent of total imports from the United States in 1913 were agricultural implements (ibid., p. 26).

13. See Donald Denoon, *A Grand Illusion* (London, 1973), pp. 65–78; G. H. L. Le May, *British Supremacy in South Africa* (Oxford, 1965), chap. seven.

14. Richard Keiser, "The South African Governor-General, 1910–1919," Unpublished Ph.D. dissertation, University of Oxford, 1975, p. 1.

15. "Closer Settlement" was often associated with the notion of "small farmers": "The idea that the land can only be economically and intelligently worked by the operations of huge concerns, more akin in staff and turnover to a small Rand Gold mine than an average farm undertaking, is entirely opposed to modern ideas of land settlement as generally expressed in this country and as in operation in other colonies." Jas. Reas, Vlakfontein, Transvaal, "Correspondence," *South African Agricultural Journal* II, 2 (August 1911), p. 225. See also A. R. E. Burton, ed., *Handbook for Settlers: Land Settlement in the Transvaal* (Pretoria, 1902), for a survey of information and advice to intending British settlers prepared by the Transvaal Department of Agriculture. What must be kept in mind, however, is that "huge farms," "Boer estates," and similar labels frequently referred euphemistically to *rentier landlordism* and the "wasteful" (from the point of view of embryonic capitalist farmers) practice of "Kaffir-farming."

16. Transvaal Colony, Native Affairs Department, *Annual Report of the Native Affairs Department, 1904* (Pretoria, 1905).

17. For example, the Transvaal Consolidated Lands Company was "one of the biggest and most important land and exploitation companies in South Africa. It had a capital of £800,000 and belonged to the Werhner-Beit [mining] group and had extensive holdings in the Northern Transvaal, acquiring 28,837 acres in 1902 alone." *African Review* (March 28, 1903).

18. Secretary for Native Affairs (SNA) 30/1390/03. Circular 79/03 ("Enforcement of Squatters Law," 6 August 1903). Cited in Paul Rich, "African Farming and the 1913 Natives' Land Act: Towards a Reassessment," *South African Labour Development Research Union (SALDRU) Farm Labour Conference*. School of Economics, University of Cape Town, September 1976. Paper No. 21.

19. SNA 35/1963/1903. Lagden to Sir G. Farrar, 22 September 1903. Cited in Rich, "African Farming," p. 6.

20. SNA 30/2571/1903. E. H. Hogge to Secretary of Native Affairs, 26 October 1903. Cited in Rich, "African Farming," p. 6.

21. SNA 30/2398/1903. Minute No. 98/03. Enforcement of Squatters' Law, 4 November 1903. Cited in Rich, "African Farming," p. 6.

22. SNA 30/1390/1903. S. W. J. Scholfield to Secretary of Native Affairs, Lagden, 15 January 1903. Cited in Rich, "African Farming," p. 6.

23. SNA 50/3090/1904. Lagden to Secretary of Native Affairs, 30 January, 1906. Cited in Rich, "African Farming," p. 9.

24. Transvaal Colony, Native Affairs Department, *Annual Report of the Native Affairs Department, 1908* (Pretoria, 1909).

25. *The Transvaal Government Gazette Extraordinary*. Pretoria, 23 May 1908. Cited in Rich, "African Farming," p. 10.

26. SNA 58/2962/05. R. Grenville to the Minister of Native Affairs, 28 April 1908. Cited in Rich, "African Farming," p. 11.

27. Union of South Africa, Select Committee on Native Affairs, *Report of the Committee on Native Affairs: Squatting*, S.C. 3-'10 (Cape Town, 1910), p. iii.

28. See C. M. Tatz, *Shadow and Substance in South Africa: A Study in Land and Franchise Policies Affecting Africans, 1910–1960* (Pietermaritzburg, 1962), p. 13.

29. *Report of the Select Committee on Native Affairs*, S.C.3-'10, p. iv.

30. *Report of the Select Committee on Native Affairs,* S.C.3-'10, Appendices, Annexure II, pp. viii-xii.

31. Tatz, *Shadow and Substance,* p. 13.

32. See Brian Willan, "The Anti-Slavery and Aborigines' Protection Society and the South African Natives' Land Act of 1913," *Journal of African History* 20, 1 (1979), pp. 84–102. The provisions of the Natives' Land Act are reproduced in full in Solomon Plaatje, *Native Life in South Africa: Before and Since the European War and the Boer Rebellion* (London, 1916), pp. 46–51.

33. See Edgar Brookes, *The History of Native Policy in South Africa from 1830 to the Present Day* (Pretoria, 1927), pp. 335–337.

34. Colin Bundy, *The Rise and Fall of the South African Peasantry* (Berkeley and Los Angeles, 1979), p. 213.

35. See Sheila van der Horst, *Native Labour in South Africa* (London, 1942), p. 291.

36. Union of South Africa, Natives' Land Commission, *Report of the Natives' Land Commission,* U.G. 22-'16 (Cape Town, 1916), Appendix X, p. 15. Hereafter cited as *Beaumont Commission.*

37. Willan, "The Anti-Slavery and Aborigines' Protection Society," p. 84.

38. See Bernard Magubane, *The Political Economy of Race and Class in South Africa* (New York, 1980), pp. 81–82.

39. Willan, "The Anti-Slavery and Aborigines' Protection Society," p. 84.

40. British Parliamentary Papers, Union of South Africa, *Correspondence Relating to the Natives' Land Act, 1913.* Cd. 7508 (London, 1914), p. 19. Hereafter cited as *Correspondence,* Cd. 7508.

41. Edward Dower, Secretary for Native Affairs, Circular Letter to all Magistrates, Native Commissioners, Sub-Native Commissioners, and all Officers of the Native Affairs Department, throughout the Union. Pretoria, 12 November 1913. Appendix III. *Correspondence,* Cd. 7508, p. 28.

42. Edward Dower, Secretary for Native Affairs, Circular Letter to all Magistrates, Native Commissioners, Sub-Native Commissioners, and all Officers of the Native Affairs Department, throughout the Union. Pretoria, 12 November 1913. Appendix III. *Correspondence,* Cd. 7508, p. 28.

43. Edward Dower, Secretary for Native Affairs, Natives' Land Act, 1913. Pretoria, 12 November 1913. Appendix IV. *Correspondence,* Cd. 7508, p. 29. In the same report, Dower explicitly stated: "these restrictions [of the Act] are temporary" (p. 29).

44. John L. Dube, Petition addressed to Prime Minister protesting provisions of the 1913 Natives' Land Act. Telegram. The Governor-General, Gladstone, to Secretary of State. Received 17 March 1914. Enclosure: Extract from "The Cape Argus" of 14 February 1914. *Correspondence,* Cd. 7508, p. 23.

45. E. L. Mathews, Union of South Africa Legislation, Report. Pretoria, 9 October 1913. *Correspondence,* Cd. 7508, pp. 20–21.

46. Edward Dower, Secretary for Native Affairs, Circular Letter to all Magistrates, Native Commissioners, Sub-Commissioners, and all officers of the Native Affairs Department throughout the Union. Pretoria, 30 June 1913. Appendix I. *Correspondence,* Cd. 7508, p. 26.

47. See Plaatje, *Native Life in South Africa,* p. 17.

48. M. L. Morris, "The Development of Capitalism in South African Agriculture: Class Struggle and the State," *Economy and Society* 5, 3 (1976), p. 302.

49. John L. Dube, Petition addressed to Prime Minister of South Africa protesting provisions of the 1913 Natives' Land Act. Telegram. The Governor-General, Gladstone, to Secretary of State. Received 17 March 1914. Enclosure: Extract from "The Cape Argus," 14 February 1914. *Correspondence*, Cd. 7508, p. 23.

50. Ibid., p. 23. Dube continued: "We have seen rents raised to the point of desperation. We have seen many of our people who by their frugality have laid by a little money in hope of buying a small piece of land where they might make a home for their families and leave something for their children now told their hopes are in vain; that no European is now permitted to sell or lease land to a native" (pp. 23–24). John X. Merriman refers to a meeting with John Dube: "Met John Dube and his friends by appointment. Very violent opposition to Sauer's Land Bill [i.e., 1913 Natives' Land Bill]. I counselled caution and moderation, I think with some effect" (Extracts from Diary, John X. Merriman, 3 May 1913. Phyllis Lewsen, ed., *Selections from Correspondence of John X. Merriman, 1905–1924* (Cape Town, 1969), p. 231.

51. Union of South Africa, Eastern Transvaal Native Lands Committee, *Report of the Eastern Transvaal Native Lands Committee: Minutes of Evidence*, U.G. 32-'18 (Cape Town, 1918), pp. 34–35.

52. Union of South Africa, Parliament, House of Assembly, *Debates of the Third Session of the First Parliament, 1913* (Cape Town, 1913).

53. Public Records Office (PRO), Colonial Office (C.O.) 551/42, 29362 (July 23, 1913). Cited in Keiser, *The South African Governor-General*, p. 143.

54. PRO, C.O. 551/59, 30888 (July 27, 1913). Cited in Keiser, *The South African Governor-General*, p. 144.

55. Plaatje, *Native Life in South Africa*, pp. 18, 24.

56. Ibid., pp. 26, 51. He continued: "Personally we must say that if any one had told us at the beginning of 1913, that a majority of members of the Union Parliament were capable of passing a law like the Natives' Land Act, whose object is to prevent the Natives from ever rising above the position of servants to whites, we would have regarded that person as a fit subject for the lunatic asylum" (p. 52); "the Orange 'Free' State, which is commonly known as 'the Only Slave State' " (p. 57); and so forth.

57. Edward Dower, Secretary for Native Affairs. Reverend J. L. Dube's Petition: Prime Minister's Reply. Enclosure: Extract from "Cape Times," 16 February 1914. *Correspondence*, Cd. 7508, p. 24.

58. Plaatje, *Native Life in South Africa*, p. 76.

59. Ibid., pp. 72, 74.

60. Ibid., pp. 103–104.

61. "Well-to-do Natives, from Grahamstown to the Transkeian boundaries, mainly derived their wealth from [ploughing-on-the-halves]. It enabled them to lead respectable lives and to educate their children. The new prohibitions tended to drive these Natives back into overcrowded reserves" (ibid., pp. 150, 153).

62. *Beaumont Commission*, U.G. 22-'14, evidence of Edwin Peniston, p. 441.

63. *Beaumont Commission*, U.G. 22-'14, evidence of Josiah Gumede, p. 533.

64. Ibid.

65. See also *Beaumont Commission*, U.G. 22-'14, pp. 479, 483, 489.

66. *Beaumont Commission*, U.G. 22-'14 (Evidence of W. Rose-Gordon, Natal, p. 443). "[Farmers] complained that these Native-owned farms with a front door upon European-owned sheep farms, and a back door in Kaffirdom, formed an excellent and convenient means whereby to annex valuable stock with little chance of detection." *Beaumont Commission*, U.G. 19-'16, Appendix VIII, p. 9.

67. *Beaumont Commission*, U.G. 22-'14, evidence of Jacobus van der Walt, Pretoria district, p. 267.

68. Rural Africans fondly referred to their accumulated herds of cattle and sheep as their 'bank.' *Beaumont Commission*, U.G.-'16, p. 292.

69. William Oakes, "The Native Again," *Farmer's Weekly*, 12 April 1916, p. 533.

70. *Beaumont Commission*, U.G. 25-'16, p. 12. Similarly, Jacob de Villiers Roos, Director of the Union Law Department, testified before a Select Committee that "a Circular was issued by our Department, at the instigation of the Native Affairs Department, asking that prosecutors under the Natives' Land Act, before commencing prosecutions, should refer to the Native Affairs Department, as otherwise *it was feared that an upheaval might result*." Union of South Africa, House of Assembly, Select Committee on Public Accounts, *Report of the Select Committee on Public Accounts*, S.C. 1-'14 (Cape Town, 1914), pp. 136–137.

71. *Beaumont Commission*, U.G. 22-'14, evidence of A. J. S. Maritz, p. 448.

72. *Beaumont Commission*, U.G. 22-'14, evidence of H. E. Essery, Lower Tugela, Natal, p. 499.

73. *Eastern Transvaal Native Lands Committee*, U.G. 32-'18, evidence of G. D. Wheelwright, p. 137.

74. *Eastern Transvaal Native Lands Committee*, U.G. 32-'18, evidence of Hugh Griffiths, p. 3.

75. *Eastern Transvaal Native Lands Committee*, U.G. 32-'18, evidence of David Worth Hook, p. 5.

76. *Beaumont Commission*, U.G. 26-'16, Minutes addressed to the Minister of Native Affairs by the Honourable Sir W. H. Beaumont, p. 3).

77. *Beaumont Commission*, U.G. 22-'16, evidence of J. S. Smit, Assistant and Sub-Native Commissioner, Klerksdorp, Appendix XI, p. 45).

78. *Beaumont Commission*, U.G. 22-'14, evidence of J. H. Gordon, Umvoti district, Natal, p. 443. ". . . the inducements to go to the Rand are far greater than we can give . . . all the young men go, and we landlords are left simply with the old men, women and girls. The result is that they get in arrear with their rent and the state of affairs is generally unsatisfactory"; *Beaumont Commission*, U.G. 22-'14, evidence of G. H. Hulett, Farmer, Eshowe district, Natal, p. 483. See also evidence of General T. Smuts, Ermelo district, Transvaal, *Beaumont Commission*, U.G. 22-'14 p. 259.

79. J 279 1/307/19, Annual Report, Ladybrand District, 1919. Cited in Rich, "African Farming," p. 20.

80. J 279 1/307/19, Annual Report, Bloemhof, 1919, p. 8. Cited in Rich, "African Farming," p. 20.

81. Johann Dicke, Pietersburg, "Natives and Land," *Farmer's Weekly*, 31 January 1917, p. 2060.

82. John L. Dube, Petition addressed to Prime Minister of South Africa protesting provisions of the 1913 Natives' Land Act. Telegram. The Governor-

General, Gladstone, to Secretary of State. Received 17 March 1914. Enclosure: Extract from "The Cape Argus," 14 February 1914. *Correspondence*, Cd. 7508, p. 23.

83. *Beaumont Commission*, U.G. 22-'16, Magistrate, Kroonstad, p. 4.

84. Union of South Africa, House of Assembly, Select Committee on Native Affairs, *Report of the Select Committee on Native Affairs*, S.C.6A-'17 (Cape Town, 1917), para. 1640, 1629.

85. *Beaumont Commission*, U.G. 22-'16, Magistrate from Winburg, p. 2. Similarly, Senator Beukes reported that "since the passing of the Act last year many land owners who had too many natives on their farms gave them notice [to quit, especially] to the native who owns a lot of stock." *Beaumont Commission,* U.G. 22-'16, p. 76. Special thanks to M. L. Morris for pointing these references out to me.

86. Plaatje, *Native Life in South Africa*, pp. 105–106.

6

The Boatmen of Ghana: The Possibilities of a Pre-Colonial African Labor History

Peter C.W. Gutkind

This chapter is a *ballon d'essai*: an exploration into early pre-colonial African labor history; an attempt to apply the approaches of social history, an intellectually adventurous still yet somewhat amorphous field,[1] to the study of a very small yet specialized and indispensable labor force whose formal beginning on the southern Ghana coast began in the last quarter of the fifteenth century. Unfortunately social anthropologists, like myself, are not trained adequately in the methods of historical research to work on widely scattered archival materials, and to sort out the epistemological, phenomenological, and ideological issues which inform the field of African historiography. Because social anthropologists have been reared on the rural traditions of allegedly encapsulated ethnic groups, complex issues in economic history (such as state formation), which invariably take the researcher beyond local communities, are still somewhat alien to our discipline.

Of course the view still prevails, but is somewhat in retreat, that the history of Africa is fundamentally an extension of European history. While archeologists working in Africa can explore its iron age with precision and cultural historians have revealed the magnificence of Nigeria's Nok sculptures, the proposition that *early* pre-colonial African labor history might develop as a worthy field in its own right will be greeted with skepticism. Incredulity is the likely response to the declared objective of tracing evidence for and the evolution of political and class consciousness[2] among the African workers required by the numerous European settlements that were first established by the Portuguese on the Ghana coast in 1482—workers in small scale, yet state-structured, societies, who, we would assume, were subsistence producers in pre-capitalist societies. To have been stimulated by, and to use as a possible point of reference, the seminal work of E. P. Thompson, Eric Hobsbawm, and Fernand Braudel (all viewed as social historians),[3] surely will elicit a reaction of benevolent indulgence as yet another flight of fancy, of overinterpretation, of an ideological determinism in face of the thinnest of evidence—particularly in the African case. Such a critique probably is justified, but the initial results of my research give me some hope that prolonged and careful archival digging will provide testimony for the proposition that Africa's labor history has substantial roots and did not commence only when a "proper" working class was established.

The history of labor in the industrial world, as well as in the so-called Third World, is not a new field. It is out of labor history that much contemporary social history has emerged.[4] A further extension, but of recent times, is socialist and "people's history."[5] If we define labor history specifically as the history of the direct producers, men and women of generations past as well as present, our focus narrows but also becomes more specific and brings us closer to what labor history should be. Labor for others, as distinguished from work for one's own or one's kin's needs, becomes an important category in the transition from subsistence to exchange and on to surplus production, from social reproduction to wage labor. Thus, William Petty observed that "labour is the father and land is the mother of wealth" and Adam Smith suggested that "the annual labour of every nation is the fund which originally supplies it with all necessities and conveniences of life which it annually consumes." However, labor in pre- or in inchoate capitalist societies still is attached to social relationships influenced by kin structures and cultural values and is not, as in more recent times, primarily determined by the forces of value or capital.

Thus the labor of direct producers is so seminal to our understanding of political, economic, and social life[6] that one is tempted to observe that the history of any people, at any time, is the history of labor particularly—of course, labor for surplus production, which is appropriated from direct producers. This view of history clearly was not acceptable to Charles Kingsley who, in his inaugural lecture at Cambridge University in 1861, had this to say:

> The new science of little men can be no science at all; because the average man is not the normal man; [and evidently there are no normal women either!] and never has been: because the great man is rather the normal man, as approaching more nearly than his fellows the true 'norma' and the standard of a complete human character . . . to turn to the mob for your theory of humanity is (I think) about as wise as to ignore Apollo and the Theseus, and to determine the proportions of the human figure from a crowd of dwarfs and cripples. The object of history is to find out what great men did with the various aspects of public life in which they were involved.[7]

Such a view of what constitutes the central core of history was not idiosyncratic to Kingsley, but common in the complacent era of Victorian England. Today, of course, we know that the laboring people of ages past, as well as today, provide a vital and critical complementarity to the study of society and its evolution from an alleged simplicity to an ever-greater and often bewildering complexity. We also know, at last, that the concept of simplicity has as little place in our vocabulary as the label tribe,[8] both having essentially a prejudicial inference. Kingsley's views are now almost universally rejected. We now accept that there is also a history of the oppressed, of megalomaniacs and exploiters.[9]

While Africanist historians, expatriate and indigenous, have generally concentrated on the colonial or immediate pre-colonial periods, emphasis gradually has shifted from the imperial histories of the major colonizing powers to a far more comprehensive approach that pays due attention to African responses to domination,[10] to coercive policies and mechanisms that created the kind of labor forces required. The issue, therefore, is not whether the study of history should be analytical or generalized, reductionist or comprehensive, ideologically informed or coldly empirical. What we must attempt is a history of substance, a cognate history, revealing processes and structures, linkages and consequences, events and their roots, all set in motion by individuals, groups, and classes expressing a harmony or conflict of interest. Always central to this reality, past or present, are those members of society who create the most basic needs and wealth needed for their own reproduction and for those who benefit from their labor. A comprehensive social history extrapolates the more fundamental structures and processes and the most essential production and exchange techniques and operations, which rest ultimately on the labor provided by what we generally have come to refer to as "the workers," the "working class," or "laboring men." Central to this kind of history is the view that class relations, and the accompanying individual and collective experience, reveal the actuality of the conditions imposed on labor. Social history demands an approach that extrapolates from below *and* from above. What is involved is not a mere juxtaposition; rather, that particular perspective (i.e., labor history) requires theoretical elaboration. Labor history is a domain but one which only has reality in a broader and more comprehensive setting that can range from the cultural and semiotic to the conditions of class conflict—history as perceived and history as lived. It is my contention that a Marxian social history is a history of reality: authentic, emphatic, and committed.[11]

Particular perspectives and models, and their claim to be definitive, must be subject to constant review. The essence of Marxist theory is, of course, the ability to deal with change, to bring about a synthesis between formative structures put in place in an earlier era and later manifestations, and between the abstract and the concrete. Marxism is not a casual monism which rests its case on a single determination but always seeks to penetrate the evolution of processes and structures, its dialectic and consequences. Thus, African labor history, distant or contemporary, cannot be forced into one oversimplified and internally unified structure being always part of a larger setting which gives it its distinctive characteristic expression and its existence.[12] History as existence, history as experience, reveals labor history as a particular collective consciousness, a history Charles Kingsley emphatically rejected, that of the "mob," of those whom he characterized as "dwarfs and cripples." Likewise, it is the consciousness of the past and a perspective on the present that gives labor history its significance.

There is, perhaps, a particular aspect of labor history which has met with a certain resistance. Because such history concentrates on the underdog, labor historians are often seen as engaged in polemicism revealing a subjective idealism which does little more than hammer home the verdict that laboring men are oppressed and always have been. While empirical history is viewed (still) as "thesis free," labor history is charged with a pre-determined ideological position. I do not intend to enter this argument, declaring myself quite simply in favor of both idealism and a clear ideological position commensurate with socialist objectives. At the same time I recognize that there is no escape from the complexity of epistemological and phenomenological questions. I also accept that methodological issues are of prime importance; at least one approach must be that speculation is a poor substitute of evidence. However, this assertion is not a tilt in the empirical direction; rather a logical analysis is required that reaches beyond appearances into actions, movements, ideas, and ideologies. I do not believe that there is in historiography a simple choice between theory and history, idealism and substantivism. The issue is perhaps more one of causality, long or short-term, historical specificity at a particular moment and in a particular setting. Empiricist ideology is deeply entrenched in western social science and has consistently ignored alternative approaches.

African history, and its labor history in particular, has yet to confront issues of theory and method. If African history has established itself in its own right and given ample proof that it is not a mere extension of European history, it has yet to free itself of the professionalism of bourgeois practitioners of the craft who have rendered much of this history mere narrative. The dominant influence of obscurantism in the social sciences certainly has had its effect on African history. The question remains: What is the principal problematic which serves as a baseline and which could launch African history on the creative venture of its own discovery and exposition?[13] Socialist historians must face the issue with the same determination as such imperial historians as Gann and

Dulgan,[14] whose right-wing perspectives have made them legendary in their own time. Socialist historians are fond of advocating a "people's history," a worthy intention if we knew precisely how to set about it, particularly as applied to Africa. However, the seminal work of the late Walter Rodney on Guyana should serve as an excellent model.[15] While such labor histories might be possible of more recent times, the obstacles to an African people's history of any depth are considerable for any period prior to the twentieth century. Primary sources are either absent or very scanty and oral history frequently is unreliable. While economic history can be pressed back a good deal further, and is vital to labor studies,[16] critical information often is lacking. Early travellers' accounts often are very useful but, as recent research has indicated, must be treated with great caution (particularly poor translations).[17] What information is available and produced by trained historians is conventional colonial historiography—the history of the colonizers, interesting but very unbalanced. More attention now is being paid to the colonized, but analytical perspectives are still in the germinal stage.

The challenge of attempting an early pre-colonial African labor history is thus an excursion into uncertainty though not one of pure speculation. Certainly, the objectives of socialist-oriented African labor history should not be glorification of the African past—or a people's history without blemishes, confusions, contradictions, false starts—or invariably noble and humanistic in outlook.[18] Reductionism, wholly antithetical to a dialectical social science, and over-simplification, must be rejected. Vulgar materialism, or idealism born of hope, do little justice to the potential of a discriminating but also resonant social history. Whether such confining restrictions are justified or not, caution is likely to explicate reality more effectively, since actions and purpose are often elusive and difficult to interpret. Labor history, as any other social or humanistic domain, is not mere narrative, and is more than a check list of events, of responses and direction. We must be able to account for the haphazard, the fortuitous, the unexpected, and the contradictory. The African past is as marked by such circumstances as anywhere else. African history, be it the history of labor or the chiefs and kings, is not organically of a single nature; nor do such histories move along a single linear path.

The relationship between political and economic structures while intimate also is variable, particularly during those periods when external agencies and ideologies actively penetrated the so-called traditional African societies, as from the sixteenth to eighteenth centuries. It was during the latter part of this timespan, particularly in the European mercantilist phase of the seventeenth century,[19] that the emerging forces of capitalism gathered momentum, first to dominate the "core" zones and later spilling into more distant "peripheral" zones creating, if not a new, certainly a distinctive and lasting division of labor and, in some cases, new specializations in production and services. Above all, such penetration had, over time, far-reaching influences on the labor process, the creation of new production processes and markets, and the rise of new class relations.

It is a matter open to much debate when it becomes both reasonable and exact to identify an African working class, and when exploitation and various forms of control and reliance on force were firmly in place.[20] Reasonably firm evidence seems to suggest that it was during the mercantile phase in Europe that West African societies, primarily those in the coastal regions, began a sequence of internal changes in production and trade leading to a new structural division of labor. Yet such a proposition should not be treated as a base line. Even prior to the fifteenth century the gold and salt trade was firmly established and extensive.[21] Such trade had generated substantial specialization of production, the commoditization of the direct producers and social relations of a distinctly hierarchical nature. It is not unreasonable to suggest that societies engaged in extensive inland trade generated a class structure that subsequent coastal contacts with the European intruders consolidated further. If firm evidence eventually becomes available to demonstrate that this proposition is correct, then we can go a step further and ask how labor was recruited, controlled, and remunerated. Was labor based on slavery, serfdom, or "wages"? In other words, would it be reasonable to speak of capitalist labor, free, or coerced? This is clearly a critical issue in early pre-colonial African labor history.

The possibility that Africa's early pre-colonial labor history can be linked to the world system model developed by Immanuel Wallerstein[22] remains to be tested. It will likely be argued that capitalist labor did not exist in Africa prior to the seventeenth century simply because the European core zones had not become fully capitalist until the middle of the seventeenth century at the earliest. While this clearly is a very critical issue, I believe that time will provide an answer, and will show that African working-class formation had very early beginnings. At present the limited evidence we have appears to suggest that capitalist objectives had begun to influence the factors of production—land, labor, and capital—from the fifteenth century on. Indeed, I would suggest that the various state structures of the West African inland and coastal formations were such that resources were centralized, and that wars were fought to obtain resources, human or physical. The evidence in support of this is quite strong, and it is reasonable to suggest that centralization of power, and hence accessibility to goods, services, and their distribution, flowed along class lines.[23] As production responded to the demands and opportunities of external trade, the time, price, and products of labor became more commoditized. Thus it is hardly surprising that early travellers such as Bosman provide us with what he considered evidence of class structure. Furthermore, when the Portuguese established themselves on the Ghana coast in 1482 they were face-to-face with chieftainships and monarchies and all their accoutrements. However, as I indicated before, economic factors may not be treated as the sole determinants—although they do impose a degree of structure and logic on social organization.

How the "African factor" influences this structure and logic is a matter which will vary over time and from one society to another. To bring this perspective into African labor history requires, perhaps, a link with social anthropology, but here the danger of obscurantism must be confronted. My own perspective is not to stress an alleged golden age, an African genius destroyed by oppressive colonizers, a generalized condition applicable beyond the African continent, but rather to emphasize that the past, in all its diversity, can help us understand the present. Thus, Walter Rodney, in *How Europe Underdeveloped Africa*, observed:

> This book derives from a concern with the contemporary African situation. It delves into the past only because otherwise it would be impossible to understand how the present came into being and what the trends are for the future. In the search for understanding of what is now called "underdevelopment" in Africa, the limits of inquiry have had to be fixed as far apart as the fifteenth century, on the one hand, and the end of the colonial period, on the other.[24]

To give substance to this approach, and to Africa's early pre-colonial labor history, I propose to give some account of the rise, the activities, the treatment, and the role played by the canoemen of Ghana. Much of this account will be fragmented because information needed is widely scattered in the archives of at least six countries, and hence is difficult to distill into a coherent exposition; much important information is not yet available, tempting the empiricist historians to refrain from any commentary, but posing a challenge to radical scholarship.

My interest in the canoemen (whose primary occupation was fishing) was aroused when I read an account of the Portuguese explorations and commercial ventures beginning in the fifteenth century when they made their way along the west coast of Africa. Once these rather courageous sailors managed to get past Cape Bojador we can well and truly say that they were on their way to round the southern tip of Africa and on to their objective of the spicelands in the east. The literature dealing with the age of discovery is vast, although much of it is strongly chauvinistic and hence of an epic and heroic nature. I do not review this literature in part because younger scholars are now taking a fresh look, and applying a much more critical perspective explicating with greater analytical skills the objectives and the consequences of exploration leading to conquest and domination of virtually all those peoples who now live in those parts of the world we refer to as the "less developed," or "underdeveloped Third World." Now we understand that in the wake of these explorations the Europeans, eager for resources, an objective disguised behind a more elevated purpose such as the familiar civilizing mission, gradually put in place what Wallerstein and others have aptly called a "world system"—a system in which capitalism came to be supreme and which is still very much in place. Thus the age of discovery laid the foundation for a new order, new economic and political structures. The roots of African labor history, as with such history elsewhere, are to be found in this major transformation, which accelerated from the sixteenth century on and by no means is complete. The history of the canoemen of Ghana began during the age of exploration.

The first Portuguese settlers arrived on the western section of the coast of Ghana in January 1482, although an earlier exploration had taken place in 1470–71.[25] Exploration of the West African coast between approximately 1440 and 1470 did not involve frequent or extensive contact.[26] The Portuguese soon discovered that the surf was exceedingly powerful (earlier travellers had termed it "the burnings" because of the haze the pounding of the waves created, while others had mistaken this for smoke rising from coastal villages), and that there were no natural harbors or adequate river estuaries and inlets, so that even with their relatively shallow draft the sailing ships had to drop anchor a considerable distance from the shore. This natural circumstance compelled the Portuguese and all those who followed them to this coast to engage the services of the canoemen, fishermen who owned the canoes and had the consummate skills to maneuver them through the surf. While the caravels and other types of sailing ships carried long boats for inshore use, they were generally unsuitable to go through heavy surf and very prone to capsizing. The use of these boats continued for a great many years and we find frequent references indicating that people and cargo were carried in these rowboat-like vessels to the edge of the surf and then transferred to canoes.

King John II of Portugal, anxious to control the gold and ivory trade, was determined to establish a permanent settlement on the coast of Ghana. When the fleet of ships left Lisbon and Sagres in 1481, they carried sundry prefabricated building materials for walls, roofs, and interiors[27] (some more recent writers have suggested this was greatly exaggerated in earlier accounts) and a garrison of 500 soldiers, many of whom fell ill and died within the first few months of the settlement of São Jorge da Mina (Elmina). In 1482, agreement was reached with Caramansa, the local potentate, and the canoemen were first engaged to carry people and cargo to the beach. How the canoemen were employed and how they were remunerated is not revealed in the archival record, but perhaps trade goods were offered and accepted, or perhaps slave labor was employed.

That the canoemen were important, indeed indispensable, was given recognition soon after the turn of the century when King Manuel (1495–1521) imposed a system of controls and a royal monopoly over many aspects of the Guinea trade, particularly in luxury goods. Restrictions had been imposed as early as 1474, when all voyages to Guinea were permitted only under royal authority. These "Manueline Ordinances,"[28] which codified a system of "monarchical monopolistic capitalism," regulated virtually all aspects of Portuguese trade to, and life ashore on, the Guinea coast. Some provisions of these ordinances were applied to the engagement, remuneration, and work of the canoemen, legislation I am tempted to characterize as labor laws. Strict rules were imposed on the captains of the sailing vessels to guard the cargo from any possible theft; canoemen were not allowed on board their ships, and contact between the crews and people ashore was not permitted. Factors, writers, and warehousemen were expected to keep a close watch on the arrival of the canoes and their departure, recording every item landed or dispatched. All African workers—whether on the beach or within the confines of the settlement—were searched, and particular care was taken in the export of gold, which was shipped in sturdy chests with numerous locks; keys were held by various servants of the crown. Canoemen frequently were suspected of attaching goods to buoys or slyly smuggling goods ashore. The penalties for violation of any of the provisions were severe and applied to all, including the governor. Despite this, it is clear from the records that virtually all the Portuguese officials engaged in private trade, which made a mockery of these laws.

Initially, the canoemen probably were a casual labor force. As Elmina was the only significant settlement, and the frequency of sailings to the Ghanaian coast amounted usually to less than six Portuguese ships a year, the number of canoemen required was very limited; no record has been found that would give us any precise number. However, records do exist that indicate that the frequency of arrivals varied from year to year. Ships departing from Portugal frequently were subject to piracy or fell victim to violent storms.[29] About the middle of the sixteenth century, however, the ships of other nations began exploration and unsuccessful attempts to establish trading centers on this coast, a development that certainly required additional labor and an increasing number of canoemen to facilitate what was known as the "floating trade." While the Portuguese, Dutch, and English, and subsequently the Danes, Swedes, French, and Brandenburgers all attempted to control the Guinea trade with legislation or chartered companies, the number of "interlopers" (those without permission or license) increased significantly from approximately the mid-sixteenth century, thereby also increasing the demand for canoemen. As the interlopers had to conduct trade in secret, at least as surreptitiously as conditions allowed, the services of the canoemen assumed even greater significance, as governors, commandants, and factors actively prevented them from working for these unlawful competitors. Unfortunately, no records could be found that revealed the conditions of their employment by interlopers, although there are occasional references to canoemen shot at sea from the ramparts of castles, and indications that attempts were made to sink their canoes, and, at times, larger canoes mounting small guns were dispatched to chase them away and prevent them from working for the interlopers.

The importance of the canoemen is revealed in the careful records kept in ledgers and account books recording on a daily basis, not only of their specific activities but also of the remuneration they received. Beginning particularly with the Dutch and English settlements in the middle of the seventeenth century, canoe activity increased very significantly, because the canoemen were employed not merely for ship-to-shore transport but also for passenger and cargo transport between the many settlements that dotted the coast. This activity assumed perhaps even greater significance because the "outstations," as the smaller settlements were called, depended totally on this type of communication.[30] The canoemen supplied these settlements with provisions of all kinds, ranging from food to building materials and trade goods; in addition they carried passengers and messages from place to place. For this work they received remuneration in kind, such as rum, cloth, or tobacco, depending on the length of their journey, the size of the crew, and, sometimes, the nature of the cargo. Thus, there was a "rate for the job," negotiated between the canoemen and the European and African employers, although the records also indicate that the canoemen often demanded more, or insisted that they had not been given their due. Often, too, the canoemen were given subsistence particularly when they broke their journey and "put in" at a settlement to rest or to wait for a storm to pass. Eventually, but not before approximately the early nineteenth century, the canoemen were paid in a variety of currencies.

The records very frequently reveal the anger expressed by governors and factors over canoemen's refusal to work for a variety of reasons: they were unwilling to pass in front of a "foreign" settlement fearing arrest or injury; the surf was too rough and would capsize the canoe; or a fellow worker had been "panyarred" (held as a pawn against a debt), mistreated by an African "bomboy" supervisor, or abused by a European; or a fear of being taken into slavery. As workers they were often linked to laborers under the ledger heading "Pay for Labor and Canoemen Hire." Indeed, the establishment lists of the English settlements break down the personnel into a number of categories such as "White Mens

Pay" and "Black Mens Pay" in addition to long lists of workers ranging from skilled artisans (carpenters, coopers, and masons) to washerwomen and garden boys. Not the least significant of their activities was the transport of slaves to the slaveships, although pay for this sordid activity never appears in the ledgers or account books. It is therefore possible that this activity, which must have occupied a large number of canoemen, might have been in the hands of "slave canoemen." We do not know all the details, but Jean Barbot[31] produced a picture showing canoemen transporting slaves. In 1753, the factor at Winnebah, writing to the government of Cape Coast Castle, reported that "unless we can secure more canoemen this part of our trade [the slave trade] will occasion difficulties for us."[32] We are not told the reason for this evident shortage of canoemen. We can only speculate to what degree this traffic in human cargo depended on the willingness of the canoemen to be engaged.

How many canoemen there were at various times is extremely difficult to determine. Certainly, the larger settlements employed far more than those attached to the "outstations," many of which had fewer than half-a-dozen, while some had none. At various times, the larger establishments such as Elmina, first under Portuguese and after 1637 under Dutch rule, and Cape Coast recorded from 30 to 40 "free canoemen." But as all the coastal settlements and villages were also important for fishing, the potential number of canoemen was likely quite large. Everywhere the canoemen were divided into two groups: slave or free. The number of slave canoemen, who were often resident within the settlements, was quite small but somewhat of a standby when free canoemen were not available. It also appears that slave canoemen were paid, although this is not recorded on a regular basis. The larger settlements as major depots dispatched canoemen to, and received them from, the outstations. Thus an entry for 18 July 1708 records the arrival at Cape Coast, then the headquarters of the Royal African Company, of 22 canoemen from various points along the coast, while the next day another 11 arrived and the following day a further 17. During the same period a total of 19 canoemen left for various settlements.[33]

The matter of numbers is important lest it be thought that this labor force was so minuscule to be of essentially little significance, however indispensable its work. But we are on firmer ground as we enter the latter part of the eighteenth century, when the records indicate more consistently the number of canoemen available to the settlements and, also, comments by factors, traders, and merchants that there was frequently a shortage of canoemen. Thus, the chief factor at the Winnebah complained in 1764 that "our trade will be greatly impeded unless we can hire more Free Canoemen. The present number of 17 is not satisfactory, but few of them wish to work for us."[34] In 1799 the establishment list for Cape Coast records a total of 41 canoemen, while in 1805 it had dropped to 30; the Dutch recorded some 57 canoemen at Elmina in 1789 and 44 in 1793. When we look at the records for the mid-nineteenth century, it becomes clear that this labor force had grown, as in 1863 there were said to be some 537 canoemen all along the coast. But it was also at this time, indeed possibly as early as 1840, that canoes were replaced by surfboats that generally carried a crew of 11 (ten paddlers and one steerman). Surfboats were of a completely different construction, specially designed to cut through the surf, far larger and hence able to carry very substantial cargo and more passengers. The matter of numbers is complicated further because African merchants, such as John Kabes, had their own canoemen, but how many were in their employ does not appear to be recorded. We learn from the records that Kabes owned a fleet of canoes both for his own use and for hire to the English and Dutch, and that if needed he also supplied the crews. While at times there was a shortage of canoemen, at other times the officials of the Royal African Company in London felt that too many were in their employ. Thus the court of assistant in London wrote to the factor at Cape Castle as follows (on 18 July 1728): "We cannot but think that a much smaller number than sixty-one canoemen may answer all you occasion, and in that case we recommend it to you always to employ as many of them only as can be spared in fishing."[35] In the same account, some figures are given about the labor force as a whole (i.e., slaves, pawns, and other workers).

> We observe the contents of your 8th, 9th, 10th and 12th paragraphs in relation to the numbers of castle working slaves and canoemen employed on the Gold Coast and at Whydah which by the lists you have sent us we find amount to no less than six hundred and seventy-seven in all a very considerable number and in our opinion more than sufficient to do all the necessary business of the company [even if it] had the whole trade of the coast to themselves.[36]

I think that the evidence suggests that the primary and most frequent activity of the canoemen was the transport of provisions and passengers between the settlements rather than ship to shore labor. Though the number of settlements increased considerably from the mid-seventeenth to the mid-eighteenth century, the increasing number of sailing ships arriving on the coast could not have occupied the canoemen on a daily basis as was the case with inshore transport. However, beginning about 1830, international trade increased considerably. Thus, when travelogues appeared with greater frequency, starting about 1850, we are treated to some very colorful accounts of sweating and gleaming bodies, strong muscles, and the good cheer of the boatmen singing as they strike their trident-shaped paddles into the violent surf. A source of amusement, excitement, yet apprehension was a practice that commenced in the twentieth century, when passengers disembarking from ocean vessels were strapped in a "mammy chair" (a wicker basket rather like a garden chair) precariously lifted over the side of the ship while swinging from a derrick and gently lowered into a rolling and pitching surfboat! When railway construction and commercial gold mining began, toward the end of the nineteenth century, the boatmen shifted huge loads of heavy equipment which frequently required two surfboats to be lashed together by means of a platform allowing for the transport of rolling stock and machinery. But even in the eighteenth century, the canoemen shifted, often annually, tens of thousands of gallons of rum, thousands of yards of cloth, and thousands of fathoms of tobacco. One also notes such items as 195,000 bricks, supplied from the hold of one sailing ship, 210,000 feet of cut lumber, tons of iron bars, and a vast range of provisions, medicines, guns, and trade goods. These are impressive figures that tell us something of the hard work assigned to the canoemen and surfboatmen of later years. It also tells us how inescapably important their labor was. Let us now turn to a brief discussion concerning the political and class consciousness of these workers.

The canoemen certainly were not a captive labor force. The vast majority pursued their primary activity of fishing, free, presumably, to reject alternative work. The free canoemen, really part of a much larger evolving labor force of skilled artisans (or apprentices training under European craftsmen) and unskilled labor, quickly realized that their services were essential to the Portuguese and those who followed them to establish slave depots and trading stations. As early as 1554, when Captain John Lok visited Cape Korsa (Cape Coast), there is a reference to canoemen refusing to do additional trips from ship to shore unless they received added remuneration of rum and tobacco, which the pilot, the renegade Portuguese Antonio Anes Pintado, was eventually forced to make available. In 1569, by which time Portuguese authority was on the wane and its trade monopoly seriously challenged, a somewhat similar incident took place at Elmina resulting in canoemen being placed in irons for refusing to work, although no explanation is given of the circumstances. In 1620, when the Dutch made serious attempts to establish themselves at Mouri, to the east of Elmina, the Portuguese tried to prevent some canoemen from working for them and managed to destroy some canoes and again placed some of the crew in irons. Clearly, labor protest resulting in serious consequences for the canoemen, while perhaps infrequent (and the archival record is very incomplete), was real and treated as such by the Europeans. But we must be careful not to overstress some events; at the same time we must not belittle those which did occur—such as a "strike" by canoemen in 1735 (brought to my attention by Margaret Priestley in a brief note entitled "An Early Strike in Ghana").[37]

In order that we may understand African labor protest we must take into account the attitudes of the European employers (as well as African merchants and entrepreneurs who had risen to prominence and were themselves employers of other Africans), how they handled the workers and the conditions of their labor. These are issues which in turn are linked to the division of labor based on race and other distinctions of status and class. Slave canoemen and laborers certainly were near to the bottom of the ladder (the destitute and outcasts were well below them), with free canoemen well above them in prestige and general bearing, often being described as independent, proud, haughty, as well as arrogant, insolent, and impertinent. I have not found any references that indicate that slave labor staged organized protest or rebellion, although in the journals and daybooks of the Royal African Company (1672–1751) there are frequent comments about disturbances in the towns close to the castles and trading stations.[38] The causes of these disturbances are varied, but a number of them allegedly were caused by labor disputes. Only cursory references are made to identify the participants. Still, some civil disturbances were serious enough to involve the use of military force.

It seems clear that many Europeans considered the canoemen to be thieves. They believed that their behavior was "rascally," thought that they could not be trusted, and complained that they "demanded beyond their work" and that they were suspected of working for interlopers, or for "the Dutch" or other nations, although they were "English canoemen."[39] Governors and factors all seemed to agree that they had to be handled firmly and that their demands for better remuneration had to be resisted. In this regard, the Europeans often brought their complaints to local caboceers (headmen, chiefs, and men of authority) to mediate disputes and to bring these "rascally" canoemen in line, to recover stolen goods and to mete out punishment under customary terms. Because canoemen, unlike most other Africans, circulated between settlements and were taken on by ships' captains who voyaged to Whydah and Benin (well to the east of Ghana), they were often subject to being pawned, beaten, or arrested in foreign lands and on occasion also taken into slavery and transported to Brazil or the West Indies, conditions that intensified their fears, demands, and protests. Both European and African traders not infrequently viewed the canoemen as potential competitors anxious to enter trade on their own account, using stolen trade goods to launch themselves. In fact, it was not unusual for the established traders to refer to the canoemen as "bandits."

Nor were charges against the canoemen, heard by the Governor-in-Council, unusual, but canoemen also managed to bring their complaints (usually referred to as "palaver") before the same body. Charges against canoemen increased from about 1750 onward and after 1850 were brought before formal magistrate courts.[40] One of the earliest "trials" I was able to find took place in 1711. The interest of this case does not lie in the fact that five canoemen were charged with theft, but in the words allegedly spoken by them to a factor and his response. The record is not one of court proceedings but rather a journal entry describing the events and transmitting this information to the Royal African Company in London. The writer, one James Oudle, records that "these canoemen, despicable thieves, think that they are more than just labour. They spoil our life and trade and then demand gold or tobacco. One Kwesi Ano even told me that he might have struck me with a knife and Quow Ada, whose wench is also a bad thief, said that the English had no right to trade in gold as this was not traded fairly on our part." The verdict was to place the canoemen in irons.[41]

But generally, attempts were made to smooth matters over and, on the whole, to keep on the good side of the canoemen. Indeed, there were occasions when the verdict went against Europeans who had failed to pay remuneration or had mistreated canoemen. Such lapses of fair treatment were usually resolved by means of fines, such as payment of double the remuneration due. Over one hundred years later, in 1833, a Dutch commandant recorded in his journal that the "rimadores [canoemen-paddlers] belong to the lower classes and [there is] constantly something unpleasant with them." He made this comment because the canoemen had refused to transport some military supplies. Indeed, we should note that the canoemen were just as indispensable in times of war (as during the prolonged campaign with Ashanti) as in peace. During the Dutch-English wars in the seventeenth century, which spilled over to the Ghana coast and resulted in considerable tension and the change of ownership of settlements, the canoemen frequently were engaged in quasi-military action, such as interference in ship-to-shore transport, or throwing torches on the decks of enemy sailing vessels. One entry records a special reward given to some canoemen who managed to set a Dutch ship alight.

How the canoemen were involved in international rivalry is a very special topic that needs a great deal of further research. The rivalry between the nations settled on this coast often was very intense (and has been well described by Harvey Feinberg, J. E. Inikori, Ray Kea, and John Vogt)[42] and the slightest disagreement could escalate to significant proportions. This was particularly true regarding rights to beach landing places and the storage of the canoes on open beaches or in sheds. Disputes were interminable and bitter; massive correspondence between governors and factors are found in all the records. It appears that the Danes occupying the eastern shores of the Ghana coast were spared at least the frequency of such disputes. For the canoemen, the periods of international conflict seem to have allowed the exercise of considerable banditry[43] and what might be seen as a *lumpen* ideology, as they often were willing to change sides. Hence, what I think we are likely to find on closer inspection of the records is that the canoemen were able to extract a price for their services during such periods.[44] Not infrequently, the canoemen were the most exposed front-line soldiers, as it were, in the rivalry that was fought as much in the offshore waters as on land. For example, canoemen were used as a sort of reconnaissance force to determine the nationality of sailing vessels, many of which arrived at night in the hope that they would not be detected, at least until daybreak. Such reconnaissance also allowed canoemen, and those Europeans who sometimes went with them, to engage in a little private trade!

A close study of the archival material indicates that it might be possible to document the rise and temporary decline of canoe activity—a sort of periodization of the labor history of the canoemen. Thus, a closer look at the period 1680–1720, when the struggle to establish European settlements was particularly intense and the role of canoemen assumed considerable importance, or the 1780s when the slave trade was very active, would be informative. In contrast, the period from 1790–1830 was somewhat slack (Ashanti-Fante hostilities between 1807 and 1830 seriously interfered with trade) but was followed by a great expansion of trade between 1834 and 1867. What this points to is that the activities of these workers must be closely dovetailed to the economic history of western commercial activity. Such a scheme would also help us greatly in documenting the accuracy of the progressive social and political consciousness, and activism, of the canoemen (and other sectors of the labor force), as well as the evolution of an increasingly complex class structure. Hence, let us turn briefly to a discussion of how the canoemen defended their rights, a test of class consciousness.

I already have given some evidence of what must justifiably be treated as *informal* labor protest, although I think that this formulation rather stacks the cards against these workers, giving the impression that they only reacted rather than took the offensive. I think the evidence supports the observation that canoemen engaged in concerted action and protest, the most common form being withdrawal of labor. In 1688, there are some eighteen references from various settlements to canoemen refusing to work. The reasons recorded, often in great detail (but always by Europeans), ranged from protests about unsafe canoes, often deliberately damaged by canoemen, to the fear that they might be panyarred by traders, or become involved in conflicts between the English and Dutch.[45] For example, occasionally canoemen refused to transport troops, and this led to the following comment made in 1794 by Navy Commander Edmund Dod: "The most disagreeable part of your letter [to John Gordon in London] is the refusal to land the Troops to dislodge the French from Amoco. . . . However disagreeable it is to me to submit to the caprice of the rascally canoemen, I propose to land the Troops tomorrow morning. . . ."[46]

Reaction to the refusal to work was clearly one of annoyance. Thus, Thomas Melville, governor of Cape Coast Castle, informed the Committee of the Company of Merchants on 1 July 1754 that since "the canoemen of that place [Annamaboe] would not work, I have sent down my own canoemen [presumably slave canoemen] to show them once more that we can do without them [presumably free canoemen]. . . ."[47] Yet three years later the factor at Commenda wrote most forcefully to the governor at Cape Coast Castle: ". . . our supplies are very short, we lack in everything. If the canoemen refuse to work this factory will cease. The canoemen are making fools of their masters; they must be forced to work as informed by the Committee. We have no supplies."[48] Another form of protest was to damage goods, allowing them to get wet, refusing to work on certain days,[49] and above all, demanding more remuneration. Thus in Dixcove in 1777 the factor reported that 11 canoemen "had threatened the traders and all the people living here. They are demanding cloth and gold and refuse to work for us. Yesterday they did the ungodly of all and did but murder the Bomboy. I gave instructions to withdraw to the fort."[50]

The examples do, I think, support the possibilities that labor and class consciousness found expression repeatedly in protest and activism. Unfortunately, there are virtually no records that would give us an insight from the canoemen's perspective. All the records were kept by the Europeans and are almost totally devoid of narrative from the workers. Only toward the end of the nineteenth century can we turn to what might be called "canoemen speak" when they produced various petitions (written by sympathetic Europeans) as during a strike of these workers at Cape Coast in 1896.

> We the boatmen of long standing labour at all hours of the day and in all conditions for very small pay. We request that our pay and conditions be improved. We need more to keep our families, our children and ourselves. We also beg leave to tell you [Governor Sir W. E. Maxwell, 1895–1898] that we shall refuse to work again to take the boats to the ships until our demands are met. We also wish to tell the shipping company that our work is very dangerous and may cause us injury or life . . . We have now decided to stop work until we are happy with the conditions because we can no longer work as we have . . . We are close among us to bring this about and beg you for good help and understanding.

The petition was signed by one Kwame Basa,"Headman of the boatmen," on behalf of 27 of them.[51]

During the early years of the twentieth century, labor protest increased significantly among many sectors of the labor force including the boatmen. The number of strikes and strikers increased to such a degree that the government established a Department of Labour in 1938.[52] A study of the archives of the Department of Labour, and records from other departments between 1920 and 1938, suggest that the boatmen were in the forefront of organized and formal strike action. It also is clear that when these strikes did occur they were settled with great speed, sometimes within hours, and rarely lasted more than two days. I think that the reasons are obvious—the boatmen had become ever more indispensable and, further, shipping companies were anxious to avoid high demurrage charges. The boatmen knew this and took advantage of it. That they were skillful at doing this becomes clear from the extensive oral history that I have collected from retired boatmen who were employed between 1924 and 1950.

Another group of important workers were the "waterside" workers or "beachboys" who carried all cargo from the surfboats to the warehouses and exports to the former. Relations between them and boatmen often were severely strained, it appears, on ethnic grounds. The latter were predominantly Fante (as had been virtually all canoemen since the end of the fifteenth century onward) while the "beachboys" were very mixed ethnically and included Kru from Liberia. Commencing just before the turn of the century, beach operations were under the control of a "beachmaster," a European employee of one of numerous shipping companies. I have collected important accounts from a number of them now living in retirement. A recent account which I received was from a pensioner, now 98, who had been a "beachmaster" from 1920 to 1927!

I would like to conclude this part of the chapter on a lighter note. On 5 February 1775, the factor at Tantumquerry sent a message via a canoeman to a captain whose sailing vessel was lying in "the roads" some distance from the shore. The factor had heard that some valuable cargo was on board. "I have been told that you have a quantity of Rasberry Brandy by you and that . . . you could spare some. On this presumption I have sent this canoe and will be very much obliged to you for 3 or 4 bottles of it."[53] No doubt he indulged his pleasure. But we do not know how the canoemen was rewarded.

To pose the question whether the canoemen composed or were part of an evolving laboring class, or were the forerunners of such a class, as early as the sixteenth century, is central to the proposition that African labor history, and labor force formation, has far deeper roots than generally is recognized. Surely, the canoemen, artisans, and laborers were "waged" employees. Despite this, were the relations of production embedded in kinship and juridicial determinants, or were they an expression of dominant economic structures? Who produced what, how, and for whom? If surplus was achieved, who created it, and who had a say over its use and distribution? What of the occupational structure, and specialized craft and artisan activity? Who controlled trade and facilitated its many complex activities? What portion of, and which goods found their way into local markets, and what were destined for regional and long-distance trade? Above all, what of the civil order, the political machinery of local and central authority? What were the needs of military institutions? Who owned the land? How did a particular social formation reproduce itself and effect the conditions of production? Was slavery central to these southern Ghanaian coastal states? How distinctive was the separation between "free" and "unfree" labor? If all work is labor, how did some work distinguish itself from other work? Could a slave ever move over, as it were, to "free" labor, to become an "owner," to being an employer?[54]

These pre-colonial societies generally are labeled as "precapitalist" and as such are said not to have incorporated the profit motive, and that their technology was at a low level that limited surplus production which could be appropriated by "capitalists" and disposed of in distant markets. Indeed, such societies were said to be anti-capitalist; the domestic economy was generally small, markets met only basic subsistence needs, and social rather than economic values were maximized.[55] Precapitalist societies do not pay wages to producers whose labor is contained and rewarded within networks of kin and their extension into wider corporate structures, and beyond that into the (ethnic) group as a whole. Such an orientation places greater weight on the *conditions* of alleged economic backwardness rather than on the *processes* of economic activities, on constraints rather than potential. The questions posed appear to raise a host of other issues that cannot be treated in detail even were the basic information available, and that generally is not the case. However, the social formation of these Ghanaian societies had a number of important features that we can identify.

In the first place they generally were hierarchical.[56] Authority rested in the power of kingship and chieftainship, although the degree of centralization varied. However, in virtually all cases, such a structure invariably resulted in some groups being on top and some below.[57] These political and economic systems were based on tributary relations both within the society and externally, on taxation extracted from agricultural producers and craftsmen, and on loyalty to chiefs and kings.[58] Thus, surplus production in crafts or other products was essential to satisfy the demands of the rulers and their extensive military establishments. Secondly, those entrenched at the upper levels of society engaged in various forms of ownership of persons for domestic use or for trade (i.e. for surplus production). Thus the basic structure of these coastal societies was class-based—perhaps no more than an incipient, rudimentary class structure but not inchoate—and involved a division of labor of peasants, craftsmen, and slaves at the lower levels and the governing class, traders, and merchants above them.[59] Yet these laboring classes, or this lower class, were constantly reconstituting themselves and thus were not homogeneous. They were divided internally into three major divisions: the peasantry grouped with the class of commoners; followed by craftsmen, artisans, and such occupational groups as canoemen and laborers; and finally slaves, these being divided between domestic slaves and those obtained in trade for exchange elsewhere.

Likewise, the non-laboring class was divided between upper and lower levels, rulers and merchants. The civic rights of the laboring classes were not the same as those in the governing class. Unfortunately the record is not clear, and certainly not consistent, regarding how the civic rights of the laboring classes differed from those of the governing class. Ray Keal[60] claims that the former's right to work, to hold political or ritual office, to own, buy, or sell slaves, or to receive any direct share of revenue collected sometimes was restricted. Kwame Arhin, on the other hand, as indicated above, insists that even domestic slaves, who certainly ranked well below free canoemen and laborers, could own property and achieve more elevated positions. Clarification is clearly needed. Fundamentally, however, I think clearly the laboring classes provided the basic needs of rulers and merchants and created surplus wealth, which was appropriated. Revenue collectors collected either a fixed tribute or what they considered reasonable. The governing class had the right to call on commoners from among slaves and free peasantry, craftsmen, and laborers for labor services. In particular, free gold producers were subject to harsh control by the rulers and merchants because this precious metal could be traded for European merchandise, particularly guns and ammunition, needed for internal security and external adventures. We know little about the response (revolts, protests, sabotage, or withdrawal of labor) of the laboring classes (other than canoemen) to their inferior position, about the demands made on their productive labor, and the conditions they had to endure. However, as I already have shown, the canoemen, generally treated as laborers, not infrequently protested their treatment, a response that significantly increased from the middle of the seventeenth century onward. Indeed, as has been noted, early in the sixteenth century King Manuel of Portugal established decrees designed to control the royal trade in gold, ivory, and peppers, by issuing regulations applicable to sea captains, merchants, factors, warehousemen, writers, craftsmen, and canoemen. These regulations, as they pertain to the control of laborers, might be viewed as labor ordinances—an important and unique development of the period.

I think it likely that this structural pattern existed prior to the arrival of the Portuguese on the Ghana coast in 1471, followed by their permanent settlement at Elmina eleven years later. Certainly, during the pre-mercantilist period, approximately 1400–1600, West Africa's economic history was tied closely to North Africa and the Mediterranean. After this period, mercantile capitalism moved to the Atlantic seaboard and the Guinea coast with the possible effect of reducing inland long-distance trade. When both slave and commodity trade increased, they became more international, with long-range consequences for the coastal regions. The establishment of permanent settlements, castles, and trading stations can be seen as the first real penetration of capitalism, an integration of these different societies into a larger system that Walter Rodney (whose scholarly interest concentrated on "Upper" rather than "Lower" Guinea) viewed as detrimental to the dynamic internal forces that might have launched West Africa (in particular) on a path of more autonomous development. However, indigenous productive and distributive forces were constrained. The interpretations remain controversial but, I think, the evidence suggests greater continuity than Rodney was willing to concede.[61] Edward Alpers has made the point, in emphasizing process rather than condition, "that the only economic history of Africa which makes any sense at all is development history," a history that explicates "the nature of the trading relations between Africa and the rest of the world over the last two millenia." However, he also acknowledges that in addition to these trading relations "indigenous African economies . . . systems of production" must be taken into account as potentially "very real obstacles to transformation."[62]

I think it is clear that regional, and certainly long-distance, trade in gold, salt, and kola, for example, already had made an impact on these coastal polities. In addition, occupational specialization was already well advanced (and more so in the western Sudan in the period 1000–1500).[63] Moreover, the natural economies based on subsistence-plus to meet internal needs had been transformed effectively with new demands on labor power or, as B. Bradby suggests, that a once closed market " 'bound' under the natural economy" was penetrated to "open up," as it were, for surplus commodity production "to extra-economic action [and] to free the labour-force from the old 'bondage.' " The use of domestic slaves (producers rather than commodities?), and the trade in slaves, "achieved expanded production" both domestically and for external trade.[64]

With the arrival of the Portuguese, followed by the Dutch and English, a further stage of commodity production gained a foothold. As trade, exchange, and circulation increased, the decline of earlier modes of operation of the economy intensified because "capitalism cannot wait centuries for a slow process of breakdown to be worked through."[65] Agriculture continued to provide subsistence—although the Atlantic slave trade might have led to a decline of food production—but the demands of towns and a more specialized division of labor drove a wedge between rural and urban life. Commodity production assumed increasing importance and various guilds for artisans and merchants made their appearance. Specialized crafts (such as canoe building to meet increasing need for inshore and shore to ship transport) were localized at particular coastal centers for example, salt at Takoradi, cloth production at Keta, beads at Elmina, and lime at Axim, although other crafts may have declined due to cheap European imports.

While the commoners were the direct producers, African merchants, a highly mobile class, provided the capital to make the system work.[66] Merchants had strong influence over the organization of production and trade although, clearly, within the context of this local African variety of mercantilism, their primary interest was in buying and selling. In the process, they established elaborate networks handling credit and collecting payments near and far, yet often these tasks were assigned to agents, factors, writers, and brokers. European traders operating from the sailing ships, or the merchants established in the settlements, frequently made capital available to African traders, who accumulated considerable wealth, such as Kwamena Ansa of Elmina and John Kabes of Kommenda, which effectively facilitated their entrepreneurship. Ahrin, reflecting on the impact of European penetration, concludes as follows:

> From the time of the first Portuguese establishment at Elmina in 1482, the European commercial establishments had both quantitative and qualitative effects on the economies of the coastal peoples. I mean by 'quantitative' effects that food producers—fishermen and craftsmen, for example—were induced to produce more than subsistence requirements in order to exploit the market opportunities offered by the castle dwellers and the trading ships. I mean by 'qualitative' influence that the market situation of the European commercial establishments led to an increase in the variety of occupations: in addition to farmers, fishermen and craftsmen there were *professional canoemen* [emphasis added] and carriers, brokers or middlemen, including gold-takers, itinerant traders or pedlars and 'servants' in the European castles and forts . . . [all leading] to the 'bug' of money-making, which resulted in stirrings of the entrepreneurial spirit.[67]

The economies of these small non-agricultural areas, incipient mini-towns that grew up alongside the castles and lesser outstations, differed substantially from the scattered settlements in the rural areas. The population varied, ranging from several hundred into the thousands and by the late eighteenth century, and certainly early in the nineteenth, Cape Coast Castle had grown to over 10,000, and Appolonia to 22,000, while Dixcove was said to have had a population of 3,000 and Makessim 10,000 toward the end of the seventeenth century. The daily life and occupations of the residents were geared almost entirely to the demands of trade, to supplying the needs of the Europeans and goods and services such as water and firewood to the ships. At various times of the year, the population increased as traders from inland arrived at the coast. As trade patterns changed, so did the composition of the population. The settlements themselves were divided into wards, each occupied by different artisans, craftsmen, and laborers. Traders, brokers, and merchants lived separately. As external trade increased, so did the activities within the settlements. Likewise, the expansion of this trade also increased the caravan trade from the north of traders who sought to purchase the imports from Europe available at the coastal warehouses. The great expansion of trade, which took place in the wake of the voyages of exploration, was spearheaded by the Portuguese.

The causes of European expansion in the late-fifteenth and throughout the sixteenth centuries are complex and would need separate treatment. Conditions arose in Western Europe leading to the rise of a new bourgeoisie, a rapid accumulation of capital, and a vast expansion of foreign trade. Significantly and essentially, the new mercantile class began to share power with the established craft guilds. Above all, a money economy began to penetrate feudal estates, transforming rent in kind into rent in money and in the process creating a new class, the hired laborer. The need for currency, gold or silver, increased markedly. The new bourgeoisie, moving slowly but with determination, propagated the fundamental objective of mercantilism—buy cheap and sell dear (in Europe the value of gold increased many times over its original purchasing price). Unequal exchange was taking place. The struggle for markets had begun and the search for new and extensive supplies of gold was intensified.

The search for gold, for luxury goods (such as ivory), and markets, the expansion or decline of trade on the West African coast, and the effects of this on the coastal settlements, particularly the rise and decline of labor, invariably were linked to cyclical changes experienced by the nations of Western Europe. The rapid expansion of explorations to Brazil and the West Indies, and the enormous resources devoted to voyages eastward, produced fluctuations of labor-force formation, of rapid increases followed by contraction, in many of the coastal settlements. For example, beginning about 1520 trade increased, creating the need for canoemen and laborers (such as beachworkers whose activities were noted earlier) while, starting about 1570 (heralding a sharp decline of Portuguese power), trade diminished but revived even before the Dutch had firmly established themselves in 1637. Yet Guinea trade did not fare well during the three Anglo-Dutch wars fought out in Europe.

Perhaps one of the most significant consequences of increased material production was the progressively unequal distribution of wealth resulting in a marked increase of freebooting, of rogues, vagabonds, and those who frequently were cited "worthless wretches"; not least manifest was the rise of rural-urban conflict. The overall composition of the coastal settlements changed rapidly after their foundation and accelerated during the seventeenth century, mostly in the size of the commoner class, those unable to look after themselves, citizens unable to pay fines, those placed in service with the "better off," those who had been panyarred, and those described by some visitors, such as W. J. Müller, as very poor, the destitute.[68] While laborers and commoners, such as wood cutters, water carriers, and charcoal producers, increased in number, so did

African artisans such as gold workers, masons, coopers, bricklayers, bead makers, and carpenters. Standing well above them were merchants and brokers and those closely attached to this class such as linguists, writers, and aspiring entrepreneurs, the latter all hoping and working for high political office within the governing class or the European establishments. Income levels varied sharply. Wealthy traders lived in considerable splendor and often distributed largess to followers.

The African settlements outside the walls of the European establishments were firmly under the control of the nobles, important brokers and merchants who took ultimate charge of all civic affairs. Their authority increased from the late sixteenth century as trade expanded in all the larger settlements. They bought, sold, and marketed; they acquired resources and exploited these with the help of slave and free labor; they controlled credit, and they also rendered judgments and ordered punishments; they collected retainers and conscripted citizens for local or distant labor and for military service. Slavery also intensified differences within these societies. The growing governing classes, particularly the important middlemen such as brokers, dominated the African settlements. The governing classes were the state, and the state was not without conflict and not without opposition, not least from among the merchants who at times challenged the power of the nobility. The latter appointed captains and caboceers to provice the link between themselves, the citizens, and the Europeans.

Opposition from among the laboring classes was sporadic and not, as far as the records reveal, organized until well into the nineteenth century. A possible exception to this were the free canoemen. As I attempted to show above, the records indicate frequent conflict, sometimes turning violent, with the European employers. The issues at stake were disagreements over payments in kind such as rum, cloth, and tobacco, working conditions in general (such as demands to take canoes through particularly dangerous surf, or the anticipation of being panyarred), false accusations of theft of cargo, and what the Europeans generally called "roguish disobedience." Well below the canoemen were the destitute, the *odofo*, described as "wretches of unruly roguery," or vagabonds "filled with theivery" and, evidently, always suspect.[69] However, efforts were made by kin or civil authorities to offer help; meager sums of court fines were allocated as aid, religious offerings helped the indigent poor, and at times, European traders (as "Christians") also helped. However, the records indicate that occasionally a few of the poor acquired wealth and perhaps power. Bandits lay in wait when merchants made their way to the coast, robbed them, and established their own enterprises, an aspiration evidently shared by the poor peasants who moved to the small towns. To be on one's own was preferred to being a retainer of a member of the upper class. Indeed, a few African traders who became powerful and rose to the rank of nobles via ceremonies of ennoblement had come from a commoner background. Thus various forms of protest and rebellion seem to have allowed for some mobility and must be considered part of the political and economic life of the coastal states. That this was recognized is codified in the term, used frequently in the records of the seventeenth century, *agyesem*, meaning revolt or social unrest. Indeed, military action was often necessary to quell disturbances.

I think the evidence does suggest that a class system was in place and that direct producers were being exploited and often mistreated; upward mobility was restricted and various forms of labor protest revealed a consciousness of class position. But the issue remains whether a working class was in the making as early as the sixteenth or seventeenth century. What does appear certain is that the division of labor was sharply drawn, resting on the distinction between the direct producers and the consumers, and that this created the normal contradictions in the social, economic, and political domains, and generated conflict.[70]

The governing classes needed gold to be exchanged for imported merchandise from Europe. Their only way to obtain this was to purchase slaves and exert pressure on direct producers, to surround themselves with retainers who were craftsmen, miners, traders, and soldiers, and to demand tribute and taxes—all of which contributed to the potential for internal strife. Within the towns, unrest could be confined as the destitute, slaves, and the laboring classes occupied different quarters. Retainers, slaves, and craftsmen worked in trade workshops in specified locations, while domestic slaves generally lived in their masters' location. Canoemen certainly lived in their own quarters (as surfboatmen operating out of Cape Coast and Elmina did until well into the twentieth century). To this day, even though all surfboat activity has ceased, residents of Cape Coast, Elmina, and Winnebah will lead the visitor to highly decorated houses which until the 1930s were said to be the meeting places for the boatmen, the headquarters of the *asafo*, a traditional structure of uncertain origin that simultaneously served as a military organization, a fraternity of young men and, perhaps, a syndicate or guild guarding the prerogatives of particular trades of artisans and goldsmiths. Today, retired boatmen still speak with pride of their *asafo*.[71]

The *asafos*, central to the political and economic life of the Fante, appear to have enjoyed a considerable degree of political power. Most coastal settlements had approximately seven *asafo* groups, each one made up of different occupational and status groups and ranked in order of their prestige in the overall hierarchy. Precisely when they appeared for the first time, what their original purpose was, and how they were structured and operated is not clearly understood. Their place in the coastal settlement becomes more evident in the eighteenth and nineteenth centuries.[72] However, it is likely that fishermen were all members of such a collectivity, which regulated the ownership of the means of production, the canoes, nets, and other tackle, as well as the composition of the crews, the rules governing their occupation, the areas to be fished and when, and the value and distribution of the catch. The internal organization of the *asafo* from the time of origin is not known. Hence how the rules were arrived at, how authority over the membership was exercised, and how a specific *asafo* related to other sectors of the laboring class and the governing class is information that it would be important to discover. It is tempting to suggest that the *asafo* operated in the manner of a syndicate or guild to protect its members and their occupation, to support their demands vis-à-vis the employers, and to provide for needed welfare services and mutual aid. Generally unsubstantiated accounts offered by retired boatmen claim that their *asafo* was the forerunner of small unions, which in recent times gave rise to the Maritime and Dockworkers Union. Despite considerable efforts to find any firm evidence for such a suggestion, none could be found.

However, the issue is critical. Clearly it is important to answer the question: Were the canoemen organized in some manner from the earliest days, and if so, how? As we move into the late-eighteenth century, it becomes more evident that the demands of the canoemen/boatmen were more coordinated, the unrest more frequent, their consciousness more evident, their withdrawal of labor more determined, and the demands and the responses of the employers more direct and explicit. What is clear is that the boatmen (often also called surfboatmen) from about 1850 on assumed a very important place in the Ghanian working class that, starting in the early part of the twentieth century, achieved a broader base incorporating railway workers, miners, dockworkers at Takoradi, construction labor, domestic servants, low-wage commercial and government employees (messengers, cleaners), and the self-employed in the small-scale, so-called informal sector. Workers in the established wage sector, and their early predecessors, had little if any control over the ownership of the means of production. The state in pre-colonial and colonial times, and subsequently, stood in direct opposition to the needs of the laboring classes. Exploitative and coercive forms of production predominated. State authority and, if need be, force were the major instruments of control coupled with ritual sanctions and ceremonial activities invoked by African employers.

Thus the division of labor and the formation of the labor process has always been geared to the relations of production and to the production of profit in excess of individual and collective needs of the producers. It is the character and objective of production that is the central and essential feature of the structure and manifestation of social relations. The view I am inclined to take is that the economic and political system of the early pre-colonial coastal settlements was essentially capitalist in character, operation, and purpose. The internal dynamic of this system helped to sustain it and to expand its penetration and range. As a relatively cohesive system, it had the capacity to pull itself out of unfavorable circumstances, such as the progressive unprofitability for European and African entrepreneurs of the slave trade, and to regear itself to the palm oil trade and other commodity production as well as developing a manufacturing and service sector.[73]

If this characterization of the pre-colonial coastal settlements—that capitalist social formations appeared substantially later, not until the eighteenth or even the early nineteenth century—is deemed incorrect, the contrary proposition might rest more securely if an effort is made to trace and analyze the complex network of trade that was in place well before the Portuguese traders arrived on the West African coast.[74] In that network, production and exchange had created local, regional, and long distance markets based on gold, iron, and salt; the distinction between the means of production (labor) and the ownership of these means was well in place particularly in the major empires and states of West Africa; these had the military means to enforce their political and economic objectives. In West Africa, a primary objective of the Portuguese explorations had been to draw the lucrative inland trade and markets to the coastal regions. If we were to give attention to the history of skilled craft production, such as metal technology, we would discover that specialization and a corresponding division of labor appeared in the Niger towns in the third century B.C. A look at the system of land tenure also would be revealing and give support to the contention that class relations divided the population between the powerful and the laboring classes. Africa south of the Sahara generally was spared the power of landowners, yet kings, chiefs, and headmen were not hesitant to act like lords of the land using that vital resources at will—or, as Jack Goody put it so effectively, "Chief would not be expected to hear complaints on an empty stomach. Their families did better than those of commoners; they rode where others walked."[75]

I think the evidence is there to suggest that substantially before the arrival of the European powers on the Guinea coast class division and unequal distribution of wealth had taken hold. As colonial authority established itself and penetrated further inland, these divisions (and the class basis of racism) crystallized. They became dominant and were the outcome of particular processes that created a typical colonial socioeconomic and political formation. I think the point is that the formation of classes is not bound up solely with the rise of capitalism, but also with the evolution of hierarchy. Class formation is an ongoing process, then as now. But to suggest this does not make it any less real in the West Africa of pre-colonial times. Thus Kwame Arhin characterized the structure of the Fante towns in the nineteenth century (and, I believe, much the same can be said of these towns in the eighteenth) as follows:

> It is, clearly, possible to speak of 'classes' in the sense of self-conscious groups distinguished by property holdings, occupation and life styles in the Fante coastal towns: membership of the different strata within the classes was a matter of achievement and enterprise. Then, even more than now, Europeans offered models of 'high class' behavious to aspirant and 'arrived' members of the propertied class.[76]

Karl Marx spoke about "the unequal development of material production" when it reaches beyond the basic requirement of social reproduction and transforms the structure of the economic base. This economic base is the repository of physical resources, of the means of production, and of labor. The physical resources, an endowment of nature, are fashioned into usable sustenance or tools that sustain the individual and the collectivity. It is only by means of labor, or work, that men can wrest from nature the sustenance and provisions needed for their individual and collective needs. As long as the objective is limited to satisfying basic needs, the labor required can be viewed as free labor. The only coercive element is based on the need to survive or the struggle between men and natural forces.

Yet even at this "simple stage," a value is attached to work, to labor, and to the worker required to produce the tools in order to obtain basic needs. But this labor is an integral part of the family, kin, and larger collectivities and regulated by various rules *internal* to the society. At a certain stage, which will vary in time and from one society to another, *external* influences and pressures redefine the value placed on labor, on production, on natural resources, and the products created by labor. Over time and depending on the nature of the external forces and how these are absorbed, rejected, or interpreted, production broadens out from the original purpose of self-sufficiency to commodity production—commodities for more extensive and wider consumption, distriubtion, marketing, and trade. Thus, labor produces value for capital. When this takes place, and it can take various forms combining the old with the new or with a more radical break with the past, labor assumes a different function in society, that is, labor to produce surplus value for capital accumulation, and thereby transforming the rate and conditions of accumulation. Rosa Luxemburg devoted years of creative effort to demonstrating how a commodity economy is inserted into social formations governed by other principles. The change is long and complex, sometimes moving forward while at other times appearing to be stagnant or even reverting to past practices and structures.

However, the most common development is the transition from so-called free labor to wage labor, which really is not free at all. While the worker is free, if not a slave, to dispose of his or her labor according to choice and willingness to make such labor available for a purpose of other than the needs for social reproduction, the worker now enters into a contract with individuals who need this labor (this commodity which labor has now become) to create wealth over and above that which is required for basic needs. Thus the contract purchases labor and the laborer is paid for the work done. While there is much debate about free and unfree labor, Marx has set out the issue quite clearly. The following passage is quoted for the sole purpose of its relevance to the understanding of canoemen.

> For the conversion of his money into capital, therefore, the owner of money must meet in the market the free labourer, free in the double sense, that as a free man he can dispose of his labour-power as his own commodity, and that on the other he has no other commodity for sale, is short of everything necessary for the realisation of his labour-power.
>
> The question why this free labourer confronts him in the market has no interest for the owner of money, who regards the labour-market as a branch of the general market for commodities. And for the present it interests us just as little. We cling to the fact theoretically, as he does practically. One thing, however, is clear—Nature does not produce on the one side owners of money or commodities, and on the other men possessing nothing but their own labour-power. This relation has no natural basis, neither is its social basis one that is common to all historical periods. It is clearly the result of a past historical development, the product of many economic revolutions, of the extinction of a whole series of older forms of social production. So, too, the economic categories, already discussed by us, bear the stamp of history. Definite historical conditions are necessary that a product may become a commodity. It must not be produced as the immediate means of subsistence of the producer itself. Had we gone further, and inquired under what circumstances all, or even the majority of products take the form of commodities, we should have found that this can only happen with production of a very specific kind, capitalist production. Such an inquiry, however, would have been foreign to the analysts of commodities. Production and circulation of commodities can take place, although the great mass of objects produced are intended for the immediate requirements of their producers, are not turned into commodities, and consequently social production is not yet by a long way dominated in its length and breadth by exchange-value. The appearance of products as commodities pre-supposes such a development of the social division of labour, that the separation of use-value from exchange-value, a separation which first begins with barter, must already have been completed. But such degree of development is common to many forms of society which in other respects present the most varying historical features.[77]

Whether the early canoemen, whose primary occupation was fishing (as such they were producers of basic needs) were more truly free labor is a conceptualization that is at best controversial and polemical—indeed, others might argue that the whole issue is irrelevant. In the end, a definitive answer will have to be teased out of more precise historical data when and if they become available. However, it is instructive to note the idea expressed in 1855 in a memo pertaining to West African labor. "In the strict sense of the term, there is no such thing as free labor in Lagos, except which is imported; and, even that of the Gold Coast canoe men, is in reality, Slavery; for very few of them, excepting the head men, are really free men.[78]

The issue of free versus unfree labor can only be resolved within the context of a broader discussion of the development of capitalism[79] in the core areas and periphery, always remembering that capitalist structures and mechanisms are never static, nor are changes linear, but proceed by fits and spurts, expansion and stagnation. Fundamental to the issue of free labor is contractualization: labor is free to accept or reject an offer, and the terms of labor no longer are determined by a preordained set of customs, status, or divine will. On the other hand, labor is not free, despite a freedom to reject a contract, because of the overwhelming control exercised by commoditization of land and labor, both being available for contract. As capitalism in the periphery creates commoditization such as wage labor, it tends to destroy alternative, nondependent means of securing a living. The accumulation of capital further commoditizes labor and its product thus creating (unfree) free labor.

This is the history—and in particular the labor history—of the early stages of commoditization of work, labor, and social relations. From the sixteenth century on, western capitalism created and nurtured different types of labor forces, different forms of labor control, and various divisions of labor. These differences, and the gradual rise of free labor, are linked to periods of expansion or stagnation, to increasing complexity of trade, and to technical advancement and application. Labor in the core areas evolved as relatively "free" and, eventually, was able to negotiate better conditions of work; labor in the periphery was (and still is) subject to coercion and the conflict between pre-capitalist structures and capitalist penetration[80] resulting in appalling working conditions and low wages. The impact of commoditization on non-capitalist societies is determined largely by what Marx termed the "solidity and internal structure" of such societies. When contractual free labor appears, that is direct producers of material production, the basis of all social, economic, and political life undergoes irreversible change. It is the true beginning of labor history. The difference between labor in early times and that which came into existence with contractual terms is more one of degree than kind. Thus, as Marx pointed out, the difference between slave labor and wage labor "lies only in the mode in which this surplus labor is in each case extracted from the actual producer, the laborer."[81]

Thus in a limited juridical sense, free labor differs from slave labor, and wage labor from that performed in non-capitalist subsistence economies. But all labor, including that of the canoemen of southern Ghana, is not free as long as it is directly under the control of capitalist enterprise, and as long as labor has no control over the distribution of its products: over markets, profits, and surplus; over decisions concerning the direction of local economies; over the import and the consequences of new techniques of production; over the decline of local crafts and the change from consumption to exchange; over the consequences of the transformation from a kin order to a social organization fashioned by the relations of production—an order based, in the words of V. I. Lenin, on the "struggle of opposites," the destruction of the old and the birth of the new. So-called free labor is nothing more than class struggle, the basis of which is the extraction of unpaid surplus labor from the (free) direct producer. Thus the key to defining what free labor is or is not, be it in pre-colonial Africa or in more recent times, is to be found in the study of production relations, or the services purchased by the owners of capital and the rewards offered the direct producers. A social formation based on capitalist social relations cannot boast that it supports free labor. The canoemen of Ghana were no exception, although in the fifteenth and sixteenth centuries, such workers could also revert to the distinctive social relations of a pre-capitalist social formation, an opportunity that existed as long as the natural economy was not yet totally at risk and slipping into decline—a development that was hastened as the rise of an indigenous bourgeoisie of traders and merchants accelerated in the seventeenth century, of men who owed their very existence to the rise of external trade.

The arrival of the Portuguese in the fifteenth century, followed by the English and Dutch, added simply a further dimension to processes of transformation which had commenced at an even earlier period during the gold and kola trade,[82] probably in the twelfth and thirteenth centuries, when extensive commercial relations produced a network of inland trade in the western Sudan. Kings, nobles, priests, elders, and clan heads had already created a sizable sector of negotiated "free" labor in the states that dotted the interior and coastal areas of West Africa. The Portuguese were very well aware of the need for African labor, as were the Dutch and English. Local production of vegetables and fowls increased to meet the needs of the local garrisons. But the need also arose to regulate the employment of a variety of African labor either as slaves or otherwise. It was this need that gave rise to various royal ordinances that the Portuguese applied to their West African (and later Indian) settlements. The settlements attracted established traders and would-be entrepreneurs from the interior who entered into contractual relations with local factors or ship's captains. At various times, from the early-sixteenth century to the end of the nineteenth century, regulations and legislation were applied to the canoemen (as well as to another group of workers, the hammockmen) setting the terms of their remuneration.[83]

In particular, during the period of the Royal African Company, the London headquarters gave each governor and factor detailed instructions how many "free canoemen" and "slave canoemen" were to be employed at their stations, how they were to be paid, and advice concerning the conditions of work. The Dutch, likewise, from 1637 on kept careful ledgers recording all remuneration to canoemen and laborers. As the size of the labor force increased in the settlements, rural-urban class distinctions began to intensify.

How significant the rural-urban distinction was is difficult to ascertain from the records. Southern Ghana was an overwhelmingly agricultural economy, yet virtually all those Africans who rose to the rank of trader, broker, and entrepreneur moved frequently from country to town, to the "waterside people" as the coastal residents were called. Many of these inland traders formed the middle-range in the political and economic hierarchy, being very much the spearhead of increasing commercialization and often employers of labor, such as carriers who headloaded goods inland. The African traders and brokers were the nexus between European capital and African labor, a function that this incipient bourgeoisie carried well into the nineteenth century,[84] but rulers and senior chiefs contained the power and influence of traders and brokers, preventing them from seriously challenging the privileges of the governing class. To that end they frequently deprived African entrepreneurs of important sources of capital, or panyarred their retainers or laborers against unpaid debts.

Those traders and brokers who did establish themselves had to find ways to serve two masters, African and European. Yet as major agents of commercialization, particularly in the kola trade, they played a significant role in the total labor process, the control of labor conditions, and the distribution of the products of labor. Thus, for example, John Kabes of Kommenda owned a fleet of canoes and also provided the canoemen. How the workers, which included the craftsmen who made the canoes, were recruited, and what remuneration they received is not recorded, as African entrepreneurs did not always keep ledgers—at least none have so far been found that record the remuneration of their African employees, canoemen or other workers. More information is available for the eighteenth and nineteenth centuries.[85] The activities of these enterprising Africans in the gold and slave trade, from the late sixteenth into the seventeenth century, have yet to be fully documented, particularly the impact of their enterprises on rural production. For example, did these Africans specialize in particular commodity trade such as firearms, firewood, charcoal production, ivory, gold, or kola? Whatever the answer might be their effect on labor force formation needs much further study. The canoemen of Ghana were an essential element in the new force which had come into existence. They were hired labor and at various times responded accordingly. As such, they serve as an example that the labor history of this part of the Guinea coast has substantial roots.

A critical labor history of Africa, pre-colonial, colonial, or post-colonial, can perhaps be defined by what it should not be rather than precisely what it ought to be. Looking at the contemporary situation, labor history has been treated all too often as the study of industrial relations or trade unions.[86] The former is concerned with bargaining and collective agreements and the latter with internal structures, social democracy, or the relation of unions to political machines. Labor history studies have been professionalized to such a degree that the role of the underclasses is often quite incidental. Workers and the work situation often are ignored in studies that ostensibly are concerned with laboring men. One such example is the otherwise interesting study by Richard Jeffries on Ghana railway workers and their union. Jeffries suggests, perhaps correctly, that "if a broadly based radical movement is to emerge, then those groups which lack the organizational mechanisms for concerted political action (as appears to be the case of the Ghana railwaymen) are likely to look for a lead to those which do and are prepared to use them, and, in Ghana, this would appear to be the proletariat alone." However, he also concludes pessimistically, "in all realism, such a prospect must be considered extremely distant."[87]

Indeed almost all trade union studies pay virtually no attention to those who the unions should serve.[88] While some labor history studies try to deal with class consciousness of various factions of labor, we yet have to adopt the sort of format which has been established in the *Journal of Peasant Studies*, which regularly has a section under the title: "Peasants Speak." We ought to re-read E. P. Thompson's *The Making of the English Working Class*,[89] Eric Hobsbawm's *Primitive Rebels*,[90] and Gareth Steadman Jones's *Outcast London*.[91] We might even return to the writings of Charles Dickens. These authors did something very important; they gave us an insight into the work situation, what workers thought and how they reacted to their conditions. Perhaps it might be useful to cite part of the introduction to *African Labor History*:

> To restore the history of the exploited masses of Africa implies the creation of an authentic tradition of struggle and therefore full information about *their own struggles*. It should not come as a surprise that the very first elements of this history have been made in the academic world. Whatever their weaknesses may be, these first efforts are preferable to silence. Theoretical formulation, the development of authentic African research, the establishment of a concrete link between this research and the needs of the present [and past] struggles and the forms of class consciousness—these are the basic elements of this program. We do not propose to substitute ourselves for those who "are making history," but we must attempt in a small way, with the best means and skills at our disposal

(academic skills being what they are), to help to bring about the creation of a tradition of working class struggle.[92]

In this introduction, the authors discuss the more recent history of African workers; little attention is paid to the pre-colonial era. My contribution is an attempt to remedy this and to suggest that African workers' struggles can be traced back to the sixteenth century and probably further if we persist in the exploration of a new field of study and have the conviction required to do so. If the evidence does not support this approach, it will have to be dropped and we must think of a better model to apply. Whatever that model is, it must take into account that a labor force was employed and that it received some sort of remuneration for its labor, that it was indispensable in the production of surplus value, and that at times it showed resistance and was punished for this. Above all, the model must take note of how the employer regulated this labor, *and* for what purpose.

Further, the model must include a clear linkage to the particular economic system that penetrated these West African coastal societies. We ought to be quite certain before we identify fundamental processes and conditions as those commensurate with proletarianization, since this condition does not invariably suggest that a clear class system has developed. Yet I also would suggest that thus far we have concentrated on a somewhat arbitrary base line without any real attempt to ask more searching questions about antecedents that might reveal information that allows us to press back a good deal further the origins of incipient class formation and proletarianization. We have, after all, concentrated a good deal of effort on the history of a class of merchants (the trade and politics school of African history), but have given almost no attention to those without whom the merchants could not have operated the way they did. It is all very well to say that the labor they had to use was drawn from the matrix of the kinship order. True, sometimes this was so, but surely more often this was not so. And did the Portuguese not supply African slaves from the Benin region to the African merchants who came to the factories? Surely this is an underclass which was used, so the records tell us, as porters and in other laboring capacities. We still need more information to understand how these workers reacted to their unenviable conditions and how they were treated.

Of course we must be careful not to make the polemical claim that these were the origins of proletarianization (although the temptation is there to do just that). It is perhaps enough for the moment simply to point out that such an underclass existed and to wait for an opportunity to document further their position in the evolution and structure of these African societies. We should not forget that these coastal societies were drawn into trade and exchange relations which, while clearly distinct and different, were an early example of the introduction of a capitalist mode of production into their body politic and economic. We know a good deal about gold production in the early days, about how gold traders demanded that workers increase production as the demand for gold increased and became a form of currency. The question we must ask is how they then increased production.

We must experiment with the kind of model and the questions which I have suggested. We should do this because we must know how structures evolved and how they worked. Who were the people who produced riches for others? These people were around, and the question is how they fitted into the whole. It is for these reasons that I have started on this project. My interest is, foremost, to dig out whatever material I can find. But I am also concerned, in the language of the moment, to set the record straight. If I may suggest so audacious an idea, I would like someone to write a "History of the Conditions of the African Working Class." I shall not be the one who can and should attempt this. But somewhere there must be a Frederick Engels among Africanists. Lots of distinguished colleagues have devoted their energy to the "History of the Western Working Class." It seems very partial that we should not devote equal energy to those workers who were indispensable and a distinctive part of pre-colonial Africa.

NOTES

Research on the history of the canoemen of Ghana has received generous support from a number of agencies to whom I owe considerable thanks. I have received support from the Wenner-Gren Foundation for Anthropological Research, the Social Sciences and Humanities Research Council of Canada, the African Committee of the Social Science Research Council (U.S.A.), the Social Science Committee, Graduate Faculty, McGill University, and in the early stages of the research, from the Centre for Developing Area Studies, McGill University. While in Ghana, I was a Visiting Research Fellow, Department of Sociology, University of Ghana, Legon, where Professor D. K. Fiawoo and his colleagues gave me most willing and generous assistance in face of real difficulties faced by all my colleagues. I must record the same for help received from all the librarians at the University of Ghana and, in particular, the reference and interlibrary loan librarians, McGill University. The services of Mr. John Hobbins went well beyond normal professional courtesy and interest in my work. Professors Myron Echenberg and Richard Rice who allowed a naive anthropologist to pick their brains, my friend and colleague Robin Cohen, Warwick University, whose knowledge of and interest in labor history is unsurpassed, Jeff Crisp and Lyn Garrett, lately at the University of Birmingham, and Greg Teal, a graduate student in our Department of Anthropology. All influenced my work and interests.

Thanks also are due to Mr. Paul Arden-Clark of the United Africa Company, London, and his colleagues in Ghana, who allowed me access to their archives.

Finally my thanks must go to many retired surfboatmen at Cape Coast, Elmina, and Accra who had the patience to answer my questions. As one of them said to another as we sat in a bar: "The European is writing about our grandfathers. Answer his questions." He was said to be over eighty years of age, and he as well as his father had labored for others. He exposed his leg which had been mangled in a surfboat accident. His compensation in 1921 had been £25!

1. Eric J. Hobsbawm, "From Social History to the History of Society," *Daedalus*, C:1 (1971), pp. 20–45; "Economic and Social History Divided," *New Society* XXIX (July 11, 1974), pp. 74–76; Gilbert Shapiro, "Prospects for a Scientific Social History, 1976," *Journal of Social History* X:2 (Winter, 1976), pp. 196–204; Fernand Braudel, "History and the Social Sciences," in Peter Burke, ed., *Economy and Society in Early Modern Europe from Annales* (London, 1972), pp. 11–42.

2. The distinction, if any, between political and class consciousness has not been sufficiently explored and I do not propose to do so in this article. However, for the time being, and whatever the implications, I propose to treat these as linked if not the same. It seems to me that class consciousness *is* political consciousness.

3. E. P. Thompson, *The Making of the English Working Class* (Harmondsworth, 1968); Eric J. Hobsbawm, *Labouring Men* (London, 1972); Fernand Braudel, *The Mediterranean and the Mediterranean World in the Age of Philip II*, vol. I (New York, 1976).

4. See for example: *History Workshop—a Journal of Socialist Historians*.

5. Raphael Samuel, ed., *People's History and Socialist Theory* (London, 1981).

6. See for example Godelier who points out that it was in the fifteenth and sixteenth centuries that words such as "travailler," "salarie," and "proletaire" first came into usage and that "When political economy emerged as a field of investigation in the 18th century, work was one of its key concepts. . . . "However, the greater part of his article is devoted to the view that the "status of work and the worker . . . is broader in scope than analysis of concrete labour processes." Maurice Godelier, "Aide-memoire for a Survey of Work and its Representations," *Current Anthropology* XXI:6 (December 1980), pp. 831–835.

7. Quoted in Gareth S. Jones, "History: the Poverty of Empiricism," in Robin Blackburn, ed., *Ideology in Social Science* (New York, 1973), p. 98.

8. Caroline Fluehr-Lobban, Richard Lobban, and L. Zangari, " 'Tribe': a Socio-political Analysis," *Ufahamu* VII:1 (1976), pp. 143–165; Immanuel Wallerstein, "The Evolving Role of the African Scholar in African Studies," *Canadian Journal of African Studies* XVII:1 (1983), pp. 9–16.

9. Steadman Jones, "History," p. 98.

10. For an outstanding study of the historians of Africa see: A. Temu and B. Swai, *Historians and Africanist History: a Critique* (London, 1981).

11. Eric J. Hobsbawm, "Labour History and Ideology," *Journal of Social History* VII:4 (1974), pp. 371–381; George Haupt, "Why the History of the Working-Class Movement?" *Review* II (Summer 1978), pp. 5–24; Elizabeth Fox-Genovese and Eugene D. Genovese, "The Political Crisis of Social History: A Marxist Perspective," *Journal of Social History* X:2 (Winter 1976), pp. 205–220.

12. For a stimulating discussion see: Gregor McLennan, *Marxism and the Methodologies of History* (London, 1981); G. A. Cohen, *Karl Marx's Theory of History: a Defence* (Princeton, N.J., 1978).

13. Peter C. W. Gutkind, Robin Cohen, and Jean Copans, eds., *African Labor History* (Beverly Hills, 1978).

14. Their publications are extensive but one example will suffice: Lewis H. Gann and Peter Duigan, *Burden of Empire: an Appraisal of Western Colonialism in Africa South of the Sahara* (New York, 1967). See also Lewis H. Gann, "Neo-colonialism, Imperialism and the 'New Class,' " *The Intercollegiate Review* (Winter 1973–74), pp. 13–27.

15. Walter W. Rodney, *A History of the Guyanese Working People, 1881–1905* (London, 1981).

16. Anthony G. Hopkins, *An Economic History of West Africa* (New York, 1973). See also numerous articles in the journal *African Economic History* commencing Spring 1976.

17. P. E. H. Hair, "Barbot, Dapper, Daviti: a Critique of Sources on Sierra Leone and Cape Mount," *History in Africa* I (1974), pp. 25–54; Albert Van Dantzig, "William Bosman's *New and Accurate Description of the Coast of Guinea: How Accurate is it?*" *History in Africa* I (1974), pp. 101–198, followed by "English Bosman and Dutch Bosman: a Comparison of Text," *History in Africa* III (1976), pp. 91–126, IV (1977), pp. 247–273, V (1978), pp. 225–256, VI (1979), pp. 265–285, VII (1980), pp. 281–291, IX (1982), pp. 295–302; Ray Jenkins, "Impeachable Source? On the Use of the Second Edition of Reindorf's *History* as a Primary Source for the Study of Ghanaian History, I," *History in Africa* IV (1977), pp. 123–147 and part II, IV (1978), pp. 81–99; I. M. Feinberg, "An Eighteenth-Century Case of Plagiarism: William Smith's *A New Voyage to Guinea*," *History in Africa* VI (1979), pp. 45–50; John D. Fage, "A Commentary on Duarte Pacheco Pereira's Account of the Lower Guinea Coastlands in his *Esemaraldo de Situ Orbis* and on Some Other Early Accounts," *History in Africa* VII (1980), pp. 47–80; Robin Law, "Jean Barbot as Source for the Slave Coast of West Africa," *History in Africa* IX (1982), pp. 155–173; A. Donelha, *An Account of Sierra Leone and the Rivers of Guinea and Cape Verde* (1625), introduction, notes, and appendices by A. Teixeira Da Mota and P. E. H. Hiar, Centro de Estudos de Cartografia Antiga, no. 19 (Lisboa, 1977).

18. Alessandro Triulzi, "Decolonising African History," in Raphael Samuel, ed., *People's History and Socialist Thought* (London, 1981), pp. 286–297.

19. Jacob Viner, "Mercantilist Thought," in David L. Sills, ed., *International Encyclopedia of the Social Sciences* IV (1968), pp. 435–443; Charles Wilson, *Mercantilism* (London, 1958); "Mercantilism': Some Vicissitudes of an Idea," *The Economic History Review* X, second series: 2 (1957), pp. 181–188; "The Other Face of Mercantilism," *Transactions of the Royal Historical Society* IX, fifth series (1959), pp. 81–101; Rudolph C. Blitz, "Mercantilist Policies and the Pattern of World Trade, 1500–1750," *Journal of Economic History* XXVII:1 (March 1967), pp. 39–55; Eli F. Heckscher, *Mercantilism*, vol. II (London, 1935); Herbert Heaton, "Heckscher on Mercantilism," *Journal of Political Economy* XLV: 3 (June 1937), pp. 370–393; D. Coleman, "Eli Heckscher and the Idea of Mercantilism," *Scandinavian Economy History Review* VI:1 (1957), pp. 3–25; Brian Schwimmer, "Mercantilism as a Social System," paper read at Symposium on Early Mercantile Enterprises in Anthropological Perspectives, Canadian Ethnological Society Meeting, Winnipeg, March 1975; Immanuel Wallerstein, *The Modern World-*

System, II: Mercantilism and the Consolidation of the European World-Economy (New York, 1980).

20. Richard Sandbrook and Robin Cohen, eds., *The Development of an African Working Class; Studies in Class Formation and Action* (London, 1975); Richard Sandbrook and Jack Arn, *The Labouring Poor and Urban Class Formation: the Case of Greater Accra*, Occasional monograph series, No. 12 (Montreal, 1977); Rob Buijtenhuis and Peter Geschiere, eds., "Social Stratification and Class Formation," *African Perspectives* (special issue), II (1978); Peter C. W. Gutkind, *The Emergent African Proletariat* Occasional Paper, no. 8 (Montreal, 1974).

21. The literature is extensive but one citation will suffice: E. W. Bovill, *Golden Trade of the Moors* (London, 1958).

22. Immanuel Wallerstein, *The Modern World-System: Capitalist Agriculture and the Origins of the European World-Economy in the Sixteenth Century* (New York, 1974), *The Modern World-System, II: Mercantilism*; "The Rise and Future Demise of the World Capitalist System: Concepts for Comparative Analysis," *Economy and Society* XVI (4 September 1974), pp. 387–415; "Trends in World Capitalism," *Monthly Review* XXVI:1 (May 1974), pp. 12–18; "From Feudalism to Capitalism: Transition or Transactions?" *British Journal of Sociology* XXVII:3 September 1976), pp. 345–354; "An Historical Perspective on the Emergence of the New International Order: Economic, Political, Cultural Aspects," in Immanuel Wallerstein, *The Capitalist-World Economy* (London, 1979), pp. 269–282.

23. Malowist in a seminal article on Mali and Songhai in the Middle Ages attempts to show how very central the trade in gold and slaves was to the consolidation of these empires. Exports and imports were of such value to the monarchs and elites that "neither sultans nor members of the dominant class were particularly interested in reorganizing the country's economy with a view to any marked expansion of production. They had no need to do this." Malowist concludes from this that agricultural expansion was neglected with the result that "both Mali and Songhai were condemned to social and economic stagnation." The "abundance of gold and slaves" was a deterrent to "social and economic progress." See: M. Malowist, "The Social and Economic Stability of the Western Sudan in the Middle Ages," *Past and Present* XXXIII (April 1966), pp. 3–15; "Rejoinder," *Past and Present* XXXVII (July 1967), pp. 157–162. However, in an equally important article, Hopkins attacked this theory and "widespread myths" about "the bulk of the population . . . assured of a relatively prosperous existence without [the peasantry] having to exert themselves unduly." Anthony G. Hopkins, "The Western Sudan in the Middle Ages: Underdevelopment in the Empires of the Western Sudan," *Past and Present* XXXVII (July 1967), pp. 149–156.

I refer to this date because the rather smaller state systems of coastal Ghana responded to external commercial links in such an active manner generating increased and diversified entrepreneurship (illustrated effectively by the canoemen), the expansion and continuity of crafts which in turn made it possible for markets and *urban* areas to expand (adjacent to the castles) and for commoditization of the economies to increase. While coastal polities rose and declined, the overall direction was one of persistence, production, and trade and not of least significance, the creation of new and more specialized labor forces.

The issue of class relations in these pre-colonial coastal societies raises the question of the place of slavery in the domestic and regional economies and their integration in production; whether the southern Ghanaian social formation may be characterized as feudal and the exact nature of state formation and state power; and how incipient capitalist penetration effected and 'articulated' with various non-capitalist structures. See: T. Buttner, "The Economic and Social Character of Pre-colonial States in Tropical Africa," *Journal of the Historical Society of Nigeria* V:2 (June 1970), pp. 275–283; Jack Goody, "Feudalism in Africa," *Journal of African History* IV:1 (1963), pp. 1–18; "Economy and Feudalism in Africa," *The Economic History Review* XXII, second series: 3 (December 1969), pp. 393–405.

24. Walter Rodney, *How Europe Underdeveloped Africa* (London, 1972), p. 7.

25. Some French writers have given support to the unsubstantiated claim that French traders and explorers were the first to reach the Ghana coast before the turn of the fourteenth century. See: P. Margry, *Les navigations françaises et la révolution maritime du XIVe au XVIe siècle* (Paris, 1867); C. de la Ronciere, *La Découverte de l'Afrique au Moyen Age* (Cairo, 1925), 10–17 rejects this claim as does E. de Santarem, *Recherches sur la priorité de la découverte des pays situés sur la côte occidentale d'Afrique* (Paris, 1842). Naturally all Portuguese writers have disputed the French claim.

Prior to these unsubstantiated French claims, the Phoenicians and Carthaginians explored the northern and northwestern coast of Africa, voyages which have been well documented. The voyage of Hanno in the fifth century B.C. is alleged to have taken him as far south as Sierra Leone. Some accounts claim that Hanno's voyages might have taken him as far as Ghana and Nigeria. It was during such voyage(s), in search of gold, that the so-called "silent trade" was alleged to have taken place (see fn. 26). However, as navigational knowledge was limited it is unlikely that such southern penetration took place. See: D. B. Harden, "The Phoenicians on the West Coast of Africa," *Antiquity* XXII:87 (1948), pp. 141–150; Robin C. C. Law, "North Africa in the Period of Phoenician and Greek Colonization c. 800 to 323 B.C.," in John D. Fage, ed., *The Cambridge History of Africa, vol. 2: from c. 500 BC to AD 1050* (Cambridge, 1978), pp. 87–147; Raymond Mauny, "Trans-Saharan Contacts and the Iron Age in West Africa," in John D. Fage, ed., *The Cambridge History of Africa, vol. 2*, pp. 272–341.

26. There are accounts of much earlier voyages (see fn. 25) during which "silent trade" is alleged to have taken place; goods intended for exchange were left on the beach by the visitors who then withdrew waiting for Africans to deposit goods of an equivalent value, an exchange procedure consuming very considerable time. However, whether such trade ever took place on the Ghana coast is very doubtful. For a general discussion of silent trade see: P. F. de Moraes-Farias, "Silent Trade: Myth and Historical Evidence," *History in Africa*, vol. I (1974), pp. 9–25; L. Sundstrom, *The Exchange Economy of Pre-colonial Tropical Africa*, with an introduction by A. C. Hopkins (London, 1974); J. A. Price, "On Silent Trade," in George Dalton, ed., *Research in Economic Anthropology*, vol. 3 (Greenwich, 1980), pp. 75–96.

27. M. N. Dias, "A organizacao da rota atlantica do ouru du Mina e as mecanismas dos resgates," *Revista de Historia* (Sao Paulo) XLIV (1960), pp. 369–398.

28. That these were applied with energy and consistency is doubtful perhaps

because they were highly formalistic and legalistic and invited being broken because conditions of life were difficult, and the temptations to get rich quickly were inviting. The Manueline Ordinances can be found in P. A. Brasio, *Monumento Missionaria Africana: Africca Occidental, 1342–1600*, ser. 2, 3 vols. (Lisboa, 1958–1964); A. Teixira da Mota, *Some Aspects of Portuguese Colonisation and Sea Trade in West Africa in the 15th and 16th Centuries* (Bloomington, Ind., 1978).

29. The passage to India was very costly to the Portuguese in ships and crews. See: James Duffy, *Shipwreck and Empire: Being an Account of Portuguese Maritime Disasters in a Century of Decline* (Cambridge, 1955).

30. Although the settlements were often within less than one mile of one another, it was extremely rare for Europeans to take to the coastal paths and treks. However, canoe activity covered the whole coast of some 400 miles.

31. Jean Barbot, *Description of the Coasts of North and South Guinea* (London, 1732).

32. To Thomas Melvil, 7 October 1753, Public Record Office (London), T70/30.

33. Royal African Company, Cape Coast Ledger, 18 July 1708, Public Record Office (London), T70/22.

34. To William Mutter, 12 February 1764, Public Record Office (London), T70/31.

35. Court of Assistants, Royal African Company to Philip Franklin, 18 July 1728, Public Record Office (London), T70/53.

36. Ibid.

37. Margaret Priestley, "An Early Strike in Ghana," *Ghana Notes and Queries* VII (January 1965), p. 25.

38. One incident which has been well described took place in 1803. See: R. Porter, "The Cape Coast Conflict of 1803: a Crisis in Relations Between the African and European Communities," *Transactions of the Historical Society of Ghana* II (1970), pp. 27–82.

39. Consistently throughout the records, canoemen are referred to as "English canoemen," "Dutch," "Danish," "Brandenburger," or "French."

40. For such cases heard in the 19th century see: Susan B. Kaplow, "Primitive Accumulation and Traditional Social Relations on the Nineteenth Century Gold Coast," *Canadian Journal of African Studies* XII: (1978), pp. 22, fn. 8.

41. James Oudle to James Phipps, 29 November 1711, Public Record Office (London), T70/2.

42. Harvey M. Feinberg, "An Incident in Elmina-Dutch Relations, Ghana Gold Coast, 1739–1740," *African Historical Studies* III:2 (1970), pp. 359–372; Ray A. Kea, "Trade, State Formation and Warfare on the Gold Coast, 1600–1826," Ph.D. dissertation, University of London, 1974; J. E. Inikori, "The Import of Firearms into West Africa, 1750–1807: a Quantitative Analysis," *Journal of African History* XVIII:3 (1977), pp. 339–368; John L. Vogt, *Portuguese Rule on the Gold Coast, 1469–1682* (Athens, Ga., 1979); Ray A. Kea, "Firearms and Warfare on the Gold and Slave Coasts from the Sixteenth to the Nineteenth Centuries," *Journal of African History* XII:2 (1971), pp. 185–213.

43. This characterization needs further exploration. A possible comparative perspective might be: Eric J. Hobsbawm, "Social Banditry" in H. A. Landsberger,

ed., *Rural Protest: Peasant Movements and Social Change* (London, 1974), pp. 142–157.

44. Unfortunately the destruction of many ships in times of war, which also attracted aggressive interlopers and piracy, as well as the heavy storms encountered during the long voyages, resulted in the loss of considerable archival materials which regularly were handed to the captains for dispatch to Europe. Many of the records inspected reveal heavy water damage.

45. E. Collins, ed., *Journal and Correspondence of H. W. Daendels, Governor-General of the Netherlands Settlements on the Coast of Guinea, part 1: November 1815 to January 1817* (Legon, 1964), pp. 137–140, 161–167.

46. Edmund Dod to John Gordon, 11 June 1794, Public Record Office (London), 170/1568.

47. Thomas Melvil to Company of Merchants, London, 1 July 1754, Public Record Office (London), T70/30.

48. To Nassau Senior, 11 December 1757, Public Record Office (London), T70/1527.

49. It was customary not to go to sea on Tuesday.

50. George Ogilvie to Richard Miles, 12 August 1777, Public Record Office (London), T70/32.

51. Petition in possession of Kofi Kabena, a retired boatman at Cape Coast, who received it from his late father who had also been a boatman.

52. Jon Kraus, "The Political Economy of Industrial Relations in Ghana," in V. G. Damachi, H. D. Seibel, and L. Trachtman, eds., *Industrial Relations in Africa* (New York, 1979), pp. 106–168; "Strikes and Labour Power in Ghana," *Development and Change* X:2 (April 1979), pp. 259–286.

53. Richard Miles to David Mill, 5 February 1775, Public Record Office (London), T70/1479.

54. Kwame Arhin discussing "rank" and "class" in nineteenth century Asante and Fante insists that "The rank of the [domestic] slave was essentially political and social, not economic," and that they enjoyed some legal rights such as ownership of property, gold, and even other slaves. Slaves destined for export overseas did not enjoy such rights. See: Kwame Arhin, "Rank and Class among the Asante and Fante in the Nineteenth Century," *Africa* XIII:1 (1983), p. 12.

55. Hopkins contests this view, rightly, yet also suggests that "it is clear that pre-colonial [West] Africa was not moving in the direction of an indigenous industrial revolution." See: Anthony G. Hopkins, *An Economic History of West Africa* (New York, 1973), p. 76. He thus challenges the conclusion arrived at by Rodney, *op. cit.* (1972).

56. The brief description which follows is drawn from many sources ranging from such early travellers as Barbot (op. cit.) and William Bosman, *A New and Accurate Description of the Coast of Guinea*, (London, 1967, 1st pub. 1705) to more recent studies of cultural and economic history such as Kea, *op. cit.* (1974).

57. Thus Bowdich, writing about the late eighteenth and early nineteenth centuries, identified an "aristocracy," the "middling orders," and the "inferior class." See: T. E. Bowdich, *Mission from Cape Coast Castle to Ashantee* (London, 1819), pp. 233, 262, 323.

58. In highly centralized societies dominated by kingship the labor process is ultimately controlled by kin or appointed agents. The surplus value belongs to

the king and is distributed according to his wish for patronage or ritual and ceremonial purpose (including military needs), reinforcing legitimacy of office and serving the collective good. In particular cases, and at particular times, such politico-economic structures possibly have something in common with the Asiatic mode of production.

59. John D. Fage, "Slaves and Society in Western Africa, c. 1445-c. 1700," *Journal of African History* XXI:3 (1980), pp. 289–310.

60. Ray A. Kea, "Social and Spatial Aspects of Production in Southern Ghana in the Sixteenth and Seventeenth Centuries," unpublished paper, n.d.

61. Rodney, *op. cit.* (1972), p. 120.

62. Edward A. Alpers, "Re-thinking African Economic History: a Contribution to the Discussion of the Roots of Underdevelopment," *Ufahamu* III:3 (Winter 1973), p. 120.

63. Raymond Mauny, *Tableau géographique de l'Ouest africain au Moyen age*, Memoires, (Daker, 1961), p. 61.

64. B. Bradby, "The Destruction of Natural Economy," *Economy and Society* IV:2 (1975), p. 138.

65. Ibid.

66. By expressing this in this manner I do not imply any leaning toward positivism!

67. Kwame Arhin, *op. cit.*, p. 15.

68. W. J. Müller, *Die Africanische auf der Guineischen Gold-Cust Gelegene Landschaft Fetu* (Graz, 1968 [1676]).

69. K. Ratelband, *Sao Jorge da Mina (Elmina) Aan de Goudkust (1645–1647)* ('s-Gravenhage, 1953), pp. 183–185, 191–192.

70. Bosman, *op. cit.* (1967), pp. 158–159; Van Dantzig, *op. cit.* (1977), p. 253.

71. Kwame Arhin, "Diffuse Authority among the Coastal Fanti," *Ghana Notes and Queries* IX (1966), pp. 66–70; Ansu K. Datta and R. Porter, "The *Asafo* System in Historical Perspective," *Journal of African History* XII:2 (1971), pp. 279–297; J. C. De Graft-Johnson, "The Fanti Asafu," *Africa* V:3 (July 1932), pp. 307–322; B. I. Chukwukere, *Cultural Resilience: the Asafo Company System of the Fanti*, Research report series, paper, 3 (Cape Coast, 1970); "Perspectives on the Asafo Insitution in Southern Ghana," *Journal of African Studies* VII:1 (Spring 1980), pp. 39–47; Arthur Ffoulkes, "The Company System in Cape Coast Castle," *Journal of the Royal African Society* VII (26 January 1908), pp. 261–277; Jarle Simensen, "Rural Mass Action in the Context of Anti-colonial Protest: The Asafo Movement of Akim Abuakwa, Ghana," *Canadian Journal of African Studies* VIII:1 (1974), pp. 25–41.

72. As far as I was able to note, *asafos* are not mentioned in any records of the sixteenth and seventeenth centuries.

73. This observation stands somewhat in contrast to what Austin, writing about Duala trade in the Cameroon, has called the "abolitionist viewpoint [which] perceives the termination of the overseas slave trade as the key landmark in the development of coastal African states; this event, it is argued, dealt a severe blow to the African ancient regimes and placed them in bitter conflict with a class of recently liberated 'new men.' " Austin appears to endorse the substantivist perspective. Ralph A. Austin, "Dutch Trading Voyages to Cameroon, 1721–1759,"

Annales de la Faculté des Lettres et Sciences Humaines Université de Yaounde II:6 (1974), pp. 25–27.

74. Catherine Coquery-Vidrovitch, "Research on the African Mode of Production," in Martin A. Klein and G. Wesley Johnson, eds., *Perspectives on the African Past* (Boston, 1972), 33–51; E. W. Vovill, *op. cit.* (1958) and *Caravans of the Old Sahara* (London, 1933).

75. Jack Goody, "Economy and Feudalism in Africa," *The Economic History Review*, second series XXII:3 (December 1969), p. 400.

76. Kwame Arhin, *op. cit.*, p. 18.

77. Karl Marx, *Capital*, vol. 1 (Moscow, 1965), pp. 169–170.

78. Campbell to Clarendon, 18 February 1855, Public Record Office (London), F.O. 84/1002. I am grateful to A. G. Hopkins for this reference.

79. James O'Connor, "Productive and Unproductive Labor," *Politics and Society* V:3 (1975), pp. 297–336; Norman A. Klein; "West African Unfree Labour before and after the Rise of the Atlantic Slave Trade," in L. Foner and E. D. Genovese, eds., *Slavery in the New World* (Englewood Cliffs, N.J., 1969), pp. 87–95.

80. Pierre P. Rey, *Colonialisme, néo-colonialisme et transition au capitalisme: exemple de la Camiloy au Congo-Brazzaville* (Paris, 1971); David Seddon, ed., *Relations of Production: Marxist Approaches to Economic Anthropology* (London, 1978).

81. Karl Marx, *Capital*, vol. 1 (New York, 1967), p. 217.

82. Paul E. Lovejoy, *Caravans of Kola: the Hausa Kola Trade* (Zaria, 1980).

83. Gold Coast, *Ordinance to Provide for the Enrollment and Regulation of Canoemen and Hammockmen*, 1852; Sierra Leone (applicable also to the Gold Coast), *An Act for the Better Regulation of Mechanics, Kroomen, Labourers, Grumettas and other Servants*, 26 April 1820, renewed 8 March 1822.

84. Kwame Arhin, *West African Traders in Ghana in the Nineteenth and Twentieth Centuries* (London, 1979); Edward Reynolds, *Trade and Economic Change in the Gold Coast, 1807–1874* (New York, 1974); "The Rise and Fall of an African Merchant Class on the Gold Coast, 1830–1874," *Cahier d'études africaines* XIV:54 (1974), pp. 253–264; Susan B. Kaplow, "The Mudfish and the Crocodile: Underdevelopment of a West African Bourgeoisie," *Science and Society* XLI:3 (1977), pp. 317–333; "Primitive Accumulation and Traditional Social Relations on the Nineteenth Century Gold Coast," *Canadian Journal of African Studies* XII:1 (1978), pp. 14–36.

85. Margaret Priestley (Bax), "Richard Brew: an Eighteenth Century Trader at Anomabu," *Transactions of the Historical Society of Ghana* IV:1 (1959), pp. 29–46: West African Trade and Coast Society: a Family Study (London, 1969).

86. Robin Cohen, *The 'New' International Labour Studies: a Definition* Working paper series (Montreal, 1980), p. 27.

87. Richard Jeffries, *Class, Power and Ideology in Ghana: the Railwaymen of Sekondi* (Cambridge, 1978), p. 208.

88. Wogu Ananaba, *The Trade Union Movement in Africa: Promise and Performance* (New York, 1979).

89. Thompson, *op. cit.* (1968).

90. Eric J. Hobsbawm, *Primitive Rebels* (New York, 1965). First published as *Social Bandits and Primitive Rebels* (Glencoe, Ill., 1969).

91. Gareth Stedman Jones, *Outcast London: a Study in the Relationship between*

Classes in Victorian Society (Oxford, 1971), and, of course, Henry Mayhew, *London Labour and the London Poor* (New York, 1968); Robert Trassell, *The Ragged-trousered Philanthropist* (London, 1955).

92. Peter C. W. Gutkind, Robin Cohen, and Jean Copans, *op. cit.* (1978), p. 26.

7

Industrialization and the Structuring of Asian Labor Movements: The "Gang of Four"

Frederic C. Deyo

Between 1960 and 1979 Hong Kong, Taiwan, South Korea, and Singapore, collectively known as the "gang of four," maintained the most rapid average annual growth rates per capita of all developing countries,[1] at over 7 percent. During those same years Hong Kong's gross domestic product (GDP) increased from U.S. $950 million to $17.4 billion, South Korea's rose from $3,810 million to $60,660 million, Singapore's rose from $700 million to $9,010 million,[2] and Taiwan's (expressed in million New Taiwan dollars) rose from $62,566 to $1,164,073.

The remarkable increase in GDP was led by expansion in labor-intensive manufacturing for world markets.[3] In the case of Hong Kong, this structural shift had occurred by 1960, whereas the shift was more pronounced during the 1960s in the other cases. South Korea's manufacturing sector increased from 14 percent to 27 percent of GDP during the 1960–1979 period, while that in Singapore and Taiwan increased from 12 percent to 28 percent[4] and from 15 percent to 43 percent[5] respectively. Corresponding increases in manufactured exports were equally significant during this period. Between 1962 and 1978 such exports increased from U.S. $642 million to $10,693 million in Hong Kong, from $10 million to $11,220 million in South Korea, and from $328 million to $4,679 million in Singapore. For Taiwan, Walter Galenson[6] calculates an index rise from 36 in 1963 to 157 in 1973. By 1978 these four countries were the largest export-manufacturers of all Third World countries,[7] a remarkable feat in view of their very small size and minimal resource endowment.

This pattern of "export-oriented industrialization" (EOI) comprises a special type of economic linkage with the world economy involving, as it does, a marriage of low-cost, abundant domestic labor to international capital, technology, and markets. The domestic ramifications of such a marriage, in turn, are many. This essay traces out these ramifications, especially as they relate to emergent labor movements, through exploration of the political changes associated with EOI during its initiation and later stages, as well as its associated economic-structural changes which impinge on the unity, power, and militance of organized labor. The analysis employs a resource-mobilization perspective that starts from the assumption that social movements and action are better explained by reference to the political, organizational, economic, and social structural resources and constraints which impinge on them than by the frustrations or issues which provide their manifest rationale.[8] Here it will be argued that Asian EOI has been associated with two factors: first, government repression of labor where prior labor politicization threatened to undermine an EOI strategy at the outset; and second, a subsequent economic-structural transformation that had the paradoxical result of reducing the independent organizational resource base of labor in all four countries, while at the same time encouraging a continuing displacement of local, enterprise-level, labor controls by state intervention in Korea and Singapore. Third, it will be shown that a later stage of EOI development has encouraged a transition from repressive to corporatist labor controls in countries where the government had intervened substantially in industrial relations at earlier stages.

Assessment of the social impact of this new development pattern for labor movements hopefully will contribute to our understanding of the way in which an EOI mode of world economic linkage and dependence relates to internal political-economic transformation.

ECONOMIC CHANGE IN THE FOUR COUNTRIES: 1950–1980

Hong Kong's early development of both entrepot and manufacturing activities under British colonial rule provided a basis for early and easy world-market oriented industrialization during the 1950s. The other three countries differed somewhat from Hong Kong in their earlier effort to industrialize through import-substitution. The problems associated with this latter development approach encouraged a shift to export-oriented industrialization in the early 1960s in South Korea and Taiwan, and in the late 1960s in Singapore. The following discussion traces the origins and pattern of export-oriented industrialization in the four countries.

Hong Kong

Hong Kong's economic history differs somewhat from that of the other three countries in that it never went through a pronounced import-substitution industrialization (ISI) stage, moving instead directly into export-oriented manufacturing at a very early stage. Hong Kong was established by Britain as a Crown Colony in 1841 and served mainly as an entrepot center linking China with Europe. Its economy therefore revolved largely around the processing, transport, and storage of outbound primary products and import of manufacturing goods.[9] Much of the manual labor force was therefore to be found in dockwork, public services, ship building and repair, light industries such as textiles and food processing, and a number of artisan and craft industries.[10]

With the end of World War II, and especially during the final stages of the Kuomintang defeat, large numbers of political refugees poured into the colony, along with many industrial entrepreneurs (especially Shanghai textile manufacturers and a few of their skilled workers)[11] seeking haven for their capital. The very small size and extreme poverty of the now-isolated colony encouraged expansion in export-oriented, rather than import-substituting, manufacturing.[12] Much of this expansion centered in small-scale, localized firms, thus reinforcing an earlier commercial pattern of recruitment of labor and mobilization and control of capital within family, clan, or other particularistic groups such as those based on linguistic or regional origin.

Korea

Following its annexation of the Korean peninsula in 1910, Japan created substantial changes in this largely agrarian new colony. Initially, in order to secure a new source of food and raw materials for the home country, there was an effort to rationalize farming technology and generally to modernize the agricultural sector. Parallel to this effort was a general discouragement of domestic industry. By the 1920s such industry as did exist was largely Japanese owned, and under strict government control.[13] Of greater importance for future industrialization was the substantial colonial investment in roads, rail lines, waterways, banking and credit associations, and electrification as part of the program of agricultural development.

It was only during the immediate pre–World War II period that substantial effort was made to develop Korean industry. During this period large-scale, heavily subsidized, and Japanese owned producers' goods industries were established in the North, and consumer goods industries flourished in the South. This development, based heavily on imported Japanese skills, capital, and technology, encouraged an early economic dualism between modern, externally focused industry on the one hand, and domestic agriculture and cottage industry on the other. In part as a consequence of the capital-intensive and limited nature of large-scale industrial enterprise, there was little movement of labor from agriculture to industrial sectors or urban areas.

Following the economic devastation of the Korean War, the politicial division of the Korean peninsula left the South a largely agrarian economy with a limited sector of small-scale, domestic-market oriented, consumer goods industry. Starting in 1953, therefore, the government, assisted substantially by United States foreign aid, embarked on a relatively short-lived ISI policy, which was to last only until the end of the decade.[14] Through foreign exchange controls, infrastructural investments, and protective import tariffs, the government successfully encouraged rapid growth in local consumer goods industries, particularly in textiles, leather products, paper, food, and rubber products. Between 1954 and 1958, by consequence, growth rates in mining and manufacturing averaged over 15 percent, as against only 4 percent in agriculture.

Import-substituting industrialization relied heavily on foreign capital. Starting from a ratio of foreign to domestic savings of 3.2/4.5 in 1953, the ratio reversed to 19.3/10.9 in favor of foreign capital by 1957. During the 1953–57 period, foreign sources accounted for over 61 percent of total investment in South Korea. Much of this capital was channeled through government-controlled banks to a few politically favored enterprises, which soon established monopolistic positions in major industrial sectors. Thus, government-sponsored industrialization perpetuated an existing industrial dualism inherited from the Japanese.

By the late 1950s growing industrial stagnation and rising unemployment called into question the long term viability of an ISI development policy. Partially in response to United States and United Nations Industrial Development Organization urging, the Korean government shifted toward an EOI approach. Thereafter, export manufacturing was encouraged through currency devaluation, elimination of many tariff and other controls over foreign trade, liberalization of import duties on those producers' goods and raw materials that were needed by export-industries, and establishment of a number of tax incentives.

Following the ISI pattern, Korean EOI remained dependent on foreign capital, in most cases channelled as loans through government development banks to local entrepreneurs who typically produced under contract for international buying groups. The continuing disproportionate government assistance to large-scale firms was based explicitly on the assumption that only established industrialists were in a position to effectively move the Korean economy ahead, and thus to provide employment for a rapidly expanding pool of job seekers. The resulting impetus given concentrated production in large urban factories later was further intensified by government development of several large export-processing zones near urban centers to accommodate foreign and domestic export-manufacturing plants along with their working populations.

Taiwan

The early period of Taiwanese development follows the Korean pattern quite closely. Like Korea, Taiwan was developed under Japanese colonial rule to an overseas source of food crops and raw materials. Like Korea, it was subject to anti-industrialization policies until World War II when it too, was transformed into an overseas site for Japanese-controlled production of fertilizer, chemicals, and petroleum.[15] Domestic light industries, often Japanese owned, were confined largely to food processing and textiles.

On the other hand, Japanese investment in rural infrastructure (roads, irrigation, schools, credit unions and cooperatives, all intended to stimulate agriculture) was, if anything, more substantial than that in Korea. Rural cottage industry was less severely limited than in Korea, and such industries as sugar refining and cement manufacture, along with home textile production, flourished.

While the early Taiwanese industrial base was damaged severely during World War II,[16] post-war growth was accelerated by an influx of Chinese industry and capital in 1948–49 as the Chinese Communist party consolidated its mainland victory over Chiang Kai Chek's Kuomintang forces. Thus, when the new nationalist government of Taiwan initiated an ISI drive in the early 1950s, it was able to put the massive inputs of United States foreign aid to effective use in expanding an already good economic infrastructure (especially roads and electrification) in order to stimulate both agriculture and industry. Especially important in this regard was government emphasis, based on hard political lessons learned on the mainland, on widely dispersed rural industry. Such an emphasis stemmed from the twin goals of providing jobs for the predominantly rural workforce and of promoting industry with immediate backward and forward linkages to agriculture.

As in Korea, the transition from ISI to EOI in the early 1960s was encouraged by declining rates of industrial growth,[17] growing and politically unacceptable levels of unemployment, and strong international pressure for trade liberalization. Unlike the Korean case, however, and following the pattern established during the 1950s, rural industrialization played an important development role. The only major exception to this generally dispersed character of industrial production was the development of several large export-processing zones within which were established export-manufacturing firms in electronics, textiles, and a few other industries.

Another important difference between Taiwanese and Korean industrialization, especially during the EOI period, is that Taiwan relied far less on foreign capital, and more on localized community and kinship networks for the mobilization of industrial capital.[18] Although the nationalist government, like its Korean counterpart, inherited from the Japanese a number of industrial enterprises, these were largely distributed (in the form of stock shares) to former landlords in compensation for landholdings redistributed to tenant farmers during the land reform programs of the early and mid–1950s.[19] Thus no basis was laid for the emergence of giant industrial monopolies as in Korea.[20]

Singapore

In some respects, Singapore's early economic history is similar to that of Hong Kong. Both were British colonial entrepot centers linking Asian land masses with Britain and the West. The economies of both emphasized commerce, finance, and shipping, along with some local consumer goods manufacture.

Beyond these similarities, however, a number of important differences emerge. First, whereas Hong Kong was cut off from the huge mainland market for consumer goods, and therefore had to move into export-oriented industrialization in the early 1950s, Singapore retained access to the larger Malaysian market until the political split between the two countries in 1965. By consequence, whereas Hong Kong did not go through a sustained ISI development phase, Singapore successfully encouraged the growth of domestic consumer goods industries to serve both Singapore and the larger Malaysian federation. This ISI development was based primarily on small-scale family enterprise rooted firmly in the many localized dialect communities of the city. Alongside this small firm sector were a number of public service organizations like those in Hong Kong, along with a scattering of large, often foreign firms in such heavy industries as chemicals, petroleum refining, and shipbuilding. Such domestic-market oriented industrial expansion was explicitly encouraged by tariff protection and government financial subsidies.

Singapore's EOI shift followed the 1965 political separation from Malaysia and the subsequent erection of mutual tariffs. This effective reduction in the domestic market for Singapore-manufactured goods forced a sudden reconsideration of the traditional ISI policy, which depended crucially on adequate domestic buying power for manufactured products. Such market considerations, along with continuing high levels of unemployment, prompted a crash program of EOI development. Given the need very quickly to create a viable and labor-absorbing export manufacturing sector, along with a lack of substantial foreign aid and loans of the sort available to both Korea and Taiwan, Singapore's ruling party used a number of tax and other incentives to attract private foreign investment into such labor-absorbing industries as electronics and textiles. The overwhelming role of foreign investment in Singapore's industrialization is seen in the fact that by 1975, foreign corporations in the manufacturing sector absorbed 76 percent of manufacturing inputs, produced 71 percent of outputs, and accounted for 65 percent of manufacturing capital formation. By 1979 wholly foreign-owned firms alone accounted for 63 percent of total industrial employment.[21] The important role of direct foreign investment led to an immediate and dramatic growth of very large manufacturing enterprises, and to their displacement of small local firms.[22]

LABOR ORGANIZATION AND CONFLICT

Before addressing the implications of Asian EOI for labor movements in these four countries, it is necessary to outline the historical trends in labor organization and action during the decades we are discussing. Most of the following discussion is based on official governmental records concerning unions and industrial disputes.

Table 7.1 suggests stagnant levels of unionization among "organizable" workers (employees) in Hong Kong during the 1960s, a finding supported by H. A. Turner, who argues that there has been little change since 1949 in the percent of the workforce organized.[23] The organizational increases of the early 1970s, which began in the context of the spillover of the Chinese Cultural Revolution and which centered mainly among public servants, continued until 1976. Data for Taiwan show a smooth, gradual increase in unionization during the mid 1970s, following a period of relative union stagnation. Quite different were the cases of South Korea and Singapore, whose unionization levels display marked fluctuations over the past two decades. Union membership in South Korea expanded slowly during 1958 and 1960, and dropped to almost nil under martial law between 1961 and 1963. Following reestablishment of unions in 1963, the percentage of employees organized declined until 1974, when there was a sharp increase. Similarly, Singapore shows rapid unionization during the early 1960s, followed by a drastic decline prior to renewed expansion during the 1970s.

Data on work stoppages (see table 7.2) display somewhat wider fluctuation, given the greater short-run impact of political and economic changes on strikes than on unionization levels. In Hong Kong, work days lost to industrial conflict, while starting out moderately high, have shown few multi-year surges of the sort found in Korea and Singapore, and show a secular decline, accompanied by a more dramatic reduction in work days lost per stoppage, during the period up to 1976. Taiwan shows consistently low levels of work days lost to stoppages during the 1960s. Unfortunately, strike data for the 1970s are not available, although there is indication of a marked increase in frequency but a decline in the size of disputes. Industrial conflict in South Korea and Singapore displays sharp, erratic fluctuations. Most significant is the drastic conflict

Table 7.1 Available Data on Unionization Trends by Country and Year

Year	Hong Kong			Taiwan		
	Total declared employee union members[1]	Union members as % of employees[2]	Union members as % of labor force[2]	Total declared union members[3]	Union members as % of employees[4]	Union members as % of employed labor force
1955				198,028		7
1956	211,313			217,613		8
1957	213,551			236,374		8
1958	226,968			249,147		9
1959	247,281			268,040		9
1960	231,960			280,173		9
1961	217,300	15		284,477		9
1962	165,000			290,588		9
1963	159,500			304,490		9
1964	142,480			324,379		9
1965	149,680			334,184		9
1966	166,900	15	12	354,382	20	10
1967	171,620			358,888		9
1968	165,580			370,391	19	9
1969	175,000	15		392,542	18	9
1970	195,000	16		488,093	21	11
1971	221,000	17	13	513,176	20	11
1972	251,729	18		560,491	21	12
1973	295,735	21		674,066	23	13
1974	317,045	22		714,786	24	13
1975	361,458	24		765,176	24	15
1976	388,077	25	20	838,408	25	15
1977	404,325	25		926,306	26	16
1978	399,995	23	20	963,987	25	16
1979	399,392		18	1,028,733	25	16
1980	384,282		16	1,103,005	26	17
1981						

Notes and Sources

1. 1956-1960: Annual Departmental Report, Registrar of Trade Unions.

   1961-1968: England and Rear (1975:86).

   1969-1971: Turner (1980:23)

   1972-1980: Annual Departmental Report, Registrar of Trade Unions.

2. 1961 and 1966: Turner, estimates.

   1969-1978: Turner (1980:23).

   1978-1980: Based on H.K. Monthly Bulletin of Statistics; 1980 based on estimate of 2,400,000 labor force from 1979 and 1981 average.

3. 1955-1964: Report of Taiwan Labor Statistics.

   1965-1980: Yearbooks of Labor Statistics.

4. Based on Quarterly Report on the Labor Force Survey in Taiwan.

Year	South Korea: Total union members[5]	South Korea: Union members as % of employees[6]	South Korea: Union members as % of labor force[7]	Singapore: Total union members[8]	Singapore: Union members as % of employees[9]	Singapore: Union members as % of employed labor force[10]
1955				139,317		
1956				157,216		
1957	246,486		4	140,710		30
1958	246,049		3	129,159		27
1959	285,461		4	146,579		
1960	33,735	37	4	144,770		29
1961	NIL			164,462		32
1962	NIL		NIL	189,032		36
1963	23,000	2		142,936		26
1964	271,579	29	3	157,050		28
1965	309,620	28	3	154,052		27
1966	336,974	27	4	141,925		
1967				130,053		
1968				125,518		
1969	444,372	22	5	120,053		
1970				112,488	23	15
1971				124,350		17
1972				166,988		22
1973				191,481		23
1974	530,900	22	4	203,561	30	24
1975	712,001	27	6	208,561	31	24
1976	823,130	28	6	221,936	31	24
1977						
1978						
1979				249,710		25
1980	1,119,572			243,841		
1981						

5. 1957-1960: Han (1974:189).

   1963-1976: Federation of Korean Trade Unions, as reported in Korea Annual.

6. Annual Report on the Economically Active Population Survey, 1976, 1977.

7. Labor Force data reported in Chen: 195.

8. Ministry of Labour.

9. Ministry of Labour.

10. Labor force figures from 1952 and 1966 from 1957 Census Report and 1966 Sample Household Survey Report respectively.

Table 7.2 Available Data on Industrial Conflict by Country and Year

Year	Hong Kong work stop-pages	Hong Kong workdays lost (000's)[1]	Hong Kong workdays per 000 labor force[2]	Hong Kong workdays per stop-page	Taiwan work stop-pages[3]	Taiwan workdays lost (000's)[3]	Taiwan workdays per 000 labor force[4]	Taiwan work-days per stop-page
1946	16	124						
1947	10	279						
1948	13	79						
1949	12	182						
1950	3	4						
1951	12	53						
1952	1	1						
1953	3	149						
1954	5	14						
1955	11	33		3000	43	3	1	70
1956	12	79			35	3	1	86
1957	3	13			55	3	1	55
1958	6	2			56	5	2	89
1959	12	30		2500	55	3	1	55
1960	9	29			52	2	1	38
1961	12	41	34		30	2	1	67
1962	12	27			64	6	2	94
1963	17	73			20	3	1	150
1964	13	43		3308	7	2	1	286
1965	9	67			15	11	3	733
1966	14	24	17		5	5	1	1000
1967	13	23		1769	5	13	3	2600
1968	25	8			20	2	1	100
1969	27	40			2	10	2	5000
1970	47	47			31	24	5	774
1971	42	26	16	619	9	2	1	277
1972	46	42			57	3	1	61
					Disputes	Workers	Workers Per Dispute	
1973	54	57			262	27,430		105
1974	19	11			494	17,319		35
1975	17	18		1058	458	16,647		36
1976	16	5	3		371	12,512		34
1977	38	11		289	380	3,858		10
1978	51	31			506	3,955		8
1979	46	40		870	503	11,383		3
1980	37	21	9	553	700	5,990		9

Notes and Sources

1. 1946-1974 are for fiscal years, April to March (Turner, 1980:88).

   1975-1977 are for calendar years (Turner, 1980:88).

   1978-1979: I.L.O. Yearbooks.

   1980: Hong Kong Monthly Digest of Statistics.

2. Labor force data from labor force sample surveys reported in I.L.O. Yearbooks.
3. 1955-1964: Report of Taiwan Labor Statistics.

   1965-1980: Yearbooks of Labor Statistics.

4. Labor force base from Galenson (1979:386).

Year	South Korea				Singapore			
	work stop-pages[5]	workdays lost (000's)[5]	workdays per 000 labor force	workdays per stop-page	work stop-pages[6]	workdays lost (000's)[6]	work-days per 000 labor force[7]	work-days per stop-page
1946					47	846		
1947					45	493	1379	
1948					20	129		
1949					3	7		
1950					1	5		
1951					4	21		
1952					5	40		
1953					4	47		
1954					8	135		
1955	20				275	946		
1956	18				29	454		
1957	45				27	109	231	4037
1958	39				22	78	162	
1959	95				40	27	55	
1960	256				45	152	304	
1961	122				116	411	804	3543
1962	---				88	165	314	
1953	70				47	388	717	8255
1964	7	2	NIL	286	39	36	65	923
1965	12	19	2	1583	30	46	80	1533
1966	12	41	4	3417	14	45		3214
1967	18	10	1	556	10	41		4100
1968	16	63	6	3938	4	11		2750
1969	7	163	17	23286	--	9		
1970	4	9	1	2250	5	3	4	600
1971	10	11	1	1100	2	5		2500
1972	NIL	NIL	--		10	18		1800
					Disputes	Workers	Workers	Per Dispute
1973	NIL	NIL	--		5	2		400
1974	58	17	1	293	10	5	6	500
1975	52	14	1	269	7	5	6	714
1976	49	17	1	347	4	3	3	750
1977	58	8	1	138	1	1		1000
1978	102	13	1	127	NIL	NIL	NIL	----
1979	105	16	1	152	NIL	NIL	NIL	----
1980	206	61	4	296	NIL	NIL	NIL	----

5. From I.L.O. Yearbooks.

6. Ministry of Labour, Annual Reports.

7. 1947 labor force total from 1947 Census.

8. This and subsequent figures include, for the first time, disputes in the export-processing zones. From Yearbook for Labor Statistics (annual); including data on workers involved.

reduction in both countries during the early 1960s. In the Korean case, stoppages increased again during the late 1960s and the late 1970s, although the pre–1961 strike surge was associated with large stoppages, whereas the later ones involved very small stoppages. Starting from extremely high levels in the 1960s, strikes have all but disappeared in Singapore with a simultaneous decline in size.

Overall, then, rapid EOI development during the 1960s and early 1970s was accompanied by stagnant levels of unionization and very low rates of work days lost to stoppages (see figure 7.1 for a comparison of these rates with those in the United States during recent years). However, while such stagnation in both organization and militancy stand in marked contrast to corresponding early periods of rapid industrialization in other countries, far more striking is the trend toward stoppages or disputes involving ever fewer workers and shorter duration in all four countries. This decline in the size of stoppages has been associated as well with increasingly defensive and unsuccessful labor action. Janet Salaff[24] and H. A. Turner[25] have pointed, for example, to the increasing tendency for strikes in Hong Kong to be short, poorly organized, and largely unsuccessful efforts to protect workers against dismissal during periods of retrenchment, a pattern that holds as well for South Korea[26] and Singapore.[27] The following discussion suggests that such a weak labor response to industrialization resulted in part from political changes, especially during initial periods of EOI, but that economic-structural changes comprise a more important explanation during later development.

THE POLITICS OF LABOR MOBILIZATION DURING THE PRE-EOI PERIOD

Given a very gradual pace of economic change and minimal economic mobilization of an industrial proletariat in all cases except that of Hong Kong (see table 7.3), the history of pre-EOI labor movements must be understood largely by reference to political rather than economic forces. In Singapore, Korea, and Taiwan the industrial workforce remained small and, with the exception of a few large government organizations, widely dispersed in rural or small family firms. On the other hand, these countries displayed substantial variation in the political context of labor. In the case of Taiwan, lack of an independence struggle or sustained challenge to the post–1949 KMT ruling elite largely precluded the political mobilization of labor. Quite different, however, were the South Korean and Singapore cases. Park Chung Hee's 1961 military coup, which was immediately followed by initiation of an EOI development strategy, followed a long period of political mobilization and increasing labor and student radicalism. This mobilization had begun with pre–

Figure 7.1 Work Days Lost to Stoppages per Thousand Workers

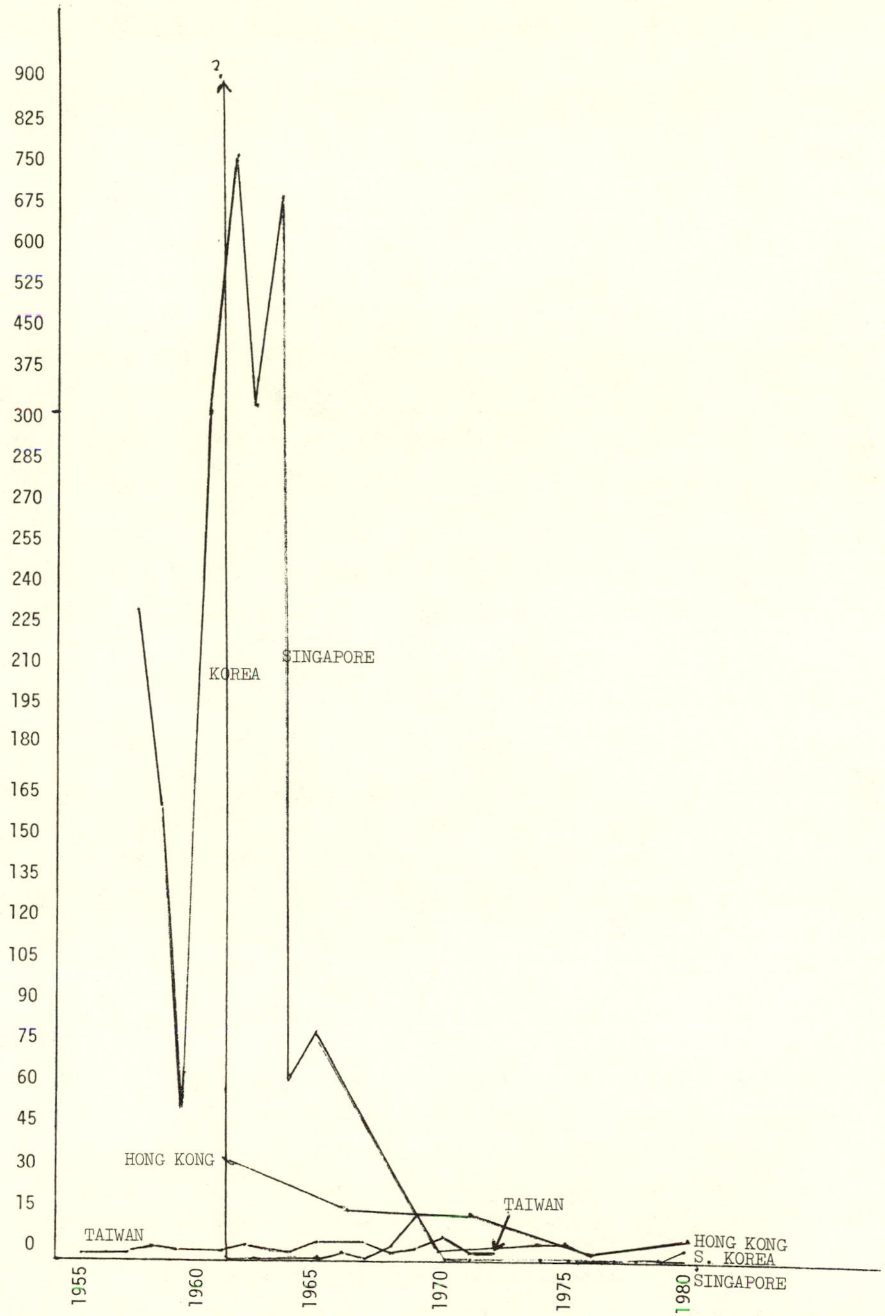

Table 7.3 Available Data on Employment Trends by Country and Year

	Hong Kong			Taiwan		
Year	manufacturing work force (000's)[1]	manufacturing as % of employed[2]	females as % of manufact. workers[3]	manufacturing work force (000's)[4]	manufacturing as % of employed[5]	females as % of manufact. workers[6]
1946		19 (1931)				
1947						
1948	61					
1949	65					
1950	90					
1951	94					
1952	93					
1953	101	30		229	8	11
1954	106					
1955	119			260	9	
1956	139			267	9	
1957	148			266	9	
1958	168			264	8	11
1959	189			268	8	
1960	229			362	11	
1961	230	39	33	376	11	
1962	279			375	11	
1963	302					12
1964	320					
1965	337			612	17	
1966	388	38	43	643	17	
1967	413			753	19	
1968	472			748	18	26
1969	524			833	19	
1970	549		51	933	20	
1971	564	42		1023	22	
1972	579			1194	24	
1973	583			1412	27	40
1974	600			1468	27	
1975	679		51	1501	29	
1976	774	40	52	1607	28	42
1977	755		51	1735	29	
1978	817		51	1901	31	43
1979	871		51	2081	32	
1980	907	42	50	2149	33	
1981				2181	33	

Notes and Sources

1. 1948-1963: Annual Departmental Reports, Commissioner of Labour. (registered employed)*

   1964-1980: I.L.O. Yearbooks (registered employed).

   1950, 1960: cited in Fan, p. 241.

2. These percentages are based on labor force sample survey data reported in I.L.O. Yearbooks, except for 1931 and 1961: Hong Kong Government Census Reports; and 1953: Chou, p. 63.

3. 1961 and 1966: labor force sample survey data reported in I.L.O. Yearbooks.

   1970 and later: based on establishment surveys reported Hong Kong Monthly Digest of Statistics.

4. 1953-1962: Report of Taiwan Labor Statistics. The sudden increase for 1960 is probably attributable to an expansion in survey coverage.

* 1961 Census figures show total number of industrial workers is over twice that derived from yearly voluntary registration. Thus, those figures should be used only to establish trends.

Year	South Korea manufacturing work force (000's)[7]	South Korea manufacturing as % of employed[7]	South Korea females as % of manufact. employed[8]	Singapore manufacturing work force (000's)[9]	Singapore manufacturing as % of employed[10]	Singapore females as % of employed[11]
1946						
1947					17	
1948						
1949						
1950						
1951						
1952						
1953						
1954						
1955						
1956	125	2				
1957	132	2			16	18
1958	125	2				
1959	140			26		
1960	487	7	27	27		
1961	513	7		28		
1962	560	8		29		
1963	604	8		37		
1964	670	9		41		
1965	800	9	30	47		
1966	833	10		53		23
1967	1021	11		58		
1968	1170	13		75	30	
1969	1232	13		101	28	
1970	1234	14	36	121	30	34
1971	1336	13		141	32	
1972	1445	13		170	35	
1973	1774	16		199	36	
1974	2012	17		234	28	
1975	2205	19	38	218	26	
1976	2678	21		234	27	40
1977	2798	22		248	27	
1978	3016	22		269	28	
1979	3126	23		293	29	
1980	2972	22	39	314	29	46
1981						

1965: Yearbook of Labor Statistics.

1966-1981: Quarterly Report on the labor force survey of Taiwan.

5. 1953-1962: employment data from Bureau of Accounting and Statistics.

6. Computed from I.L.O. Yearbook data.

7. 1956-1958: Economic Planning Board.

1959 and 1963: Economic Statistics Yearbook.

1960-1962: Chen:195 and 201.

1964-1965: Monthly Economic Statistics

1966-1974: Economic Planning Board, 1975.

1975-1979: Economic Statistics Yearbook, 1980.

8. I.L.O. Yearbooks.

9. 1959-1966: Goh (1969:142).

1967-1980: Ministry of Labour.

10. 1947, 1957: based on census data reported by Department of Statistics.

1968-1980: based on data reported by Ministry of Labour.

11. Based on household census data.

World War II underground labor resistance to Japanese rule, continued through the severe social disruptions of the Korean War, and culminated in a period first of anti-Syngman Rhee demonstrations and then of a new organizational drive and strikes during the brief period of liberal rule between the fall of the Rhee regime and the late–1961 coup.

Pre-EOI labor politicization was equally significant in Singapore. There, labor mobilization initially was encouraged by electoral competition, as Lee Kuan Yew's People's Action Party (PAP) organized Chinese labor in the late 1950s to win an electoral mandate to form the colony's first internally independent government, and then itself split into two wings, one moderate, the other socialist, each competing for labor's vote in the early 1960s. This political competition led to massive organizational efforts on the part of an increasingly politicized labor movement, as reflected in high levels of unionization and conflict during the early 1960s.

Hong Kong suggests a very different early pattern of labor mobilization. Unlike the other countries, by the late 1950s Hong Kong was already an established international manufacturing, trade, and financial center, and thus contained a substantial industrial workforce. On the other hand, following the intense political activity leading up to 1949, the 1950s saw little oppositional politicization of this potentially powerful proletariat. The natural source of such mobilization, the pro-Communist Federation of Trade Unions (FTU), continued (except during 1966–67) to maintain a low political profile in response to Peking directives, and to engage in little active organizing outside the already affiliated groups of well-off and more highly skilled male workers who had been organized very early.

STATE LABOR-REGIMES AND THE EOI INITIATIVE

An important prerequisite for the attraction of domestic, and especially foreign, capital investment[28] into labor-intensive, world-competitive, export-oriented manufacturing is the availability of low-cost, disciplined labor. In cases where a weak, internally fragmented and politically inert labor movement poses little threat to development, EOI initiative will not elicit substantial new state intervention in industrial relations. Where labor does pose a threat to investment, and where the state plays a significant role in development, state repression will be attempted as a logical concomitant of the more general development strategy. It is important in this regard to distinguish between controls imposed directly to bolster political authority on the one hand, and those oriented more specifically to economic imperatives on the other. While state labor controls usually are in response to both political and economic requirements, and while political stability may be supportive of economic development and vice versa, here we deal only with the special impetus given such labor controls by an EOI development strategy, as opposed to other development approaches, and for reasons having to do with the economic logic of this strategy. State labor controls, noted in many Third World countries, may derive from the number of other, non-EOI-related considerations, but where labor discipline is inadequate to the stringent requirements of labor-intensive EOI, state intervention becomes a crucial prerequisite for development, regardless of whether or not labor poses any direct threat to political elites.

The gradual and undramatic shift of Hong Kong's laissez-faire economy toward export manufacturing was based more on the private decisions of individual industrialists in response to new world market opportunities than on an explicit government policy initiative. Thus, EOI initiation was not accompanied by new economically-linked government intervention in industrial relations beyond continuing restrictions on political disruptions and despite moderate levels of conflict during the 1950s.

The case of Taiwan is a bit more complex. It is clear that at the point of EOI initiation labor militance was extremely low, but whether labor peace was the result of government repression or other factors is less certain. On the one hand, the government had carried over into the new Taiwanese setting most of the repressive labor legislation enacted in the context of the struggle with leftists on the mainland. While this legislation severely restricted union collective bargaining and direct action it is important to note that, despite its remaining on the books, it has remained largely non-operational. There has been little elaboration of either industrial relations machinery or implementing regulation at the local level. In any case, workers rarely challenged labor laws, which largely remained a latent control structure aimed less at economic disruption than at possible political disorder. In general, one may argue that a relatively docile labor force, along with a less substantial government role in EOI development than in Korea or Singapore,[29] reduced the impetus to substantial state intervention in industrial relations.[30]

South Korea's President Park was faced with a very different situation from that in Taiwan when he sought simultaneously to establish political control and to promote EOI development during the early 1960s. Labor at that time was highly politicized and economically militant, and threatened to undermine the new EOI policy. Thus, Park was confronted at the outset by the need to meet labor's strong challenge on both political and economic grounds. The resulting crackdown on organized labor included a strike ban, deregistration of all existing unions, and the arrest of many union activists. The immediate consequence of this repression is readily apparent in the substantial reduction in levels of both unionization and conflict during the early 1960s.

High levels of labor militancy similarly provoked government repression in Singapore. First, after the 1963 electoral victory of the PAP over the Socialist party, oppositional unions were deregistered, leaders jailed, and legislation passed that precluded political activities on the part of labor. Subsequent EOI initiation was accompanied by establishment of centralized control by a government-supported union federation over local unions and by enactment, in 1968, of two new pieces of labor legislation which are considered by some to be among the toughest outside the Socialist bloc. The new legislation, which reduced permissible levels of benefits while giving management full discretionary power in most personnel decisions, went far beyond the early depoliticization to undercutting labor's economic power as well. These two restrictive increments in labor repression are reflected in substantial reductions in levels of industrial conflict during the mid- and late–1960s.

EXPORT-ORIENTED INDUSTRIALIZATION AND LABOR MOVEMENTS: STRUCTURAL TRANSFORMATION

Export-oriented industrialization has been associated with rapid and profound change in the employment and occupational structures of all four countries. Such changes have in turn affected the unity, strength, and militancy of labor movements. In this section, it is suggested that EOI-linked structural changes have demobilized labor movements from the standpoints of independent organization and strength in all four countries. In addition, it is argued that other structural changes relating to the degree of organizational and geographical concentration of the industrial workforce have tended to undercut private sector, enterprise-level authority, and thus to enhance the potential for labor militance in Singapore and South Korea, while further reinforcing localized labor controls in Hong Kong and Taiwan, and that this difference explains the greater recent industrial relations role of the state in the former two countries.

The literature on labor militancy in the United States and Western Europe has emphasized the following structural determinants of labor organization and strikes that are explored in this study: the extent of generation of a large employed proletariat, particularly during early periods when such a proletariat forms a relatively undifferentiated mass of semi-skilled workers;[31] the concentration of employment in large industrial firms, which often increases strike frequency and work days lost to industrial conflict;[32] and the size of the city in which industry is located, with higher rates of unionization and union concentration, as well as larger and more frequent strikes, in urban centers.[33] In addition, it has usually been found that high levels of unionization are supportive of both frequent and large strikes.[34] It is important to note in this regard that the dominant literature on the determinants of labor protest views labor mobilization into large or federated unions as a significant organizational resource for strikes. In the context of a liberal, pluralistic polity, where unions in fact act as relatively independent agents of labor, such a view is justified. On the other hand, in cases of government-controlled unions, such as one finds in many Third World countries, unions in particular may be transformed from resources into control structures that constrain rather than facilitate labor action. Thus, it is easy to understand the lack of relationship, or even the negative relationship between unionization levels and industrial conflict during the post-EOI periods of South Korea and Singapore, where authoritarian governments have transformed unions into arms of government labor policy. Bearing in mind this important difference in the political context of Asian labor, we now first examine EOI-related economic structural changes that have been found to be significantly related to labor mobilization and action in the West, and second, the consequences of such changes for Asian labor.

Western industrialization typically was associated with the emergence of a growing proletariat whose organization and community context encouraged class-based mobilization against employers or the state. It is clear that in all four Asian cases industrialization has created an ever-larger industrial labor force. Korea's manufacturing workforce grew from less than 2 percent of the total in the 1950s to over 20 percent by 1980 (table 7.3), with a corresponding increase in the "industrial" workforce from 9 percent in 1960 to 30 percent in 1979. In the case of Taiwan, the percentage of the labor force employed in manufacturing grew from 8 percent in the early 1950s to 29 percent in 1977, with an increase in the industrial percentage share from 18 percent to over 40 percent. While the percentage share of Hong Kong's manufacturing workforce already had increased to nearly 40 percent by 1961, its industrial workforce continued to grow from 52 percent to 57 percent between 1960 and 1979. That of Singapore rose from 16 percent to nearly 29 percent (the industrial workforce to 38) between 1957 and 1980. In all these cases, then, industrialization has been associated with rapid creation of an industrial workforce exceeding, in percentage terms, that of most core industrial powers. Despite this rapid expansion of an industrial proletariat, the efficacy and scale of industrial protest, as measured by the size and success of stoppages, have everywhere tended to decline over time.

One possible explanation for such decline in the power of organized labor relates to continuing direct political restrictions on collective action. Such an explanation is plausible in the case of South Korea, where labor restrictions grew stricter during the 1970s in response to periodic increases in labor militancy, as well as in that of Singapore, where effective state corporatist union structures were elaborated from 1970 on. Still, this explanation fails to explain *why* such state-level controls played so important a role in these two countries; in addition, it is inadequate in the cases of Taiwan and Hong Kong. Taiwanese repressive legislation has never been effectively implemented at the local level,[35] while Hong Kong's labor legislation has, if anything, become increasingly permissive from the standpoints of labor organization and action.[36] In both cases, enterprise-level labor controls have remained relatively effective without substantial state intervention.

A second set of explanations for reduced levels of militance relates to three further political factors which are outside the purview of this essay. First, in all cases except for brief periods in Korea, elite unity has been maintained, thus reducing the likelihood of oppositional mobilization of workers. Second, EOI has been based on and further reinforces the external political and military support of Western core powers (particularly the United States), thus strengthening established elites against challenges by domestic opposition groups. And third, EOI itself has been associated with clear improvements in levels of employment and public welfare, as well as with relatively egalitarian growth,[37] and in this way has bolstered the political legitimacy of ruling elites and the development strategies they pursue.

But beyond such socio-political explanations for labor peace, EOI itself has generated transformations in the industrial-occupational structure that have had important consequences for labor organization and protest. These structural changes, relating to an expanding secondary employment sector and differences in degree of employment concentration, more directly relate to the process of EOI development itself, and go far in explaining reduced levels of effective protest and differences among these countries in the extent to which labor controls have shifted from enterprise to state.

The Secondary Employment Sector

Everywhere, Asian EOI has been associated with a disproportionate expansion in jobs characterized by low skill, low wages, and minimal employment security. The latter is a consequence of extreme market vulnerability to short-term fluctuations in world markets for light consumer goods, and is best evidenced by the massive layoffs of workers in export-industries in all four countries during the mid–1970s recession.

Recruitment into this expanding manufacturing sector has centered primarily on young, unmarried women (see table 7.3). Virtually all those labor-intensive, export-oriented industries that grew most rapidly during this period (textiles, wearing apparel, footwear, electronics, plastics) employed predominantly female production workers. By 1970, over half of Hong Kong's manufacturing workers were female, while data for Taiwan show an increase in the female share of manufacturing employment from around 12 percent at the outset of EOI in the early 1960s to 43 percent in 1978. The corresponding increase for Korea was from over 26 percent in 1960 to nearly 40 percent in 1980, while the female percentage of total manufacturing employment in Singapore increased from over 22 percent in 1966, the beginning of the EOI period, to 46 percent in 1980. In all cases females now make up a larger proportion of the manufacturing labor force than in Japan or the United States.

The rapid expansion in employment of young, unmarried females in EOI manufacturing was based on a number of considerations. First, in part because their employment ordinarily provides a secondary rather than a primary family income, and because they do not support dependents, they may be hired at relatively low wages (Diamond, 1979). Second, their competence and discipline are guaranteed by childhood socialization, which emphasizes both job-relevant skills (e.g., fine needlework) and acquiescence to male authority. Finally, and of equal importance, they tend to view work as a temporary interlude between childhood on the one hand and marriage and motherhood on the other. Their resulting status as a "part-time proletariat"[38] has the further consequences of increasing workforce flexibility in these market-vulnerable industries, and of reducing seniority-based wage increments.

The creation of an increasingly dominant secondary employment sector tends to impede independent organizational efforts by unions and to ensure that unions may be controlled easily by agencies of the government. High rates of employment turnover and low levels of skill among production workers are associated with difficulties in local unionization efforts in the context of minimal and short-term commitment to job, employer, and employment in general. In addition, such efforts become increasingly dependent on leadership from outside the ranks of workers themselves. Lack of dynamic outside leadership, as in Hong Kong and Taiwan, represents a significant depressant on labor action. Conversely, in cases of extensive government control over more active national union federations, as in Korea and Singapore, this largely ensures government control over unionization efforts themselves, thus similarly undercutting the independent organizational base for effective protest. Thus may be explained the observed pattern of ever smaller and more easily contained stoppages in all four countries, as well as the relative success with which the governments of Korea and Singapore, where restrictive regulation has been more significant, have contained militance through controls at federation and national, rather than at branch and local, levels.

Employment Concentration

It still is necessary to explain why labor controls have shifted so decisively to the state level in Korea and Singapore, while enterprise-level economic authority has remained effective in Hong Kong and Taiwan. Perhaps the most important structural explanation for this contrast relates to the extent to which development in these countries has been differentially associated with employment concentration in large factories and cities, and the ways in which differences in concentration have in turn affected traditional economic authority, labor action, and thus labor regimes as well. In order to assess the degree to which EOI in the four countries has been associated with changes in the degree of organizational concentration of workers, two rather uncertain indicators have been used. The best single indicator of such concentration is the percentage of employees in large firms, especially in the manufacturing sector. The limited data available for this measure are presented in table 7.4, and suggest a decline in concentration during the 1970s in Hong Kong and Taiwan, and increased concentration since the early 1960s in Korea.

A second, less satisfactory measure of manufacturing employment concentration is obtained by dividing total manufacturing employment by total number of manufacturing enterprises for various years. Data for this indicator again suggest declining concentration from 1950 in Hong Kong and during the 1970s in Taiwan. On the other hand, they show increasing concentration in Singapore and Korea, with a temporary reversal in Singapore resulting from the massive retrenchments accompanying the 1974 recession.

The data thus suggest that in Taiwan and Hong Kong small-scale production has played a relatively greater role in industrialization than it has in either Korea or Singapore, and thus has resulted in a relatively greater organizational dispersion of the growing industrial proletariat. This difference may be explained in part by the greater importance of "lumpy" industrial capital investment in Singapore and South Korea than in Hong Kong and Taiwan. In Singapore, direct foreign investment by large multinational corporations has led to the emergence of a significant number of very large industrial plants, especially in electronics. Korean development has relied more extensively on foreign loans than on direct investment, but here the channeling of capital through government-controlled banks to well-established industrialists[39] has had the same effect. Conversely, investment in both Hong Kong and Taiwan has generally been based more on localized mobilization of savings by local entrepreneurs, and less on foreign or government savings.[40]

A second important dimension of employment concentration relates not so much to the massing of workers in large factories as to their

Table 7.4 Indicators of Manufacturing Employment Concentration by Country and Year

	Hong Kong		Taiwan	
Year	% employees in factories 200 persons[1]	average factory size[2]	% employees in factories 100 persons[3]	average factory size[4]
1950		53		
1951		49		
1952		47		
1953		46		10
1954		46		11
1955		44		12
1956		45		12
1957		45		12
1958				12
1959				12
1960		45		12
1961			42	15
1962				
1963		41		
1964	45	42		
1965	49	42		
1966	50	41	58	23
1967	48	39		28
1968	48	40		26
1969	46	40		32
1970	44	37		
1971	40	32	64	
1972	40	30		48
1973	38	28		44
1974	38	26		39
1975		22		37
1976		21		37
1977	35	20		36
1978	30	20		36
1979	29	21		35
1980	29	20	33	

Notes and Sources

1. 1964-1974: Social and Economic Trends: 1964-1974. Census and Statistics Department.

   1977: Census and Statistics Department, 1977 Census of Industry, cited in Nyaw and Chan (1982).

   1978-1980: Hong Kong Monthly Digest of Statistics.

2. 1950-1956: Commissioner of Labor, Annual Departmental Reports: cited in Szczepanik.

   1957, 1960, 1963: Commissioner of Labour, Annual Departmental Reports. (Only covers firms equipped with power-drive machinery and employing at least 20 manual workers and which are recorded and/or registered with Labour Department.)

   1964-1974: Social and Economic Trends, ibid.

   1975-1980: Hong Kong Monthly Digest of Statistics.

	South Korea		Singapore		
Year	% employees in factories stated size[5]	average factory size[6]	% of employed in factories stated size[7]	average factory size[8]	average factory size[9]
1950					
1951					
1952					
1953					
1954					
1955					
1956					
1957					
1958					
1959	33%/100	20			
1960				50	
1961				49	
1962				47	
1963	43/100; 34/200*			43	
1964				45	
1965				47	
1966	40%/200	38		47	50
1967				49	
1968				47	
1969				59	
1970		36		69	71
1971	54%/200	36		78	79
1972		41		88	89
1973				96	96
1974	74/100; 63/200*			95	95
1975			70%/100; 58%/200	80	80
1976					83
1977		72	59%/200		83
1978					83
1979					86
1980					86

*Korea Industrial Bank Mining and Manufacturing Census Reports. Includes manufacturing and mining.

3. From Ho (1978:378).

4. 1953-1961: Statistical Abstract of the Republic of China, 1962. Due to changed registration requirements, many small firms are omitted from the records after 1969, thus explaining the sudden increase in average firm size. A fairly reliable 1970's size trend begins in 1972.

5. 1959: Economic Statistics Yearbook.
   1966 and 1971: Hasan (1976:70).

6. 1959: Economic Statistics Yearbook.
   1966, 1970-1972: Hasan (1976).

7. 1978: Department of Statistics, Report on the Census of Industrial Production: 1978, cited in Nyaw and Chan (1982).

8. The Census of Industrial Production.

9. Singapore Yearbook of Statistics.

location in large cities. In the case of Korea, industrial development has centered largely in export-processing zones located near large cities, particularly Seoul and Inchon. Data for the 1960s[41] show that the Seoul Economic Region contained over 33 percent of the manufacturing workforce of the country in 1960, and 46 percent in 1970. Like Hong Kong, Singapore's urban concentration is assured by its status as a small city-state. In addition, however, the spatial concentration of Singapore's industrial workforce has been assured by the creation of self-sufficient worker communities including living quarters, nearby factories, and recreational and commercial facilities. The experience of Taiwan has been quite different, for industry there has been encouraged to locate in rural areas; as a consequence industrialization has increasingly generated employment in small towns,[42] thus minimizing the dualism (Koo, 1976) so evident in South Korean development.[43] The only significant exception to this pattern, noted earlier, is the development of export-processing zones, which accounted for only 10 percent of export manufacture during the mid–1970s.

Such differences in employment concentration have differentially affected community structure in the four countries as well. Despite a high level of urban concentration, employment dispersal in Hong Kong's small firms has perpetuated a pattern of ethnically delineated, class-heterogeneous communities. Singapore's increasingly consolidated manufacturing structure has been associated with the growth of class-homogeneous working-class communities, especially as the government increasingly has replaced dilapidated ethnic quarters with public housing estates for specified income groups. A consequence of this policy is the massing of large numbers of factory workers and their families in high-rise accommodations near factories. A similar emergence of predominantly working-class communities has paralled the development of export-processing zones in Korea, while the greater rural dispersal of industry has had the opposite effect in Taiwan, especially in reinforcing joint-family controls over the labor force.[44]

Earlier research has suggested a positive relationship between employment concentration in large plants and urban areas and levels of militancy (though not necessarily its size or effectiveness).[45] To the extent these two forms of concentration are associated with a by-passing of traditional or personal forms of enterprise-level authority, their link with militancy may depend crucially on whether state imposed labor controls are instituted to supplant declining local ones. In the Asian context, such compensatory state controls have been implemented far more readily than in Western countries, and have thus preempted labor militance where growing employment concentration otherwise might have encouraged it. Thus, such concentration in Singapore and South Korea has been accompanied not so much by rising militancy as by a continuing and clear shift of labor controls from enterprise to state levels. Conversely, Hong Kong's small firms and localized, class-heterogeneous dialect districts, and Taiwan's rural towns, continue to ensnare workers in a web of kinship and personal obligation that guarantees their continuing loyal service for minimal reward.[46] It is important to note that even in South Korea, where repressive state labor controls have not always been successful in containing protest, such protest has, as in the other cases, been small in scale, largely defensive, poorly organized, and easily contained.

LATE EOI AND LABOR

In the context of rapid growth in the secondary labor sector, a fundamental problem facing organized labor is the lack of an independent, mobilizing, federation center that can assist in local organizing efforts as well as inform, sustain, and broaden localized conflicts, and thus increase the size and effectiveness of protest. Such a center is a particularly important resource for collective action among low-skill industrial production workers in large industrial plants, where worker solidarity is likely to be especially low.[47] In the cases of Hong Kong and Taiwan, labor peace has been ensured by largely inert labor federations and effective localized economic authority, although increasing conflict in Taiwan's export-processing zones has enhanced somewhat the coercive role of the previously moribund Chinese Federation of Labor. In Singapore and Korea, on the other hand, government control over national labor federations may play a highly significant role in ensuring that the growing potential for militance engendered by increasing employment concentration is accompanied by tight countervailing restraint on the generalization of localized disputes.

The significance of national labor federations during the 1970s has transcended their role of maintaining industrial peace, important though that role remains. Equally important now is their new "productivity" role in the context of late EOI. If early EOI development is based on the mobilization of cheap, disciplined, low-skilled labor for manufacturing, the logic of such development eventually erodes the labor supply that made it possible. At that point, upward wage pressure begins to threaten EOI itself by encouraging investors to look to other cheap-labor countries for new export platforms. By the early 1970s, all these countries had begun to experience growing labor shortages. With the exception of laissez-faire Hong Kong, the countries have sought to meet this problem through government efforts to upgrade the skills of workers and to shift investment toward higher technology fields, especially in electronics and basic engineering. In some cases, this has led to the attempted creation of corporatist union structures as means through which to achieve a fuller economic mobilization of the workforce through training programs and workforce stabilizations, following recognition that effective labor control could more fully be achieved through revitalized unions than through repression and union demobilization.[48]

In general, one would expect such a corporatist solution to be adopted where the state already plays a significant role in labor force management and where continued suppression of potential militiancy is necessary, but where elite unity ensures that revitalized unions will not be turned by opposition groups against employers or the state. That all of these conditions were met quite early in Singapore is clear. By 1970, militant and leftist unions had been deregistered and political opponents jailed or silenced. In the context of growing labor shortages and high labor force turnover, as well as of increasing employment concentration in large foreign factories, it became apparent quickly that vigorous, controlled unions were a necessary basis for stabilizing and controlling the labor force. Thus, in contrast to earlier largely repressive measures that led to a drastic decline in union membership until 1970, the ruling People's Action Party embarked on substantial new efforts to reinvigorate the union structure by offering a wide range of incentives and benefits for union members. Most important among these was the creation of retail, transportation, insurance, and other cooperative member services, along with a number of other direct benefits. In response to these service and benefit incentives, union membership climbed rapidly during the 1970s, especially in those unions most extensively involved in the new programs. In the context of subsequent efforts to introduce higher technology industry during the late 1970s, the national union federation became the major vehicle for productivity campaigns, training programs, and other efforts to further enhance the contribution of labor to development.

The move toward revitalization of a state-sponsored union structure came later in Korea, where less effective elimination of oppositional groups created a continuing threat that political liberalization and union mobilization might once again challenge ruling groups. Here, too, the growing need to upgrade skills and productivity, and a resulting desire for more effective structures through which to simultaneously control and mobilize the workforce led to a government-sponsored unionization drive starting in 1974 under the umbrella of the Federation of Korean Trade Unions (FKTU). Unlike Singapore's corporatist success, however, and largely because of elite disunity and inadequate control over FKTU leadership, the corporatist experiment was at least temporarily abandoned during the 1979–80 national political crisis.

Taiwan started from a position of less state intervention in industrial relations and moved far more hesitantly toward corporatist restructuring of the labor movement. Nevertheless, growing labor shortages and a drive toward higher technology industry encouraged the Taiwanese government, like its counterparts in Singapore and Korea, to initiate beginning in the mid–1970s a tentative revitalization of the previously moribund Chinese Federation of Labor.

It should be noted that authoritarian-corporatist, rather than more liberal, alternatives to repression have in part reflected a continuing or increased need for containment of labor protest. This is especially clear in the cases of Singapore and Korea, where increased militancy during the 1974–75 recession signalled a need for continued tight labor controls. Even in Taiwan, recent increases in labor disputes in the export-processing zones have increased the need for tighter state-level labor controls despite continued docility on the part of most industrial workers in other sectors.

CONCLUSION: EOI DEVELOPMENT AND DEPENDENT LABOR MOVEMENTS

Earlier Western industrialization saw the rise of organized labor as an autonomous, if sometimes severely repressed, effort on the part of working people to regain a measure of control over their work lives and to counter the exploitation they experienced at work. The resource base for their organizational efforts lay in a heritage of craft guilds, friendly societies, and working-class communities with their own class leadership, press, and cultural traditions.[49] The evolution of Western working-class organizations and consciousness finds few parallels in the Asian countries dealt with here. In the cases of Korea and Singapore, early pre-industrial government intervention in Asian labor relations reflected a heightened political mobilization of labor that preceded rather than followed its economic mobilization. This earlier political intervention, along with a greater state role in development planning, later were to provide a basis for pre-emptive corporatist state efforts to organize government-controlled labor organizations as instruments of development policy. As a consequence, labor movements, rather than flowing from the structural transformations of industrial change and following an evolutionary cycle of autonomous class formation and consciousness, were dependent from the very start on leadership by outside political groups (whether oppositional or official), and never were left to develop their own modes of organization and action (see Spalding, 1977, ch. 4, for a similar argument regarding Latin American labor movements).

In the cases of post–1949 Hong Kong and Taiwan, an initial lack of unified political mobilization obviated the need for as harsh political intervention in labor relations, while subsequent economic structural changes have further discouraged oppositional labor solidarity.

But the speed with which Asian industrialization has occurred, and the power of political elites in controlling labor's response to this economic change derived from the peculiar political and economic linkages of these countries to the world system. EOI has been most successful in those societies whose deep economic links to the West and Japan have been sustained by strong political bonds. Hong Kong's colonial status, and the political-military client status of Singapore, South Korea, and Taiwan *vis-à-vis* the West have provided not only the political security necessary for capital and technology flows from core countries, but support as well for ruling political groups against domestic opposition.

In addition, the peculiar patterns of EOI development itself has undercut further the independent power of labor through its association with a disproportionate expansion in the secondary employment sector, which increasingly comprises a temporary proletariat of young unmarried women whose docility ultimately is guaranteed by subordination to patriarchal family authority.[50] Thus, even in cases where industrialization has encouraged employment concentration in large factories and cities (thus enhancing the potential for militance and the need for state intervention), it has ensured at the same time that such protest would be ineffectual and easily contained. Finally, EOI has generated pressures at later stages of development for a government-sponsored reinvigoration of labor unions through creation of corporatist structures that simultaneously address the needs for control and economic mobilization.

One probably must conclude that the political economy of Asian export-oriented industrialization has severely undercut the organizational power of labor. To the extent that the new Asian industrial working class is to act as an agent of social change its power will derive, at least in the short run, largely from its ability to disrupt, provoke, or support external forces, rather than to engage in autonomous social action.

NOTES

This research was supported by grants from the Research Foundation of the State University of New York and the National Science Foundation. I am grateful to Richard Abrams, Richard Barrett, Hagen Koo, Janet Salaff, and Charles Stephenson for helpful comments on an earlier draft of the paper.

1. World Bank, 1981. *World Development Report* (Washington, World Bank).
2. World Bank, 1981.
3. Edward K. Y. Chen, *Hyper-Growth in Asian Economies: A Comparative Study of Hong Kong, Japan, Korea, Singapore, and Taiwan* (New York, 1981).
4. World Bank, 1981.
5. Republic of China, Directorate-General of Budget, Accounting and Statistics, *Monthly Bulletin of Labor Statistics*.
6. Walter Galenson, ed., *Economic Growth and Structural Change in Taiwan: The Postwar Experience of the Republic of China* (Ithaca, 1979).

7. World Bank, 1981.

8. Edward Shorter and Charles Tilly, *Strikes in France: 1830–1968* (London, 1974); John D. McCarthy and Mayer N. Zald, "Resource Mobilization and Social Movements: A Partial Theory," *American Journal of Sociology* 82:6 (1977), pp. 1212–1241.

9. E. H. Phelps-Brown, "The Hong Kong Economy: Achievements and Prospects," in Keith Hopkins, ed., *Hong Kong: The Industrial Colony* (Hong Kong, 1971).

10. Judith Agassi, "Social Structure and Social Stratification in Hong Kong," in Ian C. Jarvie and Joseph Agassi, eds., *Hong Kong: A Society in Transition* (New York, 1968).

11. Edward F. Szczepanik, *The Economic Growth of Hong Kong* (London, 1958).

12. Chen, *Hyper-Growth in Asian Economies.*

13. Sang-Chul Suh, *Growth and Structural Changes in the Korean Economy: 1910–1940* (Cambridge, 1978).

14. Hyung-Yoon Byun, Soon Chough, and Ki-Jun Jeon, "Korea," in Shinichi Ichimura, ed., *The Economic Development of East and Southeast Asia* (Honolulu, 1975).

15. Kuo-Shu Liang and Teng-Hui Lee, "Taiwan," in Shinichi Ichimura, ed., *The Economic Development of East and Southeast Asia.*

16. Ian M. D. Little, "An Economic Reconnaissance," in W. Galenson, ed., *Economic Growth and Structural Change in Taiwan.*

17. Thomas B. Gold, "Entrepreneurs, State and World System in Taiwan," in Edwin Winkler, ed., *Authoritarianism and Dependency in Taiwan* (Armonk, N.Y., 1983).

18. John C. Fei and Gustav Ranis, "A Model of Growth and Employment in the Open Dualistic Economy: The Cases of Korea and Taiwan," *Journal of Development Studies* 11:2 (1975), pp. 32–63.

19. Liang and Lee, 1975.

20. Chen, *Hyper Growth in Asian Economies*, p. 173.

21. Robert Snow, "Southeast Asia in the World System," paper presented at the 1980 Annual Meeting of the Association for Asian Studies, March 21–23, 1980, Washington, D.C.

22. Frederic C. Deyo, *Dependent Development and Industrial Order* (New York, 1981).

23. H. A. Turner et al., *The Last Colony: But Whose? A Study of the Labour Movement, Labour Market and Labour Relations in Hong Kong* (Cambridge, 1980).

24. Janet W. Salaff, *Working Daughters of Hong Kong: Filial Piety or Power in the Family* (Cambridge, 1981).

25. Turner, 1980.

26. George Ogle, "South Korea," in Albert Blum, ed., *International Handbook of Industrial Relations* (Westport, Conn., 1979).

27. Republic of Singapore, *Yearbook of Statistics, 1967–1980*; Deyo, 1981.

28. Robert Snow, "The Rise of Export-oriented Industrialization in the Philippines: The Changing Role of the Philippines in the International Division of Labor and the Role of the Subcontract Bourgeoisie," in Norman Owen, ed., *The Philippine Economy and the United States* (Ann Arbor, forthcoming).

29. Little, 1979.

30. United States, Bureau of Labor Statistics, *Labor Law and Practice in the Republic of China (Taiwan)*, Report number 404 (Washington, 1972).

31. William H. Form, "The Internal Stratification of the Working Class: System Involvement of Auto Workers in Four Countries," *American Sociological Review* 38 (1973), pp. 697–711.

32. David W. Britt, and Omer Galle, "Structural Antecedents of the Shape of Strikes: A Comparative Analysis," *American Sociological Review* 39 (1974), pp. 642–51; Shorter and Tilly, 1974; James R. Lincoln, "Community Structure and Industrial Conflict: An Analysis of Strike Activity in SMSAs," *American Sociological Review* 43 (1978), pp. 199–220.

33. Shorter and Tilly, 1974; Lincoln, 1978.

34. David Snyder, "Institutional Setting and Industrial Conflict: Comparative Analyses of France, Italy and the United States," *American Sociological Review* 40:3 (June 1975), pp. 259–78; Britt and Galle, 1974; Shorter and Tilly, 1974; Lincoln, 1978.

35. United States, Bureau of Labor Statistics, 1972.

36. Turner, 1980.

37. Pang Eng Fong, "Growth, Inequality and Race in Singapore," *International Labour Review* 111 (1975), pp. 15–28; Irma Adelman and Sherman Robinson, *Income Distribution Policy in Developing Countries: A Case Study of Korea* (Stanford, 1978); Richard Barrett and Martin K. Whyte, "Dependency Theory and Taiwan: A Deviant Case Analysis," *American Journal of Sociology* (March 1982), pp. 1064–1089; Ronald Hsia and Larry Chau, "Industrialization and Income Distribution in Hong Kong," *International Labour Review* 117 (July–August 1978), pp. 465–79; Gary Fields, "Employment, Income Distribution, and Economic Growth in Seven Small, Open Economies," paper presented at the American Economic Association Meetings, New York, December 1982.

38. Hill Gates, "Dependency and the Part-time Proletariat in Taiwan," *Modern China* 5 (1979), pp. 381–408.

39. Kyong-Dong Kim, "Political Factors in the Formation of the Entrepreneurial Elite in South Korea," *Asian Survey* 16 (1976), pp. 465–477.

40. Little, 1979, p. 476; Parvez Hasan and D. C. Rao, *Korea: Policy Issues for Long-Term Development* (Baltimore and London, 1979).

41. B. N. Song, "Production Structure of the Korean Economy: International and Historical Comparisons," *Econometrics* 45 (January 1977), pp. 147–162.

42. Samuel P. S. Ho, "Decentralized Industrialization and Rural Development: Evidence from Taiwan," *Economic Development and Cultural Change* 28 (October 1979), pp. 77–96.

43. Barrett and Whyte, 1982.

44. Bernard Gallin and Rita Gallin, "Socioeconomic Life in Rural Taiwan: Twenty Years of Development and Change," *Modern China* 8:2 (April 1982), pp. 205–246.

45. Shorter and Tilly, 1974; Lincoln, 1978.

46. A. W. Djao, "Traditional Chinese Culture in the Small Factory of Hong Kong," *Journal of Contemporary Asia* 11:4 (1981), pp. 413–25; Richard Stites, "Small-Scale Industry in Yingge, Taiwan," *Modern China* 8:2 (April 1982), pp. 247–79.

47. Shorter and Tilly, 1974.
48. Galenson, 1979.
49. E. P. Thompson, *The Making of the English Working Class* (New York, 1963).
50. Salaff, 1981.

8

Workers' Self Management and the Transition to Socialism

James F. Petras and Rita Carroll-Seguin

INTRODUCTION

The past decade has witnessed a growing interest in workers' self-management within the international labor movement. The debate over self-management has spread from the advanced industrial countries to a number of newly industrializing Third World countries. Several factors account for this growing consciousness within the working class: (1) dissatisfaction with the consequences of nationalization of the means of production and growing stratification of society; (2) the increasing discontent among workers with the alienating conditions of work and the authoritarian relations of production; (3) the rising levels of political education and the decreasing preoccupation with issues of wages and salaries; (4) the increasing understanding by labor that rapid technological changes and their introduction by hierarchical managerial authorities can lead to permanent displacement, hence the need for greater labor control; (5) in the context of ascending class conflict, workers observe the tendency for capital to disinvest, to run down plant and capital and to flee to "safe havens" making workers' control a necessity to prevent the dismantlement of enterprises; (6) and finally the increasing transnationalization of production and the increased tendency for corporate capital to relocate plants or reallocate investments has demonstrated the inadequacy of orthodox trade unionism and increased worker pressure for control over investments and decisions affecting plant location.

This forward momentum toward worker self-management has received severe jolts and backward pushes in various countries and historical periods. The violent seizure of power by terrorist rightist regimes in a number of Third World countries has led to the dismantling of workers' councils and repression of their discussion. In these circumstances, the focus of the struggle has shifted toward more immediate issues directed toward economic and political survival and elementary democratic demands. In the advanced capitalist countries, the combination of deepening economic crisis and, in some cases, rightist regimes has forced the workers' movement onto the track of defensive struggles, organizing against restrictions on trade union rights. While the initial responses to dictatorial regimes and economic crisis may appear to put the issue on the back burner, struggles that emerge as defensive responses may combine with efforts to enlarge the direct role of the workers over the production process. In fact, since the current crisis is profoundly structural and systemic, the labor movement's struggle against deteriorating conditions logically leads to reopening the issue of control over the production process. In this context, the issue of workers' self-management can re-emerge in a more dynamic context linked to a more volatile struggle against a declining social system unable to meet the elementary needs of labor.

The current context for workers' self-management is not uniformly bleak. In Greece, France, and Sweden governing parties are programmatically committed to some form of self-management. In Spain and Italy there continues to be constant syndicalist pressure to increase the role of labor within the sphere of control over production. In Third World countries, in countries as diverse as Nicaragua, Iran, Angola, and China, discussion of forms of worker participation have been broached in the recent period. In the eastern bloc, apart from the continuing discussion and practices in Yugoslavia, sections of the Polish workers' movement have raised the issue of self-management in a programmatic fashion. The discussion of workers' self-management in an increasingly global context suggests that the political conditions for its practical application have arrived. Dynamic capitalist penetration and the ensuing contradictions that have emerged in recent decades have transformed most areas of the world economy sufficiently to allow for the development of new forms of social organization of production.

Yet workers' self-management does not evolve out of the heads of idealistic thinkers. Nor is it the mere derivative of large-scale economic processes. Many efforts have been made to establish workers' self-management in isolated enterprises, largely through the initiative of individuals who were concerned with the plight of workers made redundant through plant closings or who assume that successful small-scale experiments can become pilot projects or models to successfully convince others of the rationality and practicality of workers' control.[1] A good example is a program in the General Foods plant in Topeka, Kansas. The program was an economic success—workers handled the responsibilities given to them, production increased, and labor discipline improved. But when labor made overtures toward expanding its area of responsibility, threatening several layers of management, the program was abandoned.[2] A general pattern exists in these small-scale experiments: where they are successful they threaten management and are quickly dismantled; where management retains control, little effective participation takes place and workers lose interest. Kelley (1968) discusses this phenomenon in the Glacier Metal Company experiment in England. Despite halfhearted attempts to solicit worker input and to change job titles, flattening the bureaucratic hierarchy, traditional manager-subordinate relations remained.[3] Sufficient time has elapsed to note that isolated examples of individual experiments have few sustained effects.

In the following discussion of self-management we will focus on a number of aspects of the issue: (1) the contextual determinants of self-management and its long-term prospects; (2) self-management and the transition to socialism; and (3) general problems of self-management focusing in particular on the controversies accompanying it in the context of a market economy.

ALGERIA

Introduction of Self-Management from Below

Self-management in Algeria developed out of the disorganization and lack of central authority that were part of the immediate aftermath of the Algerian independence struggle.[4] The French had withdrawn after an eight-year battle (1954–1962) leaving behind empty houses, unmanned shops, factories, and farms. They also left empty many of the administrative posts in government and most of the technical positions in industry and commerce. The exodus brought the economy to a standstill and caused massive unemployment.[5] At the same time, because the struggle had no clear class base, no coherent Algerian nationalist group had emerged to man the state apparatus. The revolutionary army, the FLN, consisted of a broad-based coalition of elements all vying for state control. Within this context, and without any direction from the state, workers throughout the country spontaneously took control of farms, factories, and shops.

The government was slow to recognize what was essentially a grass roots movement. Many factories and apartments had been vacant since April of 1962; takeovers began toward the end of June. It wasn't until August 24 that the FLN government, the *Executif Provisiore*, published a decree, "... allowing prefects to requisition abandoned industrial and agricultural enterprises and to nominate managers to administer them until the return of the owners."[6] The *Décrets de Mars* was issued by Ben Bella (who had emerged at the center of power by September 1962) the following March. In essence, it gave the government unlimited power of nationalization. At first the government only responded to UGTA (*Union General des Travailleuers*) organized labor protests or legitimated pre-existing worker management firms. Later it began a more systematic attempt to bring the dynamic sectors of the economy under state control without introducing workers' control.

Organization of Workers' Councils

The UGTA was responsible for organizing the social sector. It decided that the "*comité de gestation*," or "workers' council," was the organization form best suited to its goal of socialized production. A "Comité de Gestation" was established to advise workers on how to set up councils. Each firm was to be organized in the Yugoslav pattern. There was to be an assembly of all qualified workers which, if it were large enough, would elect a council which, in turn, would elect a committee or board of directors. In practice these groups were nothing more than rubber stamp organizations. Apart from electing the council, the assembly's only function was to vote upon plans and proposals generated elsewhere, in the beginning by the board of directors, later by government agencies.

The crucial factor was the knowledgeability and organizational capacity of the workers and this varied greatly from the masses of illiterate agricultural day workers to the small urban proletariat. Membership and election rules were never uniformly enforced. In many cases the "annual" elections were held only once and in some cases not at all. The board of directors was dominated by the state-appointed director, who was the legally acknowledged representative of the state's interests. The director was the chairman and secretary of every committee, controlling what issues were discussed and how the discussion was entered into the minutes. The director decided how membership laws were to be interpreted; in agricultural firms, for example, where seasonal workers were excluded from the assembly by law, the director could, by altering the interpretation, either pack the assembly with supporters or eliminate enemies.

Spread of Self-Management

By September the UGTA was ready to move into the countryside, where it ran into conflict with the military.

The army, the FLN, and the UGTA all attempted to harness the spontaneous seizures and organize them into a national movement, each for its own reasons. Only the UGTA had a clearly socialist position. The army controlled much of the western part of the country and, while it shared the UGTA's desire not to let the country fall back into the hands of a foreign bourgeoisie, it was in no way wedded to the concept of socialized agricultural production. Army leaders wanted to distribute individual plots of land to ex-combatants in order to secure their political base. In addition, some 2 million land-hungry peasants were returning from French "regroupment camps"[7] and army leaders were in favor of distributing land to them individually. Where self-management committees had formed, often on the largest, most modern farms best suited to collective operation, the committees were dissolved and the workers forcibly removed.[8] Thus the UGTA's efforts were limited to a tiny portion of the countryside.

The spread of workers' self-management was also limited in the industrial sector. Most of the abandoned factories and shops were in the competitive sector: small firms operating on a labor-intensive basis with very low profit margins. The growth poles of Algerian industry, natural gas and the petrochemical industry, were owned by the French government and by the multinationals. They remained unscathed by both the war and its aftermath.

From the beginning the state worked to restrict self-management to the least profitable, least productive sectors. When pressured in the latter part of his rule, Ben Bella increased the self-managed sector with a wave of nationalizations intended to increase popular support. However, most of these were tiny shops, small restaurants, and motels. There was no pattern to these nationalizations and, in the end, they formed an insignificant part of the total economy.

The economy was clearly divided into four sectors, two private and two social. The private sector was controlled in part by the Algerian petty bourgeoisie who had purchased many of the small shops and restaurants from the colonists on the eve of independence. Second, multinational corporations controlled all of the larger privately owned firms including the textile, metal, and petrochemical industries. In the social sectors there were those firms which were operated by the workers and those administrated by representatives of the state, called "*sociétés nationales*." During the first two years, all *sociétés nationales* were created by the conversion of worker-managed firms. Later, the government nationalized many profitable industries and immediately set them up as state-managed firms. Compensation often accompanied this second wave of nationalization with foreign loans supplying the funds. The pattern which evolved included the following sequence: as nationalization progressed from the shops of the petty bourgeoisie to the firms controlled by foreign capital, efficient, capital-intensive industries were managed directly by the state while the least modern, labor-intensive firms were abandoned by state bureaucrats and left for the workers to control.

Weaknesses of Algerian Self-Management

To maintain a system of self-management labor must control the state. In Algeria, labor struggled against a bureaucratic elite bent on turning the social sector into a state capitalist one. The working class and the revolutionary cadres lost the struggle because they never controlled the state. At the top administrative level where policies were created, 43 percent of the employees had been part of the previous colonial administration. At the intermediate level among those persons in charge of policy execution and routine decision making, 77 percent were ex-colonial administrators. Only at the lowest levels of government were there large numbers of FLN members and many of these positions merely paid for the political support of individual leaders.[9]

Almost immediately the UGTA and the committees entered into a losing battle against the growing tendencies toward autocratic leadership by Ben Bella and the FLN. The government began to preempt workers' control. Committees established after October were state-appointed, not elected by workers. The *Décretes de Mars* seemed to outline a socialist ideology to underpin the takeovers. In point of fact, however, only legal structures were provided; monetary and organizational support were never forthcoming. Self-management atrophied, leaving room for Boumedienne to introduce what was obviously state capitalism after he ousted Bella on June 19, 1965.

The state further weakened self-management by controlling access to capital: "The reasons for creating some form of integrated financial and marketing organization lay, initially, with a quite rational desire to integrate the socialist sector.... But the mechanisms created on this basis soon came to determine the total operation of the *comités*, making a farce of their nominal autonomy."[10] ONRA (*Office National de la Reforme Algaire*) and its subsidiaries CCRA (*Coopratifis de la Reforme Algaire*) in agriculture and the BCA (*Banque Centrale d'Algerie*) controlled revenue and credits for the socialist sector. In practice this meant that firms, already heavily in debt because of massive capital flight and destruction of capital goods that had taken place in the months before independence, were starved for capital, unable to get out of debt, unable to reach full production, and unable to increase wages. The councils were thus left open for criticism by the supporters of state capitalism on the grounds that they were inefficient. In reality it is clear that the rate of absolute exploitation actually increased under self-management.[11]

The nature of the original struggle, guerilla warfare as opposed to industrial class conflict, meant that the most committed, organized members of any would-be workers' movement toward a socialist transformation had just completed an eight-year stay in the countryside as the left wing element of the FLN. On the other hand, those who instituted workers' control were the least class-conscious workers who had stayed in the employ of the French colonizers. Workers lost interest in self-management when they were unable to obtain their primary goal: increased salaries. Large numbers of unemployed were never incorporated into the working class and were never organized, giving the self-managed sector almost no power base of popular support.

Reversal of the Reforms

In 1962 Ben Bella outlawed both the Communist and the Socialist parties. He also attempted to bring the UGTA and radical elements of the FLN under control. When he was unable to do so he merely eliminated UGTA leaders from the legislature and replaced them with his own supporters. This left the UGTA paralyzed until 1965. Local unions would strike for higher wages which government-appointed national leaders would not support. Through 1963, Bella continued to eliminate elements within the government which supported self-management.

When Bella was ousted, Boumedienne made room for the further collapse of the self-managed sector by abandoning it to market forces.[12] Shrinkage in the self-managed sector was nevertheless accompanied by expansion of the state sector. First, Boumedienne returned a number of small worker-managed shops to their previous owners, his petty bourgeoisie supporters. Next, the regime nationalized transportation, insurance, banking, and petrochemical distribution. It gained control of most of the foreign trade sector and many of the oil and natural gas related industries. These firms were brought under the direct control of state managers, their organization and operation excluding labor's participation in management.

In agriculture, the cumbersome and inefficient central bureaucracy was dismantled. However, the same set of bureaucrats took charge of the newly decentralized structures. Successful self-managed firms in construction and transport which had been in existence since the first days of independence were reorganized. The committees became powerless advisory organs. The same thing happened to every other firm in the self-managed sector large enough to pique much bureaucratic interest.

During much of 1967 union leaders and socialist members of government were imprisoned or went into exile. By the middle of 1967 UGTA leaders met in secret only, forming the nucleus of a clandestine workers' party. By 1968 state capitalism was firmly entrenched and any progress toward socialism was reversed.

Self-management in Algeria was instituted from below by workers and farmers in the period immediately following liberation. Using the Yugoslav experience as a guide, progressive elements within the government attempted, after the fact, to organize what was essentially a grass roots movement. However, the scope of self-management was limited in several ways. The state never fully supported a transition to socialism. Sectoral conflict among members of the government precluded the widespread organization of the agricultural sector. Legislation regarding the implementation of self-management was never uniformly enforced. Firms were not introduced into the self-managed sector in any systematic fashion. Only the least profitable, labor-intensive firms were represented. Credit and supplies were virtually unobtainable. Though production increased, the rate was slow enough to allow the new national bourgeoisie to blame the sector for the country's economic problems, supplying the ideological justification for the devolution of self-management into state capitalism.

CHILE

The Chilean example presents a high degree of labor participation at all levels of firm management. When workers in Chile seized the first factories they were acting from a long tradition of labor organization, electoral democracy, and state intervention in the economy. Firms in the social sector were managed jointly by state and labor representatives. Unlike the firms managed by Algerian workers, Chile's social sector contained the most dynamic sectors of industry and thus presented possibilities for real improvement in workers' living conditions. Of course, there were both external and internal constraints upon the development of industrial democracy. The history of trade unionism, so necessary in that it provided a base of organized support, carried with it an ideology which limited the participation of some members to the level of economic concerns. Externally, contradictions in Chilean society—Chile's democratic tradition which the left had utilized for decades, culminating in the election of a socialist government—precluded the forced ejection of bourgeois elements from the political arena. These elements were thus able to topple the regime. Once supporters of workers' councils lost control of the state, it was not long before they were completely dismantled.

Preconditions for Successful Implementation of Co-Management

Chile's labor organizations first developed in the late nineteenth century among miners. By the early twentieth century, several trade unions existed and a number of wider-based, more radical organizations were developing, for example, FOCH (Federacion Obrero de Chile) which was established in 1909. The first labor code was enacted in 1924 legalizing unions and strikes. Other aspects of the code were crucial to the later development of participatory democracy. Separate blue and white collar unions were created, preventing white collar workers from becoming elite union representatives. Paid union staffs were prohibited and officials, elected for a maximum of one year, had to remain at their jobs. Collective bargaining was allowed at the plant level only. Federations and strike funds were illegal. These last two measures were created in a futile attempt to keep unions weak. This attempt was only partially successful. While, perhaps, the measures retarded the development of a nationwide organization, they also hindered bureaucratic and stratification, promoting instead the involvement of the rank and file. The code also instituted profit sharing. Unions were legally entitled to 10 percent of the firm's profits. Five percent served as a wage supplement; the other five as a union fund, giving the unions a monetary base independent of the government. Until the late 1960s, most union demands were economistic, namely, they demanded higher wages. Still, the period 1958–1965 is one of increasing labor militancy. Union membership doubled. The annual number of legal strikes rose steadily from 120 in 1958 to 723 in 1965.[13]

The government's role in the economy began in a massive effort to promote import-substitution industrialization and slowly increased until, by 1970, the public sector accounted for 46.7 percent of all value added in the economy.[14] State control of industry and the nationalization of private sectors was not introduced by Allende. The initial attempts at self-management also predate him. The Unidad Popular government reacted somewhat ambivalently toward the growing movement to change social relations from below as it caused tensions between Socialist and Christian Democratic (petty bourgeois) elements within the government.[15]

Introduction of Workers' Self-Management

The first worker-owned and state-owned/worker-managed firms were actually created while Frei was in office. However, they do not represent a commitment to socialized production on the part of the government. Rather, the government allowed the social sector to expand only in response to worker protests. Only 22 small worker-owned firms were established but they were enough to encourage increased militancy among workers in the state sector. The first spontaneous factory seizures occurred in the last two years of the Frei regime. "All had less than 80 members . . . and each was a firm where the owner had abandoned the factory or the firm had gone bankrupt."[16] By the end of Frei's term in 1969, 30 such enterprises had been reorganized as state-owned/worker-managed firms, bringing the total number of firms in the state sector up to 110.

The change from the Frei to the Allende government greatly enhanced the promotion of workers' control. By September 1972 the number of state-owned/worker-managed firms had risen to 100 and by September 1973 it stood at 120 (see Table 8.1). At the same time a national organization had formed, the National Federation of Producer Cooperatives, to which 75 percent of the employees in the cooperative sector belonged. But at that point there was still a long way to go before socialist productive relations would be established. Though it was expanding, the social sector still represented only a small segment of the working class.

The social sector expanded using five legal mechanisms. The first two, intervention and requisition, were in existence prior to Allende's victory but rarely enacted. In both cases the state stepped in and operated firms because of actual or threatened declines in production. Intervention gave the state-appointed manager more power than requisition, especially over the firm's finances. The state usually intervened in response to actions taken by owners: lockouts, destruction or sale of capital goods, or outright capital flight. In many cases labor acted with the intention of forcing intervention, knowing they could, through increased agitation, pressure the state into appointing a director of their choosing. Third, the state sector expanded through the outright expropriation of the country's natural resources from multinational corporations, one of the acts which prompted international capital to organize efforts to cripple the economy and hastened the regime's demise.[17] Fourth, new firms were created and run solely by the workers. Although only eight such enterprises were ever officially created, many more were in operation awaiting final approval by the fall of the Allende government. Finally, the state, in conjunction with workers, purchased firms from owners anxious to leave a climate they perceived as less than hospitable to private property.

The *Normas Basicas*

To understand the forms industrial democracy took in Chile it is necessary to know what organizational patterns and structures emerged. To measure real participation it is also necessary to be concerned with the variety of contexts into which these structures were inserted. The manner in which the state and the workers managed firms in the social sector became the subject of a joint CUT (*Central Unica de Trabajadores*)[18] government commission which issued a set of guidelines (without force of law) during June of 1971. Called the *Normas Basicas*, these guidelines suggested that the decision-making bodies within a firm in the state sector should be comprised of both state and worker representatives. The administrative council, the principal decision-making body, was to consist

Table 8.1 Growth of the State Sector during the Allende Regime (November 4, 1970, to September 11, 1973)

Year	Number of State Enterprises	Number of State Enterprises in the Industrial Sector	Industrial Production in State Sector as Percentage of Total Industrial Production	Industrial Employment in State Sector as Percentage of Total Industrial Employment
1970	43	30	11.8	6.5
1973	420	270	40.0	30.0

Source: Espinosa & Zimbalist, 1978:42, 49, 50.

of 11 members. Six were to be from the government and five were to be elected from among workers' ranks by a general assembly of all workers. Three of the five labor representatives had to be blue collar workers. Labor representatives received no compensation for their services, served a short term, and could be recalled at any time by a majority vote of the general assembly. In reality, the 6–5 split actually favored the workers. Government representatives were often absent from the bi-weekly meetings and in many instances the representatives were selected from among the ranks of the workers.

Although more than 80 percent of the firms in the social sector had elected a functioning administrative council by the time of Allende's overthrow, a wide variation existed in the application of the *Normas Basicas*. Some sectors had a richer tradition of organized labor activity than others. Their workers were more readily engaged in self-management tasks. Unfortunately, attempts at sectoral organization met with difficulties resulting in wide variations among different firms in the same industry. But the most significant factor affecting the implementation of the *Normas Basicas* in any particular plant was the response of its union leaders. Many perceived the new organizations as rivals and wished to maintain their positions as the exclusive representatives of labor's interests. Still others could not transcend traditional trade union ideology and so remained interested only in wage and benefit issues. They were thus unable to encourage active decision making on the part of the workers.[19]

The Chilean experience with workers' self-management provides insights into the determinants of workers' attitudes toward participation. Informal interviews with a wide range of workers, from copper miners to migrant workers in squatter settlements, revealed that the workers who were more influenced by the extra-parliamentary left and whose immediate struggles were infused with a global vision of change were much more disposed to the program of self-management than those workers organized in unions led by electorally oriented trade unionists. In a related finding, Zimbalist and Espinosa found a greater receptivity to the ideas of worker self-management where the class struggle was strongest. Their findings, based upon a survey conducted in the social area in mid–1973, representing 30 percent of the industrial labor force shows that executive decision making by workers is dependent upon rank and file interest. Conversely, if the rank and file have no real power, they will quickly lose interest in any self-management scheme. Besides association with class-oriented political views, high levels of participation were also associated with better "labor discipline" and smaller differences between highest and lowest paid members of a firm. Productivity increased with participation despite an increase in the number of persons employed. Their study refuted the notion that effective worker participation led to a decline in productivity. Finally, the Chilean study demonstrated that the higher the degree of participation, the greater the rate of capital reinvestment by workers. Increase in capital stock in participatory firms was only 3.9 percent from 1959 to 1964. From 1965 to 1970 it was 4.6 percent among all firms in the self-managed sector. Among firms in the survey with more than 20 employees reinvestment averaged 15.5 percent.

Weaknesses of Self-Management in Chile and the Reversal of Reforms

Intervention and requisition were at the disposal of the working class but the opposition also had legal devices to delay, limit, or reverse takeovers. During 1971 and 1972 the government intervened and requisitioned a total of 318 firms. Sixty-five of these acts were reversed. Many more were delayed. Often a delay of only a few weeks provided sufficient opportunities for massive capital transfers. Originally Allende and his staff had planned to incorporate the largest, most dynamic industries into the state sector so that the government would control the leaders in each industry. A list of 74 of the most important privately owned firms was submitted to the legislature by Allende for nationalization. During October of 1971 a long series of parliamentary debates and juridical delaying tactics was used to prevent these acts, culminating in a constitutional impasse. By 1973 only 50 of the 74 firms had made it into the social sector.

The Chilean experience demonstrates the importance of two critical elements in the development of council socialism. On the one hand it points out the central importance of class struggle in creating the conditions for worker self-management. The necessary ingredient for effective self-management is the large-scale autonomous participation of workers. In no other country looked at in this study was there as high a degree of real participation. Workers were involved in every aspect of management. They chose product lines, made decisions about the introduction of new technology, made organizational changes, and controlled accounts. Unfortunately the Chilean experience also shows that a class society on the verge of civil war is a lethal environment for newly created workers' institutions. Existing in a pluralist framework, the Allende government never acquired sufficient control of the state or of financial mechanisms external to it to insure the longevity of the reforms. The more conservative elements of the Christian Democratic Party and right-wing extremist groups, their private property threatened, had nothing to lose in the violent curtailment of "representative democracy" and everything to gain. Through the military coup led by Pinochet in 1973, these groups were able to dismantle the social area and, through the use of terrorism and violence, erase the workers' organizations associated with self-management.

Three aspects of Chilean history made the Chilean experience with workers' control unique: (1) the existence of a system of participatory democracy; (2) a history of direct government intervention in the economy; and (3) a strong tradition of class-based collective action and trade unionism. These factors were both strengths and weaknesses. Chile had a participatory system of industrial democracy with a very strong class base. However, those factors which promoted organization and participation also meant that the classes which supported industrial democracy were never in complete control of the state and, therefore, once the state mechanism fell into the hands of class members who were opposed to participatory democracy, the organizations quickly fell apart.

BOLIVIA AND PERU

Durable workers' self-management emerges from an organized, struggle-tempered working class which struggles to develop a workers' state while organizing its self-management councils. If either or both of these conditions is not met, as has been seen in the cases of Algeria and Chile, the impulse toward a self-managed economy is short-lived. But self-management schemes do not always arise out of the experiences of the working class, however ill-formed. In many cases plans are drawn up by state functionaries with interests very different from those of workers.

Bolivian co-determination and then Peruvian industrial communities will be discussed in this section. Similarities between the two cases, which also distinguish them from the Algerian and Chilean cases, are: (1) the "top-down" organization which resulted in increased workers' involvement in management and more labor unrest; (2) the fact that both cases represent attempts on the part of corporatist, nationalist, governments to industrialize while minimizing class conflict; (3) both co-determination and the industrial communities created the unforeseen consequence of increased labor mobilization, highlighting the limited power of a corporatist regime in a developing capitalist country; (4) in both cases, lack of unity among factions of the bourgeoisie made it possible for these organizations to survive; and (5) in both cases when a single faction, which did not support self-management, established political dominance the programs were quickly dismantled.

The Bolivian experiment was limited to the tin mines. This discussion highlights the unions' dependence upon the state bureaucracy, which made it an ineffective representative of the miners' interests. Contradictions develop when workers' organizations play the dual role of guarding labor's position and serving in a capitalist managerial capacity. Finally, the nature of a movement whose existence depends upon the political space afforded it by divisions within the capitalist class is short-lived.

Moving to the Peruvian case, many of the aspects of "top-down" management noted in the Bolivian case will be seen again. In addition, the mechanisms through which labor attempts to extend the function of the apparatuses for participation supplied by the state will be discussed. The Peruvian case also demonstrates the role coercion plays in maintaining corporatist unity and in dismantling participatory organizations, in this case the industrial communities.

Bolivia

Workers' control in Bolivia was instituted "from above" to encourage increased production without escalating class conflict. Six months after the MNR government took control it nationalized the tin mines. The delay allowed time for capital flight. In addition the mines were old and not as productive as they had been. Thus, the stage was set for an escalation in class conflict as the state struggled to maintain production without incurring additional costs for labor or machinery. In response to steadily worsening living and working conditions workers' protest movements developed. The new government therefore sought to "involve" the workers in management enough to increase the amount of labor supplied without increasing wages or causing more conflict.[20]

At first the miners cooperated with the government but the honeymoon between miners and government ended when the miners realized that COMIBOL (National Tin Mine of Bolivia) officials were enriching themselves instead of financing exploration. Productivity fell and miners stopped reporting evidence of new veins. Miners' wages had not risen. An increasing segment of the payroll at each mine and in the government went to the growing white collar mine staffs and the COMIBOL bureaucracy, the ranks of which were inflated with the names of managers and bureaucrats' nonworking relatives. It was during this period that the unions and FSTMB (Federation of Bolivian Mine Workers' Unions) lost their autonomy. Union leadership, dependent upon its role in the government's co-determination program for funds, was unresponsive to worker demands, as is evidenced by the fact that miners' wages had not risen. This added to the disillusionment of the workers.

The radical miners at Siglo XX struggled to push the co-management scheme beyond what the military government intended. By design, workers originally had no power to combat managerial abuses. Miners at Siglo XX refused to participate in the original program in which workers' assemblies served only in an advisory capacity. They demanded that workers' councils be given the right to veto *any* managerial action. All expenditures had to be approved by the union. Unfortunately, the effectiveness of the veto was limited. Unions rarely had enough money to hire auditors to check mine accounts. Second, the veto also placed labor in an adversarial position in regards to management. Because of their position as watchdogs, instead of participating in management, they remained concerned with monetary issues.

Government was forced to attempt to dismantle co-management almost as soon as it began. The price of tin collapsed after the Korean War and international capital was called in to bail out the economy. Predictably, BID (Bank for Interamerican Development), and United States and West German private banks, lent the government $37.75 million on the condition that the operations of the market be unrestricted and social programs be cut. For the miners this new "liberal" policy translated into attempts to "rationalize" the operation of the labor market and production. A scheme to reorganize the co-management program was put forward by the government which would have eliminated the veto power won by the Siglo XX miners and many other benefits, including a reduction in the number of less strenuous above-ground mining jobs which served as the only available old-age, disability, and welfare services.

Through strikes, slow-downs, and protests the workers were able to defend their position and prevent the enactment of the reform for four years. During that time, political and economic tensions mounted, culminating in a coup by General Barrientos who ended the first phase of so-called co-management by sending troops into the mines in May 1965.

An analysis of this phase shows that worker militancy and organizational capacity grew in self-defense against the government's attempts to worsen conditions under the ideological guise of co-management. The councils did not, therefore, succeed in their intended role of co-opting labor. On the other hand, labor remained weak, demanding only higher wages and improved living conditions. Being but weakly organized and internally divided, labor could not serve as a mass base of support for socialized production and participatory democracy.

A wave of criticism of mine operations took place after Barrientos came to power. Everyone agreed that the mining operations had been a disaster, losing $106 million since the revolution. Labor costs had risen, no new veins had been discovered, and the price of tin had not recovered on the world market. The vested interests of the class of state functionaries who gleaned their livings from COMIBOL saw to it that the principle of nationalization was never discussed. For them the issue was not a question of returning the mines to the private sector but of extracting more value from labor and cleaning up alleged managerial inefficiency. They therefore launched a bogus campaign in an effort to renew labor's enthusiasm for self-management, promoting the idea that it was the Bolivian middle class which had somehow falsely nationalized the mines and which "maintained control of the decision making apparatuses and continued as servants of international private capitalists."[21]

Between the fall of Barrientos in 1969 and the rise of Colonel Banzer in 1971 two nationalist military figures, Ovando and Torres, ruled, providing political space for the workers' movement. In this interim the miners gained room to maneuver as their support became important to the nationalist military leaders. By this time workers' organizations had acquired enough organizational experience to participate in a substantive manner in the management of the mines. An entirely new workers' control program was introduced. "Union leaders pointed to the error of letting COMIBOL fall into the hands of the politicians . . . bourgeois bureaucrats and the military."[22] Wages were increased and the veto reinstated. The new proposal, issued May 1, 1971, described an organization which would elicit more participation from below. In the old system, top union officials automatically sat on boards. Now a general assembly was to elect all labor representatives to the board of directors. The president of COMIBOL was to be selected from a list drawn up by a directory which was elected by and comprised of miners. Managerial responsibilities of workers were to be enlarged and all members would have a vote at board meetings. In retrospect it is impossible to gauge the exact nature of the new plan which also eminated "from above." Nevertheless, workers had already demonstrated their capacity for extending the limited powers granted them. On the other hand, radical unions rejected these proposals on the grounds that they failed to deal with the basic contradiction between watching management and being co-equal with it.

The question is moot. The Banzer coup in August 1971 insured that the plan would never be implemented. A faction of the capitalist class had clearly emerged as dominant and any room to maneuver quickly disappeared. Banzer announced the removal of all veto powers and a return to "rational" labor policies. All pretense of participation was thus eliminated. As Nash concludes: "Bolivia's experience with workers' participation reveals the contradictions implicit in any compromise form of entry into management short of a socialist reorganization of the aims and structures of the industrial enterprise."[23]

Peru

Successful co-participation of labor and capital, introduced "from above" occurs only in the context of a rapidly expanding economy. Bolivia and other underdeveloped capitalist countries do not possess the resources to provide both welfare concerns to labor and incentives to capital to allow for class collaboration. Second, co-participation operates for an extended period of time when the state enters into a relationship with a highly organized, unionized labor force with its own power base, in a position to influence state policies and managerial decisions, as was the case in western Europe during the 1950s and 1960s. In France,[24] in Germany,[25] and in England[26] workers' control programs were instituted during periods of economic growth and increased demands for labor, as an answer to organized labor's challenge to the capitalist's "right" to the lion's share of profits and their "right" to control production. Workers in these countries made demands which exceeded the typical wage benefit packages. The programs established in response to those demands were often attempts to co-opt labor and quell unrest. They, therefore, offered little in the way of substantive changes. More often than not, the rank and file perceived them correctly and were less than enthusiastic participants.[27]

In contrast to the European situation, co-participation in Peru was a specific response to the burgeoning class conflict engendered by industrialization and growing peasant discontent in an underdeveloped country. Instituted "from above," it was an attempt to integrate autonomous working-class forces within the political and economic projects of the capitalist class. The Peruvian experience thus offers an example of the limitations and contradictions inherent in reforms instituted "from above" in a capitalist environment.[28]

In 1968 Juan Velasco Alvarado and his military supporters seized control of the state from his predecessor, Fernando Belaunde Terry, using a nationalist platform similar to the MNR's platform in Bolivia during the 1950s. The Belaunde regime's support for international capital had alienated many nationalist forces. Urban growth poles and foreign capital had drained the agricultural sector, leaving unrest, peasant uprisings, and land seizures. Velasco took control in order to pre-empt revolutionary mobilization among the popular classes during a period of disintegrating relations among factions of the capitalist class.[29]

At first the government underestimated the role coercion plays in maintaining corporatist unity. Peruvian leaders' control of the labor movement was often achieved through a series of tactics designed to prevent the formation of new class-based organizations, to dissolve existing ones, and to co-opt those portions of the labor movement it could not disperse. At the same time, they planned to increase productivity. The cornerstone of this ultimately unsuccessful plan was the Industrial Community, or IC. The ideology which underpinned the IC stated that labor was to share in the responsibilities and the risks of capitalist development. Supposedly, this would diffuse class conflict and decrease labor's tendency to organize. From this point of view, the program was a failure. It caused a great increase in unionization. However, the struggle that ensued was not between labor and private capital but rather between workers and the state itself, which was forced into an adversarial position vis-à-vis both labor and capital.

The Industrial Community

Velasco presented a compromise program of co-participation which alienated private capital while giving little to labor besides a small profit-sharing program. Called decree law number 18350, it was enacted in July of 1970. Part two, titles seven and eight required that 25 percent of a firm's net profits be turned over to the IC for distribution. Five percent was to be divided equally among all workers. Five percent was to be differentially distributed to *all* employees in proportion to their regular salaries and the remaining 15 percent was to be annually reinvested until the IC owned half of the enterprise.

Several critical points need to be raised here before describing the other elements of the IC. First, equality and the possibility of wage redistribution were never addressed. The 5 percent proportionately distributed included managers with large salaries so, in effect, this act perpetuated imbalances.[30] Second, law 18350 made no mention of "self-management." There was no way for workers to ever own more than 50 percent of an IC firm. Workers could, therefore, never control a majority on the board of directors. Third, no time limit for reaching the 50 percent level was ever established. By investing in and enlarging the company, management could make sure that the IC never even controlled the 50 percent allowed by law and, thus, never achieved parity on the board of directors.[31] Fourth, the ICs were supposed to promote labor discipline as an aid to industrialization. They were not supposed to reduce unemployment which averaged 35 percent of the economically active population; all industrial workers accounted for only 7 percent of the active population. Only medium and large industrial firms were included in the IC legislation. Very few workers were, therefore, included in the IC program. Further, no controls were ever created over investments in technology, exacerbating the unemployment problem by allowing IC enterprises to eliminate jobs through the introduction of capital-intensive production processes.

Other aspects of the plan were designed to minimize worker participation. IC legislation was binding upon all industrial firms with more than 6 employees. At the top of the organization was the board of directors. The board consisted of representatives of labor and private capital in proportion to the amount of stock held by each. Below the board was the workers' council consisting of six to 12 members elected by a general assembly of all workers. Participation was minimal. The general assembly only had the power to elect the council and to rubber stamp council activities. The elite within the IC were elected to the council and quickly became part of the bureaucracy. All disputes between labor and capital were mediated by the state. Council members were the only representatives of workers' interests recognized by the state. In their capacity as company board members they often left their jobs in the plant and came to have more contact with other board members than with fellow workers. The council had complete control over IC discretionary funds giving council members de facto control over all daily IC operations. It also administered the distribution of monies to workers leaving the firm in compensation for their portion of IC-owned company stock. Finally, as Espinosa and Zimbalist's model would have predicted, the rank and file, cut off from their leaders and unable to participate in decision making, quickly lost interest in the IC and returned to their unions.[32]

Organization of Peruvian Working Class

The Peruvian working class was organized prior to the initiation of the industrial communities and thus had developed sufficient class consciousness to resist efforts at co-optation. Peasant unions had been increasing in number since 1963 and they continued to grow throughout the decade. By 1968, 85 percent of all sugar cultivation was done by unionized workers.[33] At that time strikes in the agricultural sector accounted for 18.9 percent of all strikes.[34] Several haciendas were seized by workers, indicating the beginnings of spontaneous change from below.[35] When Velasco came to power, more than 50 percent of all value added in production came from unionized firms. There was a high correlation between the number of workers in a firm and the likelihood that there was a union present. In 1963, 1,461 shops had more than 20 workers. These shops employed 69 percent of the labor force in manufacturing. Among them there were 503 unions and 34 percent of the shops were unionized. The Peruvian industrial labor force was also capable of organized collective action. From 1965 to 1968 there were 392 strikes per year on the average in all sectors and 192 per year in industry.[36]

The effect of the IC on this base of organization was a pronounced increase in union activity (see table 8.2.) There were a number of reasons why the military's program promoted unionization. The industrial communities provided a legitimate platform for union organizations during the process of soliciting enough names to transform an enterprise into a union shop. The presence of the IC with its, albeit few, benefits to workers coupled with management's obvious resistance to complying with the regulations, made it clear that an independent organization was needed, capable of defending the workers' interests.[37] After 1971, unions formed outside of the industrial sector when mining, fishing, and telecommunications were added to the areas covered by IC legislation.

Table 8.2 Unionization before and after 1970 by Size of Enterprise

Number of Workers in Enterprise	Percentage of Enterprises Where a Union Was established			Percentage of Enterprises in Size Category	N	Percentage of Workers Employed by Enterprises in Size Category
	Before 1970	After 1970	By 1976			
Under 20	0	0	0	28.9	(577)	4
20-49	4	22	25	32.5	(648)	11
50-99	23	51	74	17.0	(339)	13
100-499	51	58	78	19.3	(385)	42
500+	93	41	98	2.2	(44)	30
All	17	28	38	100.0		100
N	(338)	(551)	(758)	(1938)		(190,762)

Source: Stephens: 1977:108.

In addition to the industrial communities a number of rural and industrial cooperatives were formed during the Velasco regime.[38] The experience of the industrial cooperative is informative. Though the sector was too small to be an economic or political force, it was characterized by higher degrees of participation than the rest of the social sector. These co-ops shed light on the question of workers' control over wage rates. Initially bankrupt enterprises were turned into cooperatives. By May 1976 there were 30 in Lima and they were largely successful in increasing productivity, something that usually occurs only when there is real participation. Horvat (1982) among others argues that workers tend to raise their own wages faster than productivity increases.[39] It can look like a no-win situation. External control may guarantee "correct" wage/investment ratios but lowers participation which, in turn, lowers productivity. Absence of state control, so the argument goes, may bring about an initial rise in productivity, as workers begin to act like capitalists, but will mean falling returns in the long run because of too much profit taking. Although very limited in scope, the Peruvian industrial cooperatives show this to be a false dichotomy. Constraints may be placed upon wages without limiting other aspects of self-management. In this case, the workers were, by law, limited to paying themselves no more than twice the official minimum wage. Second, these co-ops started out heavily in debt and the state would only lend them money on the condition that the borrowed amount be invested in capital stock.[40] This prevented them from doing what their capitalist counterparts had; borrow money from the government and invest it in real estate rather than in industrial development.

Labor and the IC

The IC was not able to effectively monitor the activities of management. At first the IC did not have the authority to audit the firm's accounts. Even after that right was won in January 1972, most IC officials lacked the accounting expertise to enable them to audit. And, if the company had not shown a profit, the IC was left without funds and could not hire independent auditors.

Organized labor's reaction to the IC was mixed. The Communist party-controlled CGTP provisionally supported the IC as a transitional phase in a process ending in social ownership. Other unions, fully aware of the co-optive nature of the IC, were cautious. At first, they supported profit-sharing but not worker representation on the board of directors. Later, union officials softened that position. They argued that the IC helped them to organize and therefore was not a threat. Also, the IC gave unions access to company information they would not otherwise be entitled to. A few union officials were co-opted but many left their positions as union officials to become IC representatives while retaining contacts with other union officials—a strategic gain for the unions, not for those groups that would have used the ICs to dissolve them.

Like Chile, the overall success in implementation of IC reforms depended upon the prior organizational experience of workers. First, unionized firms were more likely to have an IC. By the end of Velasco's term, 91 percent of the unionized manufacturing firms had an IC while only 58 percent of the nonunionized firms did. Second, Peruvian labor leaders were experienced in dealing with a state bureaucracy, an important skill as all collective negotiations, grievances, and contracts had to be presented by worker representatives to the Ministry of Labor for approval.[41] Workers in unionized plants had less difficulty adjusting to working within the IC guidelines than did those workers for whom the IC represented the first experience with collective action and bureaucratic relations.

Unlike Chile, where participation by unionized workers resulted in substantive changes in work organization, the number of strikes, the rate of pay, the amount of theft, and so on,[42] in Peru few real changes were made.[43] The IC's greatest effects were to aid organizing and indirectly to increase strike activity.

Often workers could not utilize IC legislation to its fullest because of ignorance. In Chile, autonomous union organizations were responsible for informing workers of their position. In this case a series of government agencies, each more conservative and less effective than its predecessor, were given the task of education. Five years after the enactment of IC legislation, "... 56% of blue collar workers simply didn't know anything about the rights granted them as members of the IC and among the 44% who knew something there were many with very rudimentary or even incorrect ideas."[44]

But as in Chile, legal provisions that were meant to fragment labor, "... ended up politicizing and strengthening the defensive power of the labor movement."[45] In Peru, unionization was increased because the limited role in the IC afforded labor by government forced labor to rely upon independent trade unions in self defense. Labor's demands were never won in IC council meetings, nor in meetings with state functionaries. Most of the issues labor was interested in were not permissible topics for discussion at board meetings. And when the worker representatives brought noncompliance problems to the OCLA (Office of Labor Communities) the agency was reduced to writing letters to the offending owner. OCLA had no legal sanctioning power. Workers' only recourse was the strike. Increases in strike activity during this period can easily be seen in table 8.3. From 1965 to 1972 strike activity was fairly constant. The ICs were first announced in 1970 and were instituted by the end of that year. From 1972 to 1975, when ICs were operating

Table 8.3 Total Number of Strikes, 1965–1975: All Sectors and Manufacturing Only

Year	All Sectors Strikes		Manufacturing Only Strikes	
	Number	Index	Number	Index
1965	397	100.0	191	100.0
1966	394	99.2	191	100.0
1967	414	104.3	207	108.4
1968	364	91.7	198	103.7
1969	372	93.7	143	74.9
1970	345	86.9	136	71.2
1971	377	95.0	184	66.3
1972	409	103.0	259	135.6
1973	788	198.5	423	221.5
1974	570	143.6	316	163.9
1975	779	196.2	427	224.1

Source: Stephens, 1977:129.

in most large firms, the number of strikes and the number of lost man-hours increased.[46] Finally, the wages and working conditions remained the primary reasons for collective action. Workers did not alter their demands to include what is normally associated with workers' control.

Capital's Reaction to the Industrial Communities

IC legislation was not designed to limit capital's prerogatives in any way, yet there was massive resistance to the IC program. No significant changes were made in the daily operations of most firms. Supervisors and managers maintained their positions. The profit-sharing scheme was an immediate nuisance to capital; however, the danger of workers ever acquiring half-ownership was minimal. Capital's immediate reaction included layoffs and disinvestment. Next, there were may irregularities in the sale of shares to ICs as they tried to capitalize the 15 percent of annual profits earmarked for reinvestment. Medium-size firms would be broken into smaller firms, each with less than 6 employees. Firms were divided into two companies, one in manufacturing, and one in the service or commercial sector, both of which were not subject to IC legislation. Profits would then be declared only in those companies which did not have an IC and where the distribution of 25 percent of the firms' earnings to labor was not required. Reminiscent of Bolivian mine managers, Peruvian factory owners would hire their relatives at very high salaries in order to capture most of the differentially distributed profits. Padded expense accounts and phantom employees were the norm.

Government Response and the Destruction of the Industrial Community

Peru differed from Chile, where obvious attempts were made to diminish the power of the bourgeoisie and from Algeria, where the bourgeoisie fled. Here, attempts were made to encourage capital investment, but to no avail.[47] Faced with capital's refusal to invest, the Velasco government buckled under and began dismantling the IC. The original plan called for labor to gradually control 50 percent of a firm, then to purchase half of the remaining 50 percent so that the workers owned 75 percent. This process was to be repeated until virtually all stock was controlled by the IC. Alarm in the private sector forced Velasco to renounce this idea and to state that 50 percent was the maximum amount the IC could ever control. Despite this and other concessions private capital refused to cooperate with Velasco's development strategy. The state was, therefore, forced to take on the task of industrialization on its own and in joint ventures with multinationals. As the state reluctantly took over more control of investment and development, public debt increased.[48] Still, the state stopped short of a direct attack on the national bourgeoisie.

Increased unionization external to the IC and an increase in the number of strikes, as well as continued noncooperation by private national capital indicate the failure of the corporatist scheme to absorb and suppress class conflict. Each side made increasing efforts to exert hegemony independently of the state mechanism. At the same time, several other factors including collapsing mineral prices, the disappearance of the anchovy, one of Peru's major exports, and debt repayment problems, forced Velasco to seek aid from the IMF which he received only after agreeing to "liberalize" trade policies and drastically reduce public spending.[49]

Spending cuts further polarized capital and labor. The redistributed profits had amounted to over one month's additional wages per year for 67 percent of all workers in IC firms. Now, inflation and unemployment eroded the previously made gains. Strikes increased and the government retaliated. It became easier to fire striking workers and when employers illegally fired workers, the government turned a deaf ear to labor's complaints. After Bermudez took control in 1976, signaling the defeat of all pro-labor forces inside and outside of the government, a state of emergency was declared and strikes were made illegal. Many union leaders were arrested and many members of government suspected of labor connections were exiled. At this point, right-wing extremist groups were no longer restricted in the use of coercion. Organizations of thugs, within the state fishing company (PESCAPERU), were used to "discipline" other unions.

Several decrees gave the government increased power over unions. The structure of the IC was altered. Representation on the board of directors had to be divided proportionally between blue and white collar workers. Fifteen percent of the firm's profits were still handed over to the IC but now they were placed in a special fund. When the fund reached the equivalent of 50 percent of the company's net worth, contributions ceased. The bulk of the fund was distributed to individual workers in the form of labor shares which carried a fixed rate of interest, were redeemable after five years, and, most important, were transferable. "Given a high enough price, a sufficient number of workers or white collar employees can certainly be found who would be willing to sell their shares back to the enterprise or to whatever intermediary."[50] This would gradually reduce worker representation on the board of directors back to zero.

The failure of the Peruvian experiment with industrial democracy illustrates the weakness of "top-down" efforts and suggests again that any scheme of participation that lacks effective mobilization of its constituents is likely to generate opposition. Deep-seated hostilities, and histories of sharp conflicts involving managerial intransigence and labor militancy are not propitious climates in which to attempt to implement co-participation schemes. The Peruvian experience demonstrates the transitory nature of co-participation. By the mid–1970s both labor and capital attempted to assert their hegemony independently of the bureaucratic state formulas for joint association. In the end, the schemes dissolved as the previous forms of class organization reemerged.

YUGOSLAVIA

The Yugoslav experience is sufficiently long and well documented to allow a detailed look at the relationship between labor, the enterprise, and the state over time. Its experience with self-management can be divided into three periods—the first from 1950 to 1965, the second from 1965 to 1974, and the third from 1974 to the present. In terms of the relationship between the enterprise and the market, the first period was characterized by central planning and a state-controlled economy. In contrast, the second period was the most "liberal." Planning was abandoned in favor of reliance upon market forces. In the last period, reliance upon market forces has been greatly reduced. However, regional governments have replaced the central government as the source of control. Important aspects of the first period include: (1) the historic genesis of workers' councils out of Yugoslavia's role in World War II and its relationship with the Soviet Union; (2) the limited scope of self-management confined, for the most part, to skilled workers and the limited purpose of self-management at this time, to encourage increased productivity; (3) the development of regional and sectoral inequalities caused by certain aspects of the relationship among the firm, the municipality, and the central government; and (4) the specific conflicts which developed into the impetus toward the introduction of the market.

In the second period: (1) the party-state retreated from economic planning; (2) the market exacerbated regional and sectoral inequalities and increased inequality of wage rates within individual enterprises; (3) the power of the municipality dwindled and was replaced by regional governments; (4) international capital came to play a greater part in firm operations; (5) individual workers began to question firm management by technicians; and (6) self-management, under the imperatives of the market, made workers responsible for production quotas, capital investment, and labor discipline. During this period, workers chose to maximize individual gains at the expense of capital accumulation. A crisis ensued in which managers, workers, and state officials called for the reimplementation of economic planning.

The 1974 constitution marks the beginning of the third period during which firms were reorganized and market forces were curbed. However, the problems which first developed during the 1950s and 1960s have yet to be dealt with.

Origin and Purpose of the Original Self-Management Scheme

Three things separate Yugoslavia from other East European countries: the anti-fascist movement which served as the base of Josip Broz Tito's regime; Tito's break with Stalin and Yugoslavia's expulsion from the Cominform in 1948; and the existence of an anti-fascist, anti-Stalinist base of popular support upon which a system of participatory democracy could be founded. Expanded participatory schemes were a method of rallying grass roots political support to Tito's isolated regime. Separation from the Soviet Union allowed for criticism of the highly centralized bureaucratic model of state planning, prior to which the original workers' councils had been completely organized from above, their only function the execution of the initial five-year plan.[51]

After 1948 self-management organizations in Yugoslavia were still subject to forms of external control. The councils were primarily designed to neutralize sources of conflict while increasing productivity. Local governments controlled the firm through taxation. Managers were left with little money to redistribute in the form of production bonuses so workers' control did not immediately result in improved living conditions. The power of the municipality over the firm was augmented by the fact that representation at the national level was based not upon plants or individual workers but rather regions: "[Which] meant that, to the degree formal organs of representation were responsive to pressure from below, they were by and large responding to territorial-based interests . . . which . . . meant ethnically-rooted ones."[52] Subsequently, territorial inequalities that had developed because of this system of regional representation would feed inter-ethnic conflicts.

Stratification with Firms and between Sectors

An examination of the workers' roles as both capitalists and exploited labor reveals three things. First, Yugoslav firms were stratified from the beginning. Skilled workers were always overrepresented on workers' councils. But this does not necessarily imply a class division between skilled and unskilled workers at this time. Most thought that the skilled workers and technicians were managing the enterprise to the benefit of the entire group. Evidence would seem to support this impression. From 1952 to 1966 the average annual rate of growth in industrial production was 8.2 percent. Employment in industry increased at a rate of 5.3 percent per year while labor productivity also rose an average of 4 percent. Illiteracy declined. Health facilities were improved and the infant mortality rate decreased.[53] Second, while inter-sectoral inequality increased, intra-firm inequality was rather low. The ratio between the highest and the lowest paid worker within a firm was restricted by law to no higher than 3:1 in fixed salaries and 5:1 in production bonuses. A longitudinal study of industrial, mining, agricultural, and service industries from 1956 to 1961[54] found the difference to be somewhat less. Salaried employees made an average for the period of only 39.3 percent more than hourly wage earners in regular salaries and bonuses. Note, however, that the trend which was to become problematic once legal restraints were removed was already apparent: this indicator had already risen from a low of 30.6 percent in 1956 to 47.7 percent in 1961. Third, the firm was run much like any capitalist enterprise. Productivity was the key word. Piece rates were often used and workers' salaries were closely linked to production.

The reactions of workers to these conditions were mixed. According to Adizes,[55] prior to 1965 workers identified with and often approved of what otherwise might be called "rate busters." Fantastic stories were told of "worker heroes" who could double and triple their production quotas. Later, workers reported missing the days when bells rang announcing that plant production quotas had been surpassed. Strike data from this period also seems to indicate that workers were either unconcerned with self-management or actually satisfied with its stratified operation. Of the 1,750 strikes that were reported between 1958 and 1969, almost all concerned personal income. Still, there were high rates of absenteeism and worker turnover during this period, seemingly indicating dissatisfaction with work and only a superficial involvement with plant management, and an interest in incomes rather than aspects of self-management.[56]

The evidence seems to bear out Espinosa and Zimbalist's contention that high absenteeism and worker turnover are associated with minimal participation. The large majority of workers did little more than elect skilled workers to positions on workers' councils because they had little prior organizational experience. In addition, many were incompletely proletarianized. "According to the 1953 census, 21% of manufacturing laborers, 38% of miners and 71% of all transport workers retained ties to the peasant community. Thirty-eight per cent of all unskilled laborers lived in villages but were employed in industry.[57] Absenteeism was highest during planting and harvest seasons.

Workers also reported that they felt their councils fairly represented their interests and they thought reinvestment and firm expansion would benefit them.[58] Workers' impressions are borne out by the workers' councils' management of discretionary funds. According to Comisso enterprise use of autonomous funds can be summarized as follows:[59]

Economic investment	41%
Consumption	27%
Charitable donations	10%
Commune funds, legal and advertising	22%

In addition, the proportion of internal financing to all other sources doubled from 1953 to 1960, from 10.9 percent to 20.8 percent.[60]

Municipality-Enterprise Relations

Having discussed the internal composition and character of the Yugoslav enterprise in the 1950s and 1960s we now turn to the relationship between the firm and the municipality—the governmental unit which interacted with the firm most frequently. This relationship is unique to the Yugoslav case. In addition to such common municipal services as roads, utilities, and the provision of zoning regulations, the municipality was responsible for economic growth, employment, and social services within its jurisdiction. The municipality was dependent upon the firm for all its income, which it garnered in the form of taxes. At the same time, the power to tax gave the municipality influence over the operations of the firm. "Recommendations" would be made to the firm's director that no inflationary wage-price increases be made which would increase the amount of tax revenue needed by the municipality. The two often worked together, especially when dealing with the federal government, or when creating wage-benefit packages to attract labor from other regions.

The regionalism that grew out of the municipality-enterprise relationship negatively affected production. Grants-in-aid and loans from development banks were all given to regional governments which in turn distributed the funds to local enterprises. In an effort to protect the local standard of living the municipality used these funds as leverage to prevent industrial specialization through the application of capital over a wide variety of industries. Often a single plant made many diverse items, making little use of economies of scale. Local-level bureaucracy expanded as did the number of "political factories." Each enterprise became less and less productive, able to rely less and less upon market mechanisms, requiring more and more preferential treatment from the municipality. The municipality was, of course, forced to comply with enterprise demands for cheap loans to insure both its tax base and the jobs of its residents. These conditions were worse in less developed regions which contained fewer dynamic industries.[61] Poorer regions thus remained underdeveloped, trapped in a cycle of inefficient production, protected markets, and low interest debt financing of the same inefficient production processes.

Uneven development during the planned phase of Yugoslav economic history aroused the discontent of the wealthier regions which saw a disproportionate portion of the national budget pouring into impoverished areas without any increase in productivity. The most developed sectors, of course, seemed to have the more successful, dynamic, competitive industries. Thus, planned allocation was villainized because it didn't lead to the highest possible national growth rate. Pressure on the party/state mechanism to allow for more reliance upon market forces came from regional/ethnic groups as well as from workers and technocrats in growing industries. The growing number of highly skilled laborers also pushed for greater autonomy and more reliance upon market mechanisms for wage and price determinations, placing their own interests above the interests of the entire class.[62] First, they argued, only increased reliance upon the market would make planning at the firm level possible. That would make improved investment decisions possible, increasing overall productivity. Second, the specific elimination of wage and price controls would be to the direct advantage of skilled workers because they were in demand by both industry and the state, and because they were concentrated in high growth sectors of the economy where prices and profitability would skyrocket once released from state control.

State, Market, and Self-Management

The central government began its retreat from economic planning prior to the 1965 reforms. The Communist party formally separated itself from various state organs. Communist party members declined as a proportion of total industrial labor force in the late 1950s and early 1960s though they were still overrepresented in industry compared to their proportions of the total labor force.[63] There was a decrease in the number of party members who were firm directors and an increase in passivity among the rank and file, resulting in a less organized labor force. Nevertheless, the party managed to maintain some degree of economic control because distribution of funds at both the local and the national level was still a highly politicized affair.[64]

State bureaucrats were not in favor of either more local autonomy or greater reliance upon the market. They were unwilling to relinquish the privileges their position afforded them and there was much debate over whether the market would allow for the achievement of social goals. The bureaucrats also argued that the modern "rational" production processes, while allowing for increased wages for some workers, did so by reducing the total number of workers employed, leaving the state, at some level, to provide for the increased number of unemployed.

Thus, three areas of conflict emerged in the early 1960s: sectoral conflict between growth industries and less productive sectors; state-industry conflict between some level of government and either individual firms or entire sectors; and intra-state conflicts among various organizational layers of government. In the struggle between the supporters of autonomous, worker-controlled firms and the supporters of central planning, firms and local governments in high growth sectors, along with those regions containing natural resources, prevailed against the supporters of the state—the bureaucrats, the least developed regions, and the Communist party.[65] The final blow came when severe economic balances—inflation, declining growth rates, unfavorable trade balances—forced the Yugoslavs into the hands of the IMF, which required "liberalization" in exchange for credit.[66]

The 1965 Reforms and the Introduction of the Market

The 1965 reforms thus represent a major shift toward greater reliance upon the market, a more decentralized government, and more control over wage rates and production decisions at the firm level. The reforms also caused deepened regional and sectoral conflicts, and increased reliance upon external financing. The central government still issued periodic plans but, unlike the original five-year plan, these were simply projections of what the economy would be like in the future, given industry's current non-directed activities. The municipality's role was limited to functions usually associated with a local government in a capitalist state: welfare, police, and infrastructure. The growth of private banks released the enterprise from the government's influence to some degree. The power of the municipal government was further reduced when the region was made the new locus of distribution of government funds.

The reforms increased inequality between regions and sectors. Not only did workers in the agricultural or peasant sectors make less money than workers in industry, the health care and social services they had access to were inferior because most of these programs had been carried out at the firm level and individual peasants and their families were not associated with any firm. The differences between regions were pronounced. In 1968 Slovenia could boast 9 percent of Yugoslavia's total land area, 8.5 percent of its population, and 15 percent of all national income. At the other extreme, Macedonia, Montenegro, Bosnia-Herzegovina, and the territory of Kosovo combined comprised 40 percent of the land, 39.5 percent of the population, but only 21 percent of the national income.[67] From 1965 to 1974, what is significant is not that interregional and intersectoral inequalities increased, but that they increased so little. The rates were only slightly higher than in the pre-reform era. The actual effects of Yugoslavia's entrance into the world market and the development of a labor market were minimized by state activity. These measures included loans from the central government to the poorer regions that went into consumption and "extra-budgetary" expenditures.[68]

Against growing inequalities came criticisms of market socialism. Some argued that sectoral and regional inequality along with increased concentration of capital and the growing differentiation among segments of the working class signaled the redevelopment of capitalism in Yugoslavia.[69] There was increasing inequality among workers with different skills within the same sector, and among workers in different sectors. They began to demand regulation of the labor market to reduce those differences.[70]

The instability of the labor market prompted Yugoslav workers to take personal wage increases at the expense of capital accumulation within the enterprise. The rate of self-financing was not fixed by law; workers could take surpluses as increases in personal income. Recently privatized banks and personal savings accounts as well as the availability of consumer durables (which only the labor aristocracy could afford) provided two alternatives to reinvestment. These alternatives had appeal for increasingly mobile laborers. Lack of central planning and the importation of new technology displaced many unskilled workers. Skilled laborers, free to change jobs as they saw fit, did so in order to maximize income. Since lifetime or even long-term employment with the same firm became an unlikely possibility and since the amount of benefit workers accrued from investments depended upon the duration of employment, it is no wonder that they sought wages at the expense of investment and productivity.

Looking at Chile, Peru, and Yugoslavia we can say that the rate of capital reinvestment in a firm depends upon the conditions under which the investment is to be made. Neither capital nor labor will willingly invest in an enterprise where their ability to control their investment is limited. Capital flight occurs when nationalization threatens capitalist prerogatives. Increased private savings and consumption serve as alternatives to investment for a mobile work force.

Workers' Participation after the 1965 Reforms

Looking at survey data it is difficult to ascertain exactly how successful self-management was in terms of real participation and in terms of benefits received by labor after 1965. Extensive research by Kamusic in 1968 revealed that a large majority of workers at all levels were in favor of further growth of self-management when growth of state authority was posed as the alternative. On the other hand, when, in the same study, workers were asked whether or not workers' councils and organizations functioned better after the 1965 reform, results were much less conclusive. Close to 30 percent of the respondents said conditions were indeed better, 45 percent thought there was no change, and 25 percent thought conditions were actually worse.[71] There is also evidence that indicates a growing dissatisfaction with the management of technicians and experts. The legitimacy of technocratic control declined because of growing inequalities and because workers were simply more organized and more conscious of their position than they were in the 1950s. Strikes escalated from 1965 to 1975 as workers turned away from self-management and back to trade unions[73]. Trade union policies also changed. In the expanding economy of the 1960s they struggled for the introduction of market forces because wages were being depressed by the state. In the decline of the 1970s they reversed their position, favoring more controls to keep wages from falling and to decrease growing inequality. The situation would have been worse except that social pressure from unions counteracted the polarizing effects of the market.[73]

Retreat from Market Socialism

As the economic downturn got under way, workers and managers, regardless of their differences over distribution of incomes, all came to agree that more state control was necessary. They advocated state intervention at the republic level only. The regional government could be controlled. According to theory, in a market economy, downturns eliminate inefficient producers. However, less than 400 workers per year lost their jobs due to bankruptcy because of government intervention at the regional level solicited by individual enterprises.[74]

The crisis of 1972 was the product of these forces. A political stalemate had developed. Decentralization meant distribution of power among social forces with inherent conflicts of interest. Firms and republics fought over jobs and production lines. The firm was the republic's only source of revenue and the republic served as the firm's access to credit and state aid. Inter-republic conflicts over the distribution of national wealth and inter-sectoral conflicts over the need for more or less state control were irreconcilable because of the lack of a strong central government.

The stalemate was finally broken by constitutional amendments in 1972 and by the new constitution in 1974. First, these documents restricted enterprise autonomy. A portion of all surplus was legally earmarked for investment. The amount that could be distributed as wages was specified. Republics were given some control over investment capital. Critical of the patterns of uneven development, in favor of more planning and less market, the constitution nevertheless promoted a weak central government. Decisions at the national level could only be made with the consent of the representatives from all the republics. With the Communist party in control of arbitration, stalemates are no longer a problem. However, the new decision-making process is slow and unwieldy. So many different areas and sets of interests have to be coordinated that fragmentation continues to be a problem.

Firms still have a great deal of freedom and as long as increased productivity continues to be the enterprise's goal, self-management will not solve the problems Yugoslavia shares with many capitalist countries. Managers will continue to find it difficult to be both productive and community-minded. The 1974 constitution specifically charges the firm with the responsibility for developing health and unemployment programs, yet the state is still the primary provider of these services. Unemployment continues to be a major problem as investment is funneled into capital-intensive projects. Since air and water are not considered production assets they come under no one's control and pollution is the consequence.[75]

The constitution also left unsolved many of the problems with participatory democracy within the enterprise. Yugoslavia is unique in that it has institutionalized the participation of the population in all spheres of life. Assemblies are elected by workers and their organizational experience has increased as has their degree of participation. Still the firm today is dominated by the technocracy.

Evidence indicates that workers' control programs cannot survive in non-socialist states. But even within them, the successful implementation of a program of workers' control, by itself, will not bring about the development of an egalitarian socialist state. In this regard the Yugoslav case has been informative. A social formation with a fairly well developed and, at least at the firm level, a fairly democratic system of self-management nevertheless suffers from sectoral and regional underdevelopment, regional nationalisms, stratification and fragmentation within the working class—all of which will be exacerbated by the current world economic crisis. The system of participatory democracy in Yugoslavia is not responsible for all the economic and political problems; the relationship is an interactive one. Self-management has served to fragment the working class and to encourage workers in individual firms to operate like capitalists. The "mixed" economy, in its various forms, within which these firms operate, has increased the inequalities between sectors and regions, thus supporting the fragmentation process. Meanwhile it has only been the party/state mechanism which has mitigated the inequalities that result from "market socialism." Increasingly, the party/state has been able to do very little to counteract the market, so that today, some of the worst aspects of capitalism have emerged. High unemployment, increased exploitation, and pollution are being repeated in the market socialism, worker-managed, economy of Yugoslavia.

The process of formation of a self-management-based socialism must avoid the policy of favoring the dynamic sectors of industry and direct itself to the incorporation and activation of the class as a whole. This is the primary direction to which socio-economic development must concern itself within the semi-industrialized countries of the Balkans and Mediterranean. To do otherwise is to attenuate the socialist commitment in society at large—especially among the large sectors of the non-working class excluded from self-management, and among those thousands of small firms whose workers' conditions of employment are still shaped by market and entrepreneurial considerations.

CONCLUSION

The emergence of a class consciousness directed toward the direct control over the productive process is not an inevitable result of class struggle, but rather the specific outcome of political leadership and organization which is actively committed to this form of social organization. The successful struggle for workers' control can only be undertaken within the broader context of a process of transformation from private to social ownership. The attempt to introduce workers' control in the context of private ownership leads to dynamic disequilibrium—the uncertainty of power relations causes capital to disinvest and block the development of productive forces. On the other hand, workers' control allows the working class to check the operations of capital but provides little leverage to initiate new policies and to reorganize the productive relations.

The previous discussion underlies the importance of the *manner* in which collectivization and worker self-management are instituted: changes initiated from below provide the experiences of solidarity that are so necessary for sustaining the new organs of production. Changes implemented through elite action from above impose new structures on a passive labor force, reproducing the old patterns of hierarchical authority and labor passivity. Hence, in the transition from the old form of class control to the new, only the collective action of the producers can produce an authentic transformation of social relations.

The emergence of autonomous class organizations which embrace broad sectors of the working class and which transcend the narrow or fragmented trade union structure have become the arenas within which democratic forms of collectivism have emerged. The factory council movements in Europe, the industrial belts in Chile, the workers' assemblies in Bolivia and Yugoslavia provide the kind of open political arena in which the exercise of power from the 'bottom-up' is possible.

Attempts to implement workers' self-management through executive fiats, or through other mechanisms that do not involve the workers in the process of transformation, have generally produced negative results. The most likely outcome has been the nonparticipation of the workers and the usurpation of "representative" positions by a small coterie of former trade union officials. This top-down approach is usually accompanied by the reproduction of previous structures of hierarchical authority, now dubbed with the label "worker" something or other. The logic of this system is that the consciousness of the workers remains concerned with economistic issues, and the levels of conflict and nonresponsiveness to productivity goals remain the same as before.

The transition to self-managed socialism is first and foremost a mortal threat to the whole organization of production and political control under capitalism. For the ruling class and its state, and in the case of the Third World, its imperialist allies, the attempt by workers to seize control over the means of production is the signal for a historic confrontation. All the political, propagandistic, and coercive apparatuses are mobilized to counter this effort. The capitalist class moves to sabotage production, the bankers close off credit, the owners of transport paralyze the circulation of goods, and the military is prepared for decisive action. What is striking about this confrontation is not only the specific action taken by the ruling class but the high levels of consciousness and organization that it reflects. The repression is aimed not only at turning back the particular movement for workers' control but at obliterating the organization and consciousness in the working class. Hence, the reaction of the capitalist class to the organization of a worker self-management system frequently finds expression in historically new and deeper levels of violence and repression, to dissolve the memory of self-affirming labor and to replace it with the wage slave.

The anticipation of this historical response pattern of the capitalist state requires that the workers' movement combine local rank and file movements for self-management at the point of production with a broader social and political movement to control the financial and other networks of the economy. The movement must take control over the state or have sufficient influence to combat efforts by capital to bring the military or coercive apparatus into the struggle. Control over networks and the state become essential elements in allowing the self-management movement to develop.

The failure of the self-management movement to gain control over these areas can lead to the reversibility of changes. The historic experiences in Chile, Czechoslovakia, Hungary, and Poland demonstrated that even where widespread organization of workers' councils have been established and even where they have secured the support of substantial sectors of the working class and have begun to function effectively in production, they have been reversed. The seizure of power by the capitalist class and/or by a bureaucratic elite has reversed the changes, displaced the workers in power, and either privatized or bureaucratized the self-management sector.

In the context of the transition to worker self-management, the *permeability* of a "pluralist society"—more accurately a class society verging on civil war—presents the most serious threat of destruction of the new worker institutions. The existence within a society of a class of displaced landlords, capitalists, bankers, generals, and so on (with little to lose and everything to gain from a putsch or civil war) creates a *dangerous class* capable of and committed to the destruction of the emerging democratic foundations of the new system. In these circumstances, the diffusion of power through decentralized structures based upon open-ended political discussion is an invitation to self-destruction. In the transition period, therefore, the system must combine centralized political direction with secure democratic control from below, excluding those classes which are unwilling to accept the political boundaries of the self-managed state. Clearly, there are dangers in centralized political authority, but the dangers of the decentralized pluralist state are even more transparent. The only guarantee that the tension between self-management at the level of production and centralized political rule at the national level can lead to creative results is through strict adherence to democratic procedures and to controls between the two levels.

What this discussion suggests is that self-management is an unstable form between capitalism and socialism. It threatens capitalist prerogatives, but is not securely anchored within a state structure capable of consolidating the new social power. The historical experiences cited earlier regarding the transition from capitalism to socialism suggest that while workers' control may precede the transition, it cannot by itself insure successful consummation. Without a successful transformation of the political structure and a comprehensive restructuring of the economy, worker-controlled enterprises are likely to be undermined.

Our survey of several historical experiences demonstrates that class struggle and organization are essential in creating the political experience and social solidarity necessary for the transformation of effective self-management councils. Conversely, councils established as a consequence of parliamentary, bureaucratic, or executive efforts fail to elicit the active and sustained activity of the ostensible beneficiaries of the reforms. In summary: the institutionalizatoin of worker self-management presupposes control over the state. The transformation of the state presupposes the existence of a revolutionary party linked to workers' councils. The realization of socialism requires councils of self-managing workers.

NOTES

1. See Matejko, "From Peasant to Worker in Poland," *International Review of Sociology*, 7:3, pp. 25–55, and G.D.H. Cole, *Socialist Thought*, vol. 1, "The Forerunners: 1789–1850" (London, 1953).

2. *Business Week*, March 8, 1974.

3. J. Hyatt, "Workers' Capitalism: Free Distribution of Stocks to Employees Spurred by a New Tax Law Provision." *Wall Street Journal*, April 29, 1975; and C. Agyris, "Personality and Organization Theory Revisited," *Administrative Science Quarterly* 18 (June, 1975), pp. 141–167.

4. The following narrative of events makes extensive use of I. Clegg's *Workers' Self-Management in Algeria* (London, 1971).

5. "It has been estimated that if oil and natural gas are excluded, there was a drop in overall production of 28% in the period 1959–1963, while in the tertiary sector there was a drop . . . of 36% . . . " in Clegg, *Workers' Self Management*, p. 79.

6. *Ibid.*, p. 47.

7. Colonial forces removed local populations and placed them in these camps in order to make strategic locations less valuable to the FLN.

8. Clegg, *Workers' Self-Management*, pp. 50–51.

9. *Ibid.*, p. 116.

10. *Ibid.*, p. 70.

11. In agriculture, during the first year after the revolution, pre-independence production levels were met despite a 60 percent decrease in machinery. In industry, the initial blows—loss of machinery, absence of a skilled workforce, lack of capital, insecure access to supplies—were devastating, setting production figures back more than ten years. Still, there was a steady increase in production from 1963 to 1968 when 1958 levels were once again obtained. Unemployment during this period remained constant and there was virtually no investment in new technology. Salaries were not increased. The few who were employed worked harder and longer for the same amount of money.

12. Clegg, *Workers' Self-Management*, p. 134.

13. J. Espinosa and A. Zimbalist, *Economic Democracy: Workers' Participation in Chilean Industry 1970–1973* (New York, 1973), p. 42.

14. S. Ramos, *Chile: Una Economia de Transicion?* (Santiago, 1972), p. 78.

15. M. Raptis, *Socialism, Democracy and Self-Management* (London: Allison & Busby, 1980).

16. Espinosa and Zimbalist, *Economic Democracy*, p. 42.

17. J. Petras and M. Morley, *The United States and Chile: Imperialism and the Overthrow of the Allende Government* (New York, 1975).

18. CUT was formed in 1953 and controlled by the Communist party after 1958. The CUT program dropped the necessity of a socialist state from its platform in 1959 and was legalized in 1971.

19. Espinosa and Zimbalist, *Economic Democracy*, pp. 53–56.

20. If productivity is measured by the amount of crude ore extracted rather than refined ore, then labor productivity did increase the "honeymoon" phase of miner-government relations.

21. J. Nash, "Workers' Participation in Nationalized Mines of Bolivia 1952–1972," in vol. 3 of *Participation and Self Management*, E. Pusic, ed. (Zagreb, 1972), pp. 157–72.

22. *Ibid.*, p. 166.

23. *Ibid.*, p. 169.

24. A.M. Ross and P. T. Hartman, *Changing Patterns of Industrial Conflict* (New York, 1960).

25. F. Deppe et al. *Kutik der Mitbestimmung* (Frankfurt, 1969).

26. W. Kendall, "Workers' Participation and Workers' Control: Aspects of the British Experience," in vol. 3 of *Participation and Self Management*, E. Pusic, ed., pp. 57–69.

27. For a general discussion of co-participation, workers' control and co-management in Europe see also: C. D. King and M. Van de Val, *Models of Industrial Democratic Consultation, Codetermination and Workers' Management* (The Hague, Netherlands: Mouton, 1978); A. Meister, ed., *Socialisme et Autogestion* (Paris, 1964); and M. Best and W. Connolly, *The Politicized Economy* (Boston, 1976).

28. For a discussion of the limits of corporatism see also: A. C. Stepan, *The State and Society: Peru in Comparative Perspective* (Princeton, N.J., 1978); C. McClintock, "Self Management and Political Participation in Peru 1967–1975: the Corporatist Illusion" *Sage Professional Papers* (Beverly Hills, Calif., 1977); J. Petras et al., *Class, State, and Power in the Third World* (London, 1981).

29. His program called for the nationalization of IPC, a subsidiary of Standard

Oil of New Jersey, without compensation, angering the U.S. based MNC's and banks, and risking an economic blockade similar to the one applied to Chile under Allende. Less aggressively, he expropriated coastal sugar plantations and the U.S. owned Cerro de Pasco mining company for which compensation was paid. Velasco, however, had no interest in a movement toward socialism. He was interested in promoting U.S. investment in copper as long as some of the profits could be captured for Peruvian development. See J. Malloy, "Dissecting the Peruvian Military: Review Essay," *Journal of Inter-American Studies and World Affairs*, 15:3, pp. 375–382; C. A. Astiz, *Pressure Groups and Power Elites in Peruvian Politics* (Ithaca, N.Y., 1969); and A. Quijano, "Nationalism and Capitalism in Peru: A Study of Neo-Imperialism," *Monthly Review*, 23:3 (1971).

30. Espinosa and Zimbalist found a strong relationship between income equality within a firm and degree of workers' participation.

31. Only one IC representative was given a seat on the board initially. The number of representatives was supposed to grow in proportion to the portion of total stock owned by the IC up to 50 percent and half the board of directors at which point there would be "co-determination" and the chairman of the board would be elected by a simple majority.

32. E. H. Stephens, *The Politics of Workers' Participation: The Peruvian Approach in Comparative Perspective* (New York, 1980).

33. *Ibid.*

34. Petras et al., *Class, State, and Power in the Third World*, p. 225.

35. J. Matos Mar et al., *El Peru Actual: Sociedad y Politica* (Mexico, 1970); and S. C. Bourque and D. S. Palmer, "Transforming the Rural Sector: Government Policy and Peasant Response," in *The Peruvian Experiment*, A. F. Lowenthal, ed. (Princeton, N.J., 1975).

36. Stephens, *The Politics of Workers' Participation*, p. 129.

37. *Ibid.*, p. 108.

38. Petras et al., *Class, State, and Power in the Third World*, pp. 222–237; and C. McClintock, "Self Management and Political Participation in Peru."

39. B. Horvat, *The Political Economy of Socialism*, vols. 1 and 2 (Armonk, 1982).

40. J. Vanek, *The Labor Managed Economy* (Ithaca, N.Y., 1977).

41. Stephens, *The Politics of Workers' Participation*, p. 107.

42. Espinosa and Zimbalist, *Economic Democracy*, pp. 127–175.

43. Stephens, *The Politics of Workers' Participation*, pp. 101–144.

44. *Ibid.*, p. 112.

45. Espinosa and Zimbalist, *Economic Democracy*, p. 36.

46. See D. Sulmont for a discussion of the labor movement during this time, "El desarrollo de la clase obrera en el Perú," Lima: Pontifica Universidad Católica, Centre de Investigaciones Sociales, Economicas, Politicas y Antropologicus, 1974, and *El Movimiento obrero en el Perú, 1900–1956*, (Lima: Pontifica Universidad Católica, 1975).

47. A government bond program aided the transfer of private capital out of the depleted agricultural sector in an effort to foster investment in industry. However, most private investment went into real estate and the remainder was ploughed back into already existing enterprises. In 1973, 76 percent of private industrial investment went into already existing enterprises, and in 1974, 66.2

percent. Yet private investment was barely enough to cover replacement. Stephens, *The Politics of Workers' Participation*, p. 148.

48. S. Hunt, "Direct Foreign Investment in Peru. New Rules for an Old Game," in *The Peruvian Experiment*, ed. A. F. Lowenthal (Princeton, N.J.: Princeton University Press, 1975).

49. B. Stallings, "Peru and the US Banks: Who Has the Upper Hand?" paper prepared for a conference on US foreign policy and Latin America, Studies of the Social Science Research Council, Washington, D.C., March 27–31, 1978, and *Latin American Economic Report* (1967), p. 18.

50. Stephens, *The Politics of Workers' Participation*, p. 234.

51. E. Commisso, *Workers' Control under Plan and Market* (New Haven, 1979), p. 42.

52. *Ibid.*, p. 47.

53. *Ibid.*, pp. 55–57.

54. G. Macesich, *Yugoslavia: The Theory and Practice of Development Planning* (Charlottesville, Va., 1964), p. 24.

55. I. Adizes, "On Conflict Resolution and an Organizational Definition of Self Management," in vol. 5 of *Yugoslav Workers' Self-Management*, M. J. Broekmeyer, ed., (Dordrecht, 1970), pp. 17–43.

56. V. Jovanov, "Protest Work Stoppages," *Socialist Thought and Practice* 26 (July–Sept. 1967).

57. Commisso, *Workers' Control under Plan and Market*, p. 61.

58. Meisler, *Socialisme et Autogestion*, p. 99; M. Barrat-Brown, "Yugoslavia Revisited," *New Left Review* 1 (January-February 1969), pp. 39–43; and J. Kolaga, "A Yugoslav Workers' Council," *Human Organization* 20: 1 (1961), pp. 27–31.

59. Commisso, *Workers' Control under Plan and Market*, p. 59.

60. S. Pejovich, *The Market Planned Economy of Yugoslavia* (Minneapolis, 1966), p. 70.

61. Commisso, *Workers' Control under Plan and Market*, p. 49.

62. From 1958 to 1965 the percentage of highly skilled workers among all industrial workers increased from 5.2 percent to 8.9 percent. The percentage of industrial workers with university degrees climbed from 6.1 percent to 14 percent, Commisso, *Workers' Control under Plan and Market*, p. 54.

63. J. Kolaja, *Workers' Councils: The Yugoslav Experience* (London, 1965), p. 21.

64. Meisler, *Socialisme et Autogestion*, p. 32; and A. R. Johnson, *The Transformation of Communist Ideology* (Cambridge, 1972), p. 210.

65. The government depressed the prices of resources so these regions would profit from the inevitable rise in prices that would result from the introduction of market mechanisms.

66. C. Payer, *The Debt Trap* (New York, 1975), p. 132.

67. M. Kamusic, "Economic Efficiency and Workers Self Management," in *Yugoslav Workers' Self-Management*, M. J. Broekmeyer, ed., pp. 76–116.

68. Commisso, *Workers' Control under Plan and Market*, p. 101.

69. There was a wave of bank mergers and from 1965 to 1967, 12 percent of all firms merged. For more on this see: P. Sweezy and L. Huberman, "Peaceful Transition from Socialism to Capitalism?" *Monthly Review Press* 14 (March, 1964), pp. 569–589; C. Bettelheim and P. Sweezy, *On the Transition to Socialism* (New York, 1971), and Barrat-Brown, "Yugoslavia Revisited."

70. N. Pasic, "Self Management as an Integral Political System," vol. 4 of *Yugoslav Workers' Self-Management*, M. J. Broekmeyer, ed., pp. 1–29; and N. Matejko, "The Socialist Principle of Workers' Control," in vol. 3 of *Participation and Management*, E. Pusic, ed., pp. 25–55.

71. Kamusic, "Economic Efficiency and Workers Self Management," p. 84.

72. Jovanov, "Protest Work Stoppages."

73. Commisso, *Workers' Control under Plan and Market*, p. 105.

74. *Ibid.*, p. 87.

75. I. Adizes, "On Conflict Resolution and an Organizational Definition of Self Management," in vol. 5 of *Yugoslav Workers' Self-Management*, M. J. Broekmeyer, ed., pp. 17–34.

Annotated Bibliography

Agulhon, Maurice. *Une ville ouvrière au temps du socialisme utopique: Touloun de 1815 à 1851*. Paris: Mouton, 1970. Agulhon's important study of working-class radicalism in Toulon argues that Mediterranean sociability patterns played an important role in forming institutions that could mobilize workers to protest.

Alt, John. "Beyond Class: The Decline of Industrial Labor and Leisure." *Telos* 28 (Summer 1976). Most studies of popular leisure make few connections between the world of work and the world of leisure, and in particular they tend to see any connection as one way—from work to leisure. John Alt's study does attempt to make these connections, from a theoretical Marxist point of view. As the title implies, however, Alt, like Stedman Jones, sees older artisanal forms of working-class leisure as in decline in the twentieth century. They are replaced by a "mass culture of consumerism."

Aminzade, Ronald. *Class Politics and Early Industrial Capitalism: A Study of Mid-Nineteenth Century Toulouse, France*. Albany: State University of New York Press, 1981. An important study of the development of class consciousness among workers in Europe during the first half of the nineteenth century.

Amsden, John, and Brier, Stephen. "Coal Miners on Strike: The Transformation of Strike Demands and the Formation of a National Union." *Journal of Interdisciplinary History* 7 (Spring, 1977): 583–616.

Arenberg, Conrad, and Kimball, Solon. *Family and Community in Ireland*. Cambridge: Harvard University Press, 1940. This classic is a beginning for anyone interested in migration and class formation. Although not about the U.S. it sets out the model of stem migration and sheds light on the process by which the Irish came to the United States.

Baldamus, William. *Efficiency and Effort*. London: Tavistock Institute of Human Relations, 1961.

Barton, Josef. *Peasants and Strangers: Italians, Rumanians, and Slovaks in an American City, 1890–1950*. Cambridge: Harvard University Press, 1975.

Belleville, Pierre. *Une nouvelle class ouvrière*. Paris: Julliard, 1963. A pioneering work that sketched the formation of a new "post-industrial" working class in France.

Bendix, Reinhard. *Work and Authority in Industry: Ideologies of Management in the Course of Industrialization*. New York: John Wiley, 1956. According to Bendix, employer strategies play an important role in determining the formation of the labor movement; each employing class gets the workforce it deserves.

Berg, Maxine. *The Machinery Question and the Making of Political Economy, 1815–1848*. Cambridge: Cambridge University Press, 1980.

Bernard, Pierre. "Attitudes au travail et action ouvrière." *Sociologie du travail* 4 (Oct.-Dec. 1962): 349–366.

Bezucha, Robert J. *The Lyon Uprising of 1834: Social and Political Conflict in the Early July Monarchy*. Cambridge: Harvard University Press, 1974. Bezucha's study of Lyonnais worker militancy highlights the importance of coalitions between small masters and artisans in the outbreak of social revolution.

Blauner, Robert. *Alienation and Freedom: The Factory Worker and His Industry*. Chicago: University of Chicago Press, 1964.

Bodnar, John. *Immigrants and Industry: Ethnicity in an American Mill Town*. Pittsburgh: University of Pittsburgh Press, 1977.

———. *Workers' World: Kinship, Community and Protest in an Industrial Society, 1900–1940*. Baltimore: Johns Hopkins Press, 1982.

Bodnar, John; Weber, Michael; and Simon, Roger. "Migration, Kinship and Urban Adjustment, Blacks and Poles in Pittsburgh, 1900–1930." *Journal of American History* (Dec. 1979): 548–565.

Bolton, D. "Unionization and Employer Strategy: The Tanganyikan Sisal Industry, 1958–1964." In P. Gutkind, R. Cohen, and J. Copans, eds., *African Labor History*. Beverly Hills, Calif.: Sage Publications, 1978.

Booth, Douglas E. "Karl Marx on State Regulation of the Labor Process: The English Factory Acts." *Review of Social Economy* 36 (October 1978): 137–158.

Braverman, Harry. *Labor and Monopoly Capital: The Degradation of Work in the Twentieth Century*. New York: Monthly Review Press, 1974. Braverman's widely influential work argues that the reorganization of work in the twentieth century has achieved a proletarianization of white collar workers and forged a large and increasingly homogenous "new" proletariat.

———, ed. *Technology, the Labor Process and the Working Class*. New York: Monthly Review Press, 1976. A collection of essays that focus on Braverman's book.

Brenner, Robert. "Agrarian Class Structures and Economic Development in Pre-Industrial Europe." *Past and Present* 70 (1976): 30–74.

———. "The Origins of Capitalist Development: A Critique of Neo-Smithian Marxism." *New Left Review* no. 104 (1977): 25–92. An important Marxist critique of the dependency theorists.

Bryceson, Deborah. "The Proletarianization of Women in Tanzania." *Review of African Political Economy* 17 (Jan.-April 1980): 4–27.

Bundy, Colin. *The Rise and Fall of the South African Peasantry*. Berkeley and Los Angeles: University of California Press, 1979. Bundy analyzes the manner in which African landholders responded to economic pressures and opportunities in the mid- to late-nineteenth century in South Africa's rural areas. In surveying the four provinces (in addition to one case study of the Herschel district), he argues that African "peasants" (actually petty commodity producers) took advantage of expanding markets for agricultural commodities and consequently reproduced and survived on an ever-expanding basis until the so-called "employers' offensive" after 1890. The commercialization of "white farming" undercut the African "peasantry," bringing about its decline and deterioration as a class.

Burawoy, Michael. *Manufacturing Consent: Changes in the Labor Process under Monopoly Capitalism.* Chicago: University of Chicago Press, 1979. Burawoy, a sociologist who took an industrial job and studied workers as a "participant observer," combines his own shop-floor observations with his profound knowledge of industrial and Marxist sociology to create a provocative analysis of the influence of the labor process on working-class political life. Burawoy argues that the influence of the labor process on workers has been underestimated by Marxists and non-Marxists alike. Labor process explains not only militancy but the quiescence of the modern-day American working class.

Burawoy, Michael, and Skocpol, Theda. *Marxist Inquiries: Studies of Labor, Class, and States.* Chicago: University of Chicago Press, 1982. Marxist sociologists discuss labor process and class in a special issue of the *American Journal of Sociology.*

Calhoun, Craig. *The Question of Class Struggle: Social Foundations of Popular Radicalism during the Industrial Revolution.* Chicago: University of Chicago Press, 1982. A new critique of Thompson which attempts to resurrect the traditional view of social protest in England before 1819. Unlike most other participants in the debate this book lacks both clearly drawn arguments and new evidence. There is a lot of smoke and heat here but little light.

Caplow, Theodore. *The Sociology of Work.* Minneapolis: University of Minnesota, 1954. A systematic treatment of the labor process by an important American sociologist.

Castoriadis, Cornelius. "On the History of the Workers' Movement." *Telos* 30 (Winter 1976–77), pp. 3–42.

Clawson, Dan. *Bureaucracy and the Labor Process: The Transformation of U.S. Industry, 1860–1920.* New York: Monthly Review Press, 1980.

Clayre, Alasdair. *Work and Play: Ideas and Experiences of Work and Leisure.* London: Weidenfeld and Nicolson, 1974.

Clayton, Anthony. "The 1948 Zanzibar General Strike." *Research Report No. 32.* Uppsala: Scandinavian Institute of African Studies, 1976. The 1948 strike is a little-known but important event.

Clayton, Anthony, and Savage, D. C. *Government and Labour in Kenya, 1895–1963.* London: Frank Cass, 1974. An overview of labor from the establishment of the colony. Clayton and Savage are particularly concerned with the evolution of official labor policy, although in addition they provide a wealth of detail on working conditions, economic conditions, and employer attitudes in the colony.

Cohen, Gary A. *Karl Marx's Theory of History: A Defense.* Oxford: Clarendon Press,

1978. Of importance to anyone interested in both a Marxist critique of Edward Thompson's co-determinist concept of class and a Marxist analysis of structuralism.

Commons, John R. "American Shoemakers 1648–1875: A Sketch of Industrial Revolution." In *Labor and Administration*. New York: A. M. Kelley, 1913. A clear statement of Commons's celebrated argument concerning the effect of the expanding market on labor organization.

Cooper, F. *From Slaves to Squatters: Plantation Labour and Agriculture in Zanzibar and Coastal Kenya, 1890–1925*. New Haven: Yale University Press, 1980. This is the first history to focus on labor in the former slave-holding region; it is an excellent examination of the particularities of that economy and the responses of ordinary Africans to it.

———. "Africa and the World Economy." *African Studies Review* 24, nos. 2–3 (June-Sept. 1981): 1–93. An important review of the literature which emphasizes the need to look at the proletarianization process in African labor history.

———. "The Problem of Slavery in African Studies." *Journal of African History* 20, no. 1, (1979): 103–125.

Couvares, Francis G. "The Triumph of Commerce: Class Culture and Mass Culture in Pittsburgh." In *Working-Class America*, Michael H. Frisch and Daniel J. Walkowitz, eds., (Urbana: University of Illinois, 1983): 123–152.

Cronin, James E. *Industrial Conflict in Modern Britain*. London: Croom Helm, 1979.

Cunningham, Hugh. *Leisure in the Industrial Revolution*. Discusses the impact of the industrial revolution on "traditional" forms of recreation. This book seeks to correct earlier notions of a decay in popular amusements with a discussion of the transformation and replacement of traditional forms by new, more commercialized forms.

Davenport, T.R.H. *South Africa: A Modern History*. London: Macmillan, 1980. While this work is not directly related to agriculture, it provides a valuable survey of the political and economic history of South Africa.

Dawley, Allan. *Class and Community: The Industrial Revolution in Lynn*. Cambridge: Harvard University Press, 1978. An important study of the effect of technological change in working-class protest and consciousness.

Deere, Carmen Diana. "Women's Subsistence Production in the Capitalist Periphery." Reprinted in *Peasants and Proletarians: The Struggles of Third World Workers*, Robin Cohen et al., eds. New York: Monthly Review Press, 1979. A pioneering and by now classic article on the intersection between male wage labor and female subsistence production, which demonstrates that the exploitation of unpaid female labor through the household unit ultimately cheapens the cost of wage labor for capital.

Deyo, Frederic. *Dependent Development and Industrial Order: An Asian Case Study*. New York: Praeger, 1981. A study of the implications of export-led, foreign-dominated industrialization for labor in Singapore during the last two decades. Deyo concludes that such industrialization was initially associated with the political suppression of organized labor, but that later efforts to encourage greater investment in high technology manufacturing led to a shift toward state-sponsored corporatist labor regimes.

Dobb, Maurice. *Studies in the Development of Capitalism.* Rev. version. London: Routledge and Kegan Paul, 1983. Although much of the material in this book is now outdated, Dobb's interpretation remains provocative and interesting.

Elkans, Walter. *Migrants and Proletarians: Urban Labour in the Economic Development of Uganda.* London: Oxford University Press, 1960. This is a classic work but it tends to present the migrant worker as tradition-bound and quiescent, a view that has been undermined by the work of van Onselen in particular, but also that of Stichter, Illife, Perrings, Gordon, Peace, and Lubeck.

England, Joe, and Rear, John. *Chinese Labor under British Rule: A Critical Study of Labor Relations and Law in Hong Kong.* Hong Kong: Oxford University Press, 1975. A discussion of workers and trade unions under British colonial rule. England and Rear find that union weakness is in part attributable to the employment policy of employers, and in part to the fragmentation of the union movement. Such fragmentation, they argue, is in turn rooted in political differences within labor, Hong Kong's small enterprise structure, and national labor legislation which encourages splinter unions.

Fawzi, Saad ed din. *The Labour Movement in the Sudan, 1946–1955.* London: Oxford University Press, 1957. A quite valuable work on a little known subject.

Foster, John. *Class Struggle and the Industrial Revolution: Early Industrial Capitalism in Three English Towns.* New York: St. Martin's Press, 1974. Foster's book presents an imaginative and original interpretation of class conflict in English textile towns during the Industrial Revolution.

Franke, R. H., and Kaul, J. D. "The Hawthorne Experiments: First Statistical Interpretation." *American Sociological Review* 43 (1978): 623–643. This redoing of the evidence from the landmark Hawthorne experiments argues that the original researchers misinterpreted their findings and that the effects of repression and industrial depression were the major reason for increases in productivity.

Fried, Marc. *The World of the Urban Working Class.* Cambridge: Harvard University Press, 1973.

Friedenson, Patrick. *Histoire des usines Renault.* 2 vols. Paris: Editions de Seuil, 1972.

Friedland, William. *Vuta Kambi: The Development of Trade Unions in Tanganyika.* Stanford: Hoover Institute, 1969. The most comprehensive work on East Africa outside Kenya. This study presents the emergence of trade unions during the 1950s and 1960s within the conceptual framework of institutional transfer.

Friedmann, Georges. *The Anatomy of Work: Labor, Leisure, and the Implications of Automation.* Glencoe, Ill.: Free Press, 1954. A classic study of the labor process.

———. *Industrial Society: The Emergence of the Human Problems of Automation.* Glencoe, Ill.: Free Press, 1955. The earliest and still one of the most devastating critiques of Taylorism.

Friedmann, Georges, and Naville, Pierre. *Traité de sociologie du travail.* 2 vols.

Paris: Armand Colin, 1964. A useful survey of approaches to the study of the labor process in Europe.

Furedi, F. "The Kikuyu Squatters in the Rift Valley: 1918–1929." in *Hadith 5*, B. A. Ogot, ed., 177–194. Nairobi: EALB, 1975.

Galenson, Walter. "The Labor Force, Wages, and Living Standards." In *Economic Growth and Structural Change in Taiwan: The Postwar Experience of the Republic of China*, Walter Galenson, ed. Ithaca: Cornell University Press, 1979. A discussion of employment and wage trends during Taiwan's industrialization period, as well as the institutional linkages between labor unions, firms, and the ruling party. Galenson shows that Taiwanese industrial development has substantially reduced earlier high levels of unemployment, while at the same time increasing the standard of living for large numbers of persons.

Golab, Caroline. *Immigrant Destinations.* Philadelphia: Temple University Press, 1978.

Goldthorpe, John et al. *The Affluent Worker: Industrial Attitudes and Behavior.* New York: Cambridge University Press, 1976. Goldthorpe's study of English workers and their attitudes towards work is widely influential.

Goodman, David, and Redclift, Michael. *From Peasant to Proletarian.* New York: St. Martin's Press, 1982. An argument for looking at Latin American proletarianization as a highly differentiated process within the context of a world system approach.

Gordon, David M.; Edwards, Richard; and Reich, Michael. *Segmented Work, Divided Workers: The Historical Transformation of Labor in the United States.* Cambridge: Cambridge University Press, 1982. This survey presents a number of interesting arguments about the process of class formation among American industrial proletarians.

Gorz, Andre. *Essays on the New Working Class.* St. Louis: Telos, 1975. During the 1960s Gorz was one of the most eloquent of the theorists of the "new working class."

———. *Farewell to the Working Class: An Essay on Post-Industrial Socialism.* Boston: South End Press, 1982. This work presents Gorz's chastened reflections.

Gouldner, Alvin. *Patterns of Industrial Bureaucracy: A Case Study of Modern Factory Administration.* Glencoe, Ill.: Free Press, 1954. An important study of industrial relations that opened the way for many modern studies of the labor process.

———. *Wildcat Strike.* New York: Harper and Row, 1965.

Gramsci, Antonio. *Selections from the Prison Notebooks.* New York: International, 1971. The idea of "dominant culture" borrows much from Antonio Gramsci's notion of "hegemony." Although the sections on "The Modern Prince" and "State and Civil Society" are most often cited, the section on "Notes on Italian History" is most suggestive.

Greenberg, Stanley. *Race and State in Capitalist Development: Comparative Perspectives.* New Haven: Yale University Press, 1980. Arguing from a "circulationist" (i.e., the exchange perspective) view, Greenberg describes the growth of "labour-repressive agriculture" in the South African countryside. His position is the obverse of M. L. Morris.

Grillo, R. D. *African Railwaymen: Solidarity and Opposition in an East African Labour*

Force. London: Cambridge University Press, 1973. An anthropological work focusing on ethnic, status, and other personal relationships among one group of fairly stabilized Ugandan workers.

Gutkind, P.; Cohen, R.; and Copans, J., eds. *African Labor History.* Beverly Hills, Calif.: Sage Publications, 1978.

Gutman, Herbert. *Work, Culture and Society in Industrializing America.* New York: Knopf, 1976. An important series of articles on the connection between work experience, working class culture, and protest.

Hammond, J. L., and Hammond, Barbara. *The Town Labourer.* New York: Doubleday, 1968. (First written in 1925 and subsequently revised; last edition in 1938). This is a classic discussion of the industrial working class in the English Industrial Revolution. Its interpretation has been much debated, and while later scholarship makes revision of the Hammonds' work necessary it is still worth reading.

Hanagan, Michael P. *The Logic of Solidarity: Artisans and Industrial Workers in Three French Towns: 1871–1914.* Urbana, Ill.: University of Illinois Press, 1980.

Hartmann, Heidi. "Capitalism, Patriarch and Job Segregation by Sex." *Signs* 1, no. 3, part 2 (Spring 1976): 137–169. A provocative and interesting article which traces capitalism and the sexual division of labor within modern industry to "partriarchy." Her argument lacks adequate documentation.

Hinton, James. *The First Shop Stewards' Movement.* London: Allen & Unwin, 1973. Hinton's study shows that issues of workers' control were an important element in the wave of worker militancy in England toward the end of World War I.

Hirsch, Susan E. *Roots of the American Working Class: The Industrialization of Crafts in Newark, 1800–1860.* Philadelphia: University of Pennsylvania Press, 1978. An important study of the effects of deskilling on everyday working-class life.

Hobsbawm, E. J. "Custom, Wages, and Work Load in Nineteenth Century Industry." In *Labouring Men,* E. J. Hobsbawm, ed. New York: Anchor, 1964. Hobsbawm elaborates some fascinating and bold theories concerning the effects of class struggle on industrial relations.

———. *Workers: Worlds of Labor.* New York: Pantheon, 1984.

Humphries, Jane. "Class Struggle and the Persistance of the Working Class Family." *Cambridge Journal of Economics* 1 (1977): 241–258. This is a highly original and interesting attempt to depict the role of the family within working class protest movements, but as in her other writings, Humphries does not document her arguments in a convincing fashion.

———. "The Working Class Family, Women's Liberation, and Class Struggle: The Case of Nineteenth Century British History." *Review of Radical Political Economics* 9, no. 3 (1977): 25–41.

Iliffe, John. "The Creation of Group Consciousness: A History of the Dockworkers of Dar-es-Salaam." In *The Development of an African Working Class,* R. Sandbrook and R. Cohen, eds. This small gem views the emergence of workers' consciousness from "the bottom up."

Jackson, Robert Max. *The Formation of Craft Labor Markets.* New York: Academic Press, 1984. Jackson presents an original and persuasive interpretation of the relationship between technological change, craft labor markets, and unionism among American workers.

Jacques, Martin, and Mulhern, Francis, eds. *The Forward March of Labour Halted?* London: Verso, 1981. This collection contains Eric Hobsbawm's famous 1978 "Marx Memorial Lecture" and the comments of British leftists. Hobsbawm's remarks are not original, but the pessimism of these remarks by the foremost Marxist labor historian (and arguably the world's foremost labor historian) occasioned a lot of comment at the time.

Janmohamed, K. "African Labourers in Mombasa, c. 1895–1940." In *Hadith 5*, B. A. Ogot, ed., 154–176. Nairobi: EALB, 1975.

Johnson, Christopher H. *Utopian Communism in France: Cabet and the Icarians, 1839–1851.* (Ithaca, New York: Cornell, 1974). Johnson's study of utopian communism makes clear that skilled workers threatened by trade crises were a dominant force in working-class support for Communism.

Jones, Gareth Stedman. "Working Class Culture and Working Class Politics in London, 1870–1900: Notes on the Remaking of the Working Class." *Journal of Social History* 7 (Summer 1974): 460–508.

Joyce, Patrick. *Work, Society and Politics: The Culture of the Factory in Later Victorian England.* New Brunswick, N.J.: Rutgers University Press, 1980. Joyce argues that the manufacturer's dominant position in the factory allowed him to dominate all aspects of working-class life.

Katznelson, Ira. *City Trenches: Urban Politics and the Patterning of Class in the United States.* Chicago: University of Chicago Press, 1981. Katznelson explores why it is that shop-floor consciousness remains confined to the workplace and does not penetrate ethnic communities in the United States.

Kerr, Clark; Dulop, John T.; and Meyer, C. A. *Industrialism and Industrial Man.* Cambridge: Harvard University Press, 1960. This book has been a favorite target of criticism since the 1960s.

King, K. "Education and Social Change: The Impact of Technical Training in Colonial Kenya." In *Hadith 6*, B. A. Ogot, ed., 145–164. Nairobi: EALB, 1976.

Kornblum, William. *Blue Collar Community.* Chicago: University of Chicago, 1974. This study of South Chicago steelworkers is full of rich detail on the relationship between the organization of work and sociability.

Kornhauser, Arthur; Dubin, Robert; and Ross, Arthur M. *Industrial Conflict.* New York: McGraw-Hill, 1954. The essays in this book have exerted enormous influence on the sociology of work and in labor history.

Laurie, Bruce, and Schmitz, Mark. "Manufacturing and Productivity: The Making of an Industrial Base." In *Philadelphia: Work, Space, Family and Group Experience in the 19th Century.* Theodore Hershberg, ed. Oxford: Oxford University Press, 1981. An impressive article which reminds us that the profitability of economies of scale varied enormously within nineteenth century industry throughout most of the century. Industrialization can hardly be described as the triumphal march of factory organization throughout existing industrial structures.

LeMasters, E. E. *Blue Collar Aristocrats: Life Styles at a Working Class Tavern.* Madison: University of Wisconsin, 1975. A more recent study of the effect of occupational community on consciousness is LeMasters' participant observation of construction workers in a Wisconsin tavern.

Lipset, Seymour Martin; Trow, Martin A.; and Coleman, James S. *Union Democracy: The Internal Politics of the International Typographical Union.* Glencoe, Ill.: Free Press, 1956. A classic study of occupational community and its implications for consciousness.

Lockwood, David. "Sources of Variation in Working-Class Images of Society." In *Working-Class Images of Society.* Martin Bulmer, ed. London: Routledge & Kegan Paul, 1975. Lockwood's article presents a useful introduction to the study of the occupational community and its implications for consciousness.

McGlaughlin, Virginia Yans. *Family and Community: Italian Immigrants in Buffalo, 1880–1930.* Ithaca: Cornell University Press, 1977.

Mackenzie, Gavin. *The Aristocracy of Labor: The Position of Skilled Craftsmen in the American Class Structure.* Cambridge: Cambridge University Press, 1973. An important study of American working-class life, an important critique of the "bourgeosification" explanation of American skilled workers' behavior.

Malcolmson, Robert W. *Popular Recreations in English Society 1700–1850.* Cambridge: Cambridge University Press, 1973. Malcolmson studies the interrelationship between work and leisure in the pre-industrial period.

Marglin, S. A. "What Do Bosses Do? The Origins and Functions of Hierarchy in Capitalist Production." *Review of Radical Political Economics* 6: 33–60. A widely influential interpretation of the origins of the factory system: Marglin argues that it was not technology but the need for increased labor discipline that provided the original motor for the factory system of the English Industrial Revolution.

Marx, Karl. *Capital.* 3 vols. New York: International Publishers, 1967. Chapters 14 and 15 of volume one of *Capital* contain some of Marx's most important thoughts on historical changes in the labor process.

Mayo, Elton. *The Human Problems of an Industrial Civilization.* New York: Macmillan, 1933. The classic of American industrial sociology.

Meachem, Standish. *A Life Apart: The English Working Class 1890–1914.* Cambridge: Harvard University Press, 1977.

Menetra, Jacques-Louis. *Journal de ma vie.* Paris: Montalba, 1982. The memoirs of this eighteenth-century French glassworkers are a goldmine of information on the outlook and experiences of pre-industrial skilled workers.

Montgomery, David. *Beyond Equality: Labor and the Radical Republicans: 1862–1872.* New York: Vintage, 1967. An influential work that explores the origins of a specifically proletarian radicalism in American history.

———. *Workers' Control in America: Studies in the History of Work, Technology and Labor Struggles.* Cambridge: Cambridge University Press, 1979. This collection presents a number of Montgomery's seminal contributions to the debate over the role of labor process in worker militancy in nineteenth-century America.

Morris, M. L. "The Development of Capitalism in South African Agriculture: Class Struggle in the Countryside." *Economy and Society* 5, no. 3 (1976): 292–343. Morris argues—using, variously, Hindness and Hirst, Balibar,

Poulantzas, Marx, and Lenin—that the "labour-tenant system" that emerged in the South African countryside after the 1920s was indeed capitalist production. His argument marks a significant break with those who ignore production relations and concentrate exclusively on exchange (in the tradition of Barrington, Moore, Wallerstein, Frank, Amin, Emmanuel, etc.). Morris centers his analysis on the contradiction that forced the "Labour tenant system" into decline by the 1940s.

Moss, Bernard. *The Origins of the French Labor Movement: The Socialism of the Skilled Worker.* Berkeley: University of California Press, 1976. A fine overall portrait of French worker political activity in the course of the nineteenth century.

Mottez, Bernard. *Systèmes de salaires et politiques patronales.* Paris: CNRS, 1966. An important book that shows how the forms of wage payment are part of larger patterns of industrial relations.

Nolan, Mary. *Social Democracy and Society: Working-Class Radicalism in Dusseldorf, 1890–1920.* Cambridge: Cambridge University Press, 1981.

Ogle, George. "South Korea." In *International Handbook of Industrial Relations,* Albert Blum, ed. Wesport, Conn.: Greenwood Press, 1979. This article summarizes the major findings and discussion in the author's earlier dissertation on labor legislation and organized labor in South Korea. He focuses especially on the ways in which the government attempted, with varying degrees of success, to control and suppress labor unions during the 1950s and 1960s.

Palmer, Bryan D. *A Culture in Conflict: Skilled Workers and Industrial Capitalism in Hamilton, Ontario, 1860–1914.* Montreal: McGill-Queen's University Press, 1979.

Petras, James; Morley, Morris; and Smith, Steven. *The Nationalization of Venezuelan Oil.* New York: Praeger, 1977.

Pounds, N.J.G. *An Historical Geography of Europe 1500–1800.* Cambridge: Cambridge University Press, 1979. This book is a fund of information concerning the progress of industrialization across the European continent.

Price, Richard. "The Labour Process and Labour History." *Social History* 8, no. 1 (Jan. 1983): 57–75.

———. "Structures of Subordination in Nineteenth-Century British Industry." In *The Power of the Past: Essays for Eric Hobsbawm.* Pat Thane, Geoffrey Crossick, and Roderick Floud, eds., 119–142. Cambridge: Cambridge University Press, 1984.

Prothero, Iorwerth. *Artisans and Politics in Early Nineteenth-Century London: John Gast and His Times.* Baton Rouge, La.: Louisiana State University Press, 1979.

Rancière, Jacques. *La nuit des prolétaires.* Paris: Fayard, 1981. Rancière argues that historians have too critically accepted the proposition that pride in work and labor processes have determined worker consciousness.

Roy, Donald. "Efficiency and the Fix: Informal Intergroup Relations in a Piecework Machine Shop." *American Journal of Sociology* 60 (1954): 255–266. The handful of articles by Donald Roy remain among the best works on the organization of work and shop-floor culture produced in the United States.

———. "Quota Restrictions and Goldbricking in a Machine Shop." *American Journal of Sociology* 57 (1952): 426–442.

Sabel, Charles F. *Work and Politics: The Division of Labor in Industry*. Cambridge: Cambridge University Press, 1982.

Salaff, Janet. *Working Daughters of Hong Kong*. Cambridge: Cambridge University Press, 1981. An excellent study of the impact of industrialization on family structure in Hong Kong. On the basis of case studies of several young female factory workers, Salaff argues that industrialization has not so much undermined family loyalty on the part of young working women as created new economic resources for the strengthening of traditional family bonds.

Salaman, Graeme. *Community and Occupation: An Exploration of Work/Leisure Relationships*. London: Cambridge University Press, 1974. Salaman has carried out research on the nature of occupational community among British railway workers.

Sandbrook, R. *Proletarians and African Capitalism: The Kenyan Case, 1960–1972*. London: Cambridge University Press., 1975. This is a full and solid study of both the internal politics of the union movement and union-government relations in the 1960s.

———. "The State and the Development of Trade Unionism." In *Development Administration: The Kenyan Experience*, G. Hyden, R. Jackson, and J. Okumu, eds., 252–294. Nairobi: Oxford University Press, 1970.

Sandbrook, R., and Cohen, R., eds. *The Development of an African Working Class*. London: Longman, 1975.

Scott, Roger. *The Development of Trade Unions in Uganda*. Nairobi: East African Publishing House, 1966.

Singh, M. *History of Kenya's Trade Union Movement to 1952*. Nairobi: East Africa Publishing House, 1969. For early attempts at unionization, the indispensible primary source is the memoirs of Makhan Singh, who was so instrumental in spurring the development of militant African trade unionism.

Smelser, Neil. *Social Change in the Industrial Revolution*. Chicago: University of Chicago Press, 1959. A powerful, early attempt to synthesize the relationship between working-class families and industrial change in Western European society. Much of the literature in the field, and principally much of Edward Thompson's work, can be viewed as a response to Smelser.

Special Task Force to the Secretary of Health, Education, and Welfare. *Work in America*. Cambridge: MIT Press, 1973. Much quoted.

Stearns, Peter. *Lives of Labor: Work in a Maturing Industrial Society*. New York: Holmes and Meier, 1975. An important interpretation of the roots of worker militancy by an influential American labor historian.

Steinberg, Stephan. *The Ethnic Myth: Race, Ethnicity, and Class in America*. New York: Atheneum, 1981. A critical view of the whole issue of ethnicity as seen by American historians and sociologists, and an analysis of how the issue of ethnicity has reified culture.

Stichter, Sharon. *Migrant Labour in Kenya: Capitalism and African Response 1895–1975*. London: Longman, 1982. This work provides an overview of labor from the establishment of the colony in the 1890s. Stichter examines the spread of African wage-earning alongside the competing growth of peasant economies, and the early history of protest actions by both migrant and urbanized workers, emphasizing the efforts of workers to exert control over the conditions of their work.

———. "Trade Unionism in Kenya, 1947–1952: The Militant Phase." In *African Labor History*, P. Gutkind, R. Cohen, and J. Copans, eds., 154–174. Beverly Hills, Calif.: Sage Publications, 1978.

———. "Workers, Trade Unions, and the Mau Mau Rebellion." *Canadian Journal of African Studies*, 2 (1975): 259–275.

Stone, Katherine. "The Origins of Job Structure in the Steel Industry." *Review of Radical Political Economics* 6, no. 2 (Summer 1974): 61–97.

Thernstrom, Stephan. *The Other Bostonians: Poverty and Progress in the American Metropolis, 1880–1970.* Cambridge: Harvard University Press, 1973.

Thompson, E. P. *The Making of the English Working Class.* New York: Vintage, 1966. This classic, first published in 1963, has strongly influenced almost all subsequent studies of class formation and proletarianization.

Touraine, Alain. *La Conscience ouvrière.* Paris: Editions du Seuil, 1966. Touraine's work has been extremely influential in shaping discussions of the labor process in Europe.

———. *L'Evolution du travail ouvrier aux usines Renault.* Paris: CNRS, 1955. Touraine's clearest statement of the effect of changes in the labor process on the workers' movement.

Trempé, Rollande. *Les mineurs de Carmaux, 1848–1914.* Paris: Les éditions ouvrières, 1971. Trempé's study of the organization of work in coal mining and of the effects of changes in the structure of work on militancy is superb.

Turner, H. A. et al. *The Last Colony: But Whose?* Cambridge: University of Cambridge, 1980. A broad historical assessment of the changing political and economic position of unions and labor in Hong Kong. Turner argues that industrialization in this small colony has been associated with a progressive diminution of the power of organized labor in new manufacturing sectors, but with a rise in the power of labor in the public services and other nonindustrial workers.

Walker, Charles R. *Steel: The Diary of a Furnace Worker.* Boston: Atlantic Monthly Press, 1923. A record of an early "participant observer" in an early twentieth-century American steel works.

———. *Steeltown, An Industrial Case History.* New York: Harper Brothers, 1964.

Walker, Charles R., and Guest, Robert H. *The Man on the Assembly Line.* Cambridge: Harvard University Press, 1962. A classic study of labor process.

Ware, Norman. *The Industrial Worker, 1840–1860.* Boston: Houghton-Mifflin, 1924. A classic by one of the leading figures in American labor history. This book is still wonderful reading.

Warner, Lloyd, and Low, J. O. *The Social System of the Modern Factory.* New Haven, Conn.: Yale University Press, 1947.

Weber, Max. *General Economic History.* New Brunswick, N.J.: Transaction, 1981. This book contains some of Weber's most important writings on labor process and the rise of industrial capitalism.

Williams, Raymond. *Marxism and Literature.* Oxford: Oxford University Press,

1977. Ostensibly an introduction to basic concepts, this book is more fundamentally a condensation and reinterpretation of ideas Williams has been developing since *Culture and Society*.

Wolfe, Eric. *Europe and the People without History*. Berkeley: University of California Press, 1982. Attempt to define and analyze the interrelation between different parts of world economy.

van der Horst, Sheila. *Native Labour in South Africa*. New York: Frank Cass, 1971. Originally published in 1942 (and then again released in 1971), this book is a classic liberal account of the African labour movement in South Africa. While it has been superseded by more recent works, van der Horst's book contains valuable bibliographical references and provides a general survey of labor conditions still useful today.

van Zwanberg, R. *Colonial Capitalism and Labour in Kenya, 1919–1939*. Nairobi: East African Literature Bureau, 1975. Though uneven and sometimes overstated, the book contains useful information for the mid-colonial decades.

Index

About the Contributors

RITA CARROLL-SEGUIN is a Ph.D. student in sociology at the State University of New York at Binghamton. Her interests lie in the methods and processes of stratification. Currently she is studying Southeast Asian refugee resettlement in advanced industrial nations.

OLIVER CARSTEN is a Research Associate in Social Science at the University of Michigan. Currently he is writing *Work and the Lodge: Working-Class Sociability in Meriden and New Britain, Connecticut, 1850–1940*, a book on the interrelationship of work patterns and leisure-time activities.

JOHN CUMBLER is Associate Professor of History at the University of Louisville and has served as Visiting Senior Lecturer at the Centre for the Study of Social History at the University of Warwick, and as Visiting Scholar in the Department of Urban Studies and Planning at the Massachusetts Institute of Technology. He has published numerous articles in the fields of urban, labor, and social history, and is the author of *Working-Class Community in Industrial America* (1979) and editor of *A Moral Response to Industrialism* (1982). Currently he is working on the social history of economic decline.

FREDERIC C. DEYO is Associate Professor of Sociology at the State University of New York College at Brockport; previously he taught at the University of Singapore. He has published extensively on workers and trade unions in Thailand and Singapore, and is the author of *Dependent Development and Industrial Order* (1981), which deals with industrialization and trade unions in Singapore. Currently he is completing a book on industrial relations in Taiwan, Singapore, South Korea, and Hong Kong.

PETER C. W. GUTKIND is Professor of Anthropology at McGill University, where he has been since 1963. He has held appointments at a number of African universities and in the West Indies. His interest is in urbanization and urbanism in Africa, particularly in the historical roots of class formation and consciousness. He is the author of a number of books and numerous articles and editor of the Sage Series on African Modernization and Development and he has served as President of the African Studies Association (USA).

MICHAEL HANAGAN is Assistant Professor of History at Columbia University. He is the author of numerous articles and of *The Logic of Solidarity: Artisans and Industrial Workers in Three French Towns, 1871–1914* (1980) and editor (with Charles Stephenson) of *Proletarians and Protest: The Roots of Class Formation in an Industrializing World* (1986). Currently he is working on a history of class formation, family formation, and worker militancy in nineteenth-century France.

ALF LUEDTKE is Research Associate at the Max-Planck-Institute für Geschichte in Göttingen, West Germany. He has conducted research on forms and practices of domination, especially in the context of the establishment of the "modern state" in Western Europe and in Germany in particular. More recently, he has focused on the experiences and politics of the dominated, especially industrial workers in Germany in the nineteenth and twentieth centuries. He also is interested in interdisciplinary exchange, especially dealing with notions and theories of social analysis and interpretation, between social anthropologists and historians. He is author of *Gemeinwohl, Polizie und Festungspraxis: Staatlich Gewaltsamkeit und innere Verwalung in Preussen, 1815–50* (1982) and (with others) of *Klassen und Kultur: Socialanthropologische Perspektiven in der Geschichtsschreibung* (1982). Since 1972 he has served as editor of *Sozialwissenschaftliche Informationen für Unterricht und Studium*, a journal of history and social science.

MARTIN MURRAY is Associate Professor of Sociology at the State University of New York at Binghamton. He is author of *The Development of Capitalism in Colonial Indochina, 1870–1940* (1981) and editor of *South African Capitalism and Black Political Opposition* (1982). Currently he is involved in research projects concerning the formation of the rural proletariat in the South African countryside, 1890–1940, and on the contemporary political situation in South Africa and the composition of Black opposition to the apartheid regime.

JAMES F. PETRAS teaches sociology at the State University of New York at Binghamton. He is the author of many articles and several books, including *The Crisis of Capitalism and Socialism in the Late Twentieth Century* (1978) and *Class, State and Power in the Third World* (1982).

CHARLES STEPHENSON is a member of the Department of History at Central Connecticut State University. He served as editor (with Elizabeth Pleck) of the Series in American Social History (State University of New York Press) (1979–1982), and as Chair of the Network on Workers and Industrialization (1978–1982). He edited (with Robert Asher) *Life and Labor: Dimensions of American Working-Class History* (1986), and *Ethnicity and the American Worker* (1986), and (with Michael Hanagan) *Proletarians and Protest: Studies in Class Formation in an Industrializing World* (1986). Currently he serves as editor (with Robert Asher) of the American Labor History Series for the State University of New York Press. He is author of numerous articles and of *The Real Democrats: The Democrats of Texas in Texas Politics in the 1950s* (1986). Currently he is completing a study of migration and economic development in America, 1870–1930.